Nelson Advanced Science

Tools, Techniques and Assessment in Biology

A Course Guide for Students and Teachers

John Adds • Erica Larkcom
Ruth Miller • Robin Sutton
With a contribution by Sue Howarth

First published in 1999 by:
Nelson Thornes (Publishers) Ltd

Reprinted in 2001 by:
Nelson Thornes Ltd
Delta Place
27 Bath Road
CHELTENHAM
GL53 7TH
United Kingdom

02 03 04 05 / 10 9 8 7 6 5 4

A catalogue record for this book is available from the British Library

ISBN 0 17 448273 6

Illustrations by page make-up Hardlines, Charlbury, Oxfordshire
Printed and bound in China by L.Rex Printing Co., Ltd.

Acknowledgements
The authors and publishers would like to thank the following for permission to use copyright photographs:
Science Photo Library: Figures 2.13, 2.14(b)
Neil Thompson: Figures 4.6, 4.9 and 4.11
John Adds: Figure 5.8(c)
Dean Madden, National Centre for Biotechnology Education: Figure 5.3
Techne (Cambridge) Ltd: 5.6(a)
Bio-Rad Laboratories Ltd: Figure 5.7
Erica Larkcom: Figure 5.8(a), 5.9, 5.15(a) and (b)
Philip Harris Ltd: Figures 5.8(b), 6.10, 6.11 and 6.18
Science and Plants for Schools, Homerton College, Cambridge: Figures 5.11, 5.12
Mark Hanley Browne: Figure 5.13
John Walmsley: Figure 6.19
Electronmicroscopy Unit, Royal Holloway, University of London: Figure 2.12

Figure 3.5 is reproduced by permission of the *Journal of Biological Education*.
Figure 5.1 has been published on the National Centre for Biotechnology Education (NCBE) website (http://www.ncbe.reading.ac.uk) and in a slightly different form in the *Journal of Biological Education*. The authors and publishers are grateful to Dean Madden of NCBE for permission to reproduce this material.
Figure 5.4 is compiled from data in Short, J. M. et al. (1988) *Nucleic Acids Research*, 16, pp7583-7600.
Figure 5.5(a) and 5.6(b) are based on material in Walker, R. W. and Rapley, R. (1997), *Route Maps in Gene Technology*, published by Blackwell Science.
Figure 5.5(b) is based on Figure 10.3 from Alberts, B., Bray, D., Johnson, A., Lewis, J., Raff, M., Roberts, K. and Walter, P., (1998) *Essentials of Cell Biology*, published by Garland.
Figure 5.6(b) is based on material from Madigan, M. T., Martinko, J.M. and Parker, J. (1997) *Brock's Biology of Microorganisms*, published by Prentice Hall.
The authors and publishers are grateful to Dean Madden and John Schollar of NCBE, Peter Finegold of the Wellcome Trust, Richard Price of SAPS and Dr Mary MacDonald for all their help in the preparation of Chapter 5.

Contents

Introduction

Tools, Techniques and Assessment in Biology supports the Biology texts published in the Nelson Advanced Modular Science series. These are based on the London Examinations (Edexcel) AS and A level modular syllabuses (specifications) in Biology and Human Biology, Chemistry and Physics. *Tools, Techniques and Assessment in Biology* provides a guide which offers support throughout the A level Biology course, and its aim is to help students to develop their skills in practical work as well as giving advice on how to approach the examination. It is appropriate for all A level Biology syllabuses(specifications) and equivalent courses at this level.

Written for students and for teachers, *Tools, Techniques and Assessment in Biology* explores the essential tools and techniques which you will use in your practical work during the A level course, in the laboratory and in the field. This guide also introduces you to some newer techniques which will certainly become part of Biology courses at this level in the 21st century. It gives the rationale behind the procedures, the 'why' and the 'how' of your practical investigations, leading you through to the treatment and interpretation of results to ensure development of a biological understanding in a wider context. It includes advice on necessary safety procedures and risk assessment, in the laboratory and in the field. This resource is a course guide rather than a 'recipe' book, with all the instructions or protocols for you to follow. It is amply illustrated with details of a wide range of experiments and case studies, with actual data. These serve to exemplify the descriptions being given and can act as models to help you to work out what to do in your own practical investigations.

There are cross references in the margin of the book which take you from one part to other related sections of the book and to the Appendices. Appendix I provides references to other useful books. Appendix II provides references for suppliers of practical equipment and materials together with further information on kits: Appendix III summarises ways of sampling vegetation and Appendix IV gives a review of statistical methods. Appendix V refers to key skills and shows how the practical work described provides opportunities to develop and collect evidence for key skills, as identified by QCA. Key skills opportunities are highlighted in the margin throughout the text.

Tools, Techniques and Assessment in Biology takes you from basic laboratory practice - using equipment and taking measurements - through to more sophisticated quantitative techniques. These include colorimetry, counting cells, an example of a bioassay and an introduction to datalogging. Microscopes are tools of particular value to biologists and you are given the background of how they are used with examples of how to record your observations accurately in biological drawings. A comprehensive and detailed survey of fieldwork techniques complements the coverage of laboratory practical work. With the help of a 'statistical planning chart' you are taken step by step through a full range of statistical tests, how to select, implement and integrate them with your practical investigations, from the hypothesis and planning through to analysis and interpretation of your results. You are given specific advice on writing the reports of your investigations – the style, how to present your data and how to handle the discussion. The 'more advanced' tools and techniques bring you face to face with operations which are now used in research, in

INTRODUCTION

industry or in diagnostic procedures in medical or forensic science - manipulations with DNA, tissue culture, simulation of industrial fermentations or using an immunological assay - and inclusion of 'fast plants' lets you do meaningful experiments with plants on the laboratory bench. The authors hope this guide will help you to do interesting and successful practical work - with an emphasis, always, on how you can safely do your own investigations which enable you to explore biological processes and enhance your understanding of Biology.

The authors

Erica Larkcom B.A., M.A., C.Biol., M.I.Biol., former Subject Officer for A level Biology, now Deputy Director, Science and Plants for Schools, Homerton College, Cambridge

John Adds B.A., C.Biol., M.I.Biol., Dip. Ed., Chief Examiner for A level Biology, Head of Biology, Abbey College, London

Ruth Miller B.Sc., C.Biol., M.I.Biol., Chief Examiner for AS and A level Biology, former Head of Biology, Sir William Perkins's School, Chertsey, Surrey

Robin Sutton, B.Sc., Ph.D., Ecologist working for the Field Studies Council as Assistant warden at Rhyd-y-Creuau, The Draper's Field Centre, Betws-y-Coed, North Wales

Note to teachers on safety

When practical instructions have been given we have attempted to indicate hazardous substances and operations by using standard symbols and appropriate precautions. Nevertheless you should be aware of your obligations under the Health and Safety at Work Act, Control of Substances Hazardous to Health (COSHH) Regulations and the Management of Health and Safety at Work Regulations. in this respect you should follow the requirements of your employers at all times.

In carrying out practical work, students should be encouraged to carry out their own risk assessments, i.e. they should identify hazards and suitable ways of reducing the risks from them. However they must be checked by the teacher or lecturer. Students must also know what to do in an emergency, such as a fire.

Teachers and lecturers should be familiar and up to date with current advice from professional bodies.

Laboratory techniques

Laboratory practice – measurements and manipulations

Practical work is an important aspect of your studies in biology. It includes making observations of living organisms in their natural environment, investigating physiological processes in organisms and tissues, and carrying out experiments to study the properties of isolated enzymes. The use of a microscope is essential for the study and understanding of the structure of cells and tissues, and this is described in Chapter 2. The main purpose of this chapter is to introduce you to some basic laboratory techniques and the use of simple apparatus.

Many experiments in biology require you to make quantitative observations, with careful measurements, rather than qualitative descriptions. For quantitative work, it is important to use the appropriate units. The Système International d'Unités (SI units) is used to provide a system of units which is free from ambiguity and any possibility of misinterpretation. SI units should always be used in quantitative work.

Table 1.1 gives the prefixes which are common to all SI units, and which are likely to be encountered in your practical work.

The unit of **mass** is the kilogram (kg), although sometimes it may be more convenient to use the gram (g). Be careful to distinguish between mass and weight: mass is a measure of the quantity of matter present, whereas the weight of an object is the force it exerts on anything which supports it. This force is normally due to the fact that an object is being attracted towards the Earth by the force of gravity. For most purposes in biology, the term mass should be used rather than weight, for example, fresh mass, not fresh weight.

Length is expressed in metres, or fractions or multiples of the metre, as shown in Table 1.2.

Table 1.1 *Some SI prefixes and their symbols*

Multiple or fraction	Prefix	Symbol
10^6	mega	M
10^3	kilo	k
10^{-1}	deci	d
10^{-2}	centi	c
10^{-3}	milli	m
10^{-6}	micro	μ
10^{-9}	nano	n

Table 1.2 *SI units used to measure length*

Name of unit	Multiple or fraction of a metre	Symbol
kilometre	10^3	km
metre		m
centimetre	10^{-2}	cm
millimetre	10^{-3}	mm
micrometre	10^{-6}	μm
nanometre	10^{-9}	nm

The SI unit of **area** is the square metre (m^2), although in ecological studies, the hectare (ha) is often used. One hectare = 10^4 square metres.

A convenient unit of **volume** in biology is the cubic decimetre (dm^3), which is equivalent to one litre. The preferred smaller units of volume are the cubic centimetre (cm^3) and the cubic millimetre (mm^3). The microlitre (μl), which is numerically equal to one cubic millimetre, is sometimes used for very small volumes, although it is a non-SI unit.

Concentrations are expressed as moles per cubic decimetre, although this unit cannot be used for substances if their molecular mass is not known with certainty, for example, most proteins. In this case, it is usual to express their concentrations in units of mass per unit volume, usually grams per cubic decimetre. In biology, concentrations are often expressed in terms of percentages. As an example, to make up a 2 per cent solution of sucrose, 2 g would be dissolved in distilled water, then the total volume of the solution made up to 100 cm^3, in a volumetric flask, by adding more distilled water. This is referred to as a 2 per cent weight for volume (2% w/v) solution.

The SI unit of **time** is the second (s), but it is often convenient to use larger units, such as minutes, hours, days or years. The SI unit of **pressure** is the pascal, (Pa), but for many purposes the kilopascal (kPa) is more convenient. Traditionally, pressures have been measured in terms of millimetres of mercury (mm Hg). Blood pressures are still sometimes quoted in mm Hg, rather than in pascals. One kilopascal equals 7.5 mm Hg, so to convert mm Hg to kPa, divide by 7.5.

Temperature is expressed as degrees Celsius (°C). The SI unit of **energy** is the joule (J), which is defined as the work done when a force of 1 newton (1 N) acts through 1 metre in the direction of the force. In nutrition, the calorie is still often used as a measure of heat energy. One calorie is the heat energy required to raise one gram of water by 1 °C. One calorie = 4.184 joules. Be careful not to confuse the calorie with the 'Calorie' – which is really a kilocalorie (kcal).

Table 1.3 *Some SI units and their symbols*

Physical quantity	Unit	Symbol
mass	kilogram	kg
length	metre	m
time	second	s
area	square metre	m^2
volume	cubic decimetre	dm^3
concentration	moles per cubic decimetre	$mol\ dm^{-3}$
pressure	pascal	Pa
energy	joule	J

Notice that in Table 1.3, the symbol for moles per cubic decimetre is written as mol dm^{-3}. We use **negative indices** when symbols are combined, for example, metres per second would be written as m s^{-1}, kilograms per square metre as kg m^{-2}.

Basic laboratory equipment

You should be familiar with the following items of laboratory equipment, which will be needed for many investigations, including enzyme experiments:

- test tubes and boiling tubes
- Bunsen burner, tripod and gauze
- beaker
- measuring cylinder
- thermometer
- graduated pipettes
- plastic syringes
- Pasteur pipettes
- spotting tile
- stop watch or stop clock
- Chinagraph pencil or spirit marker pen.

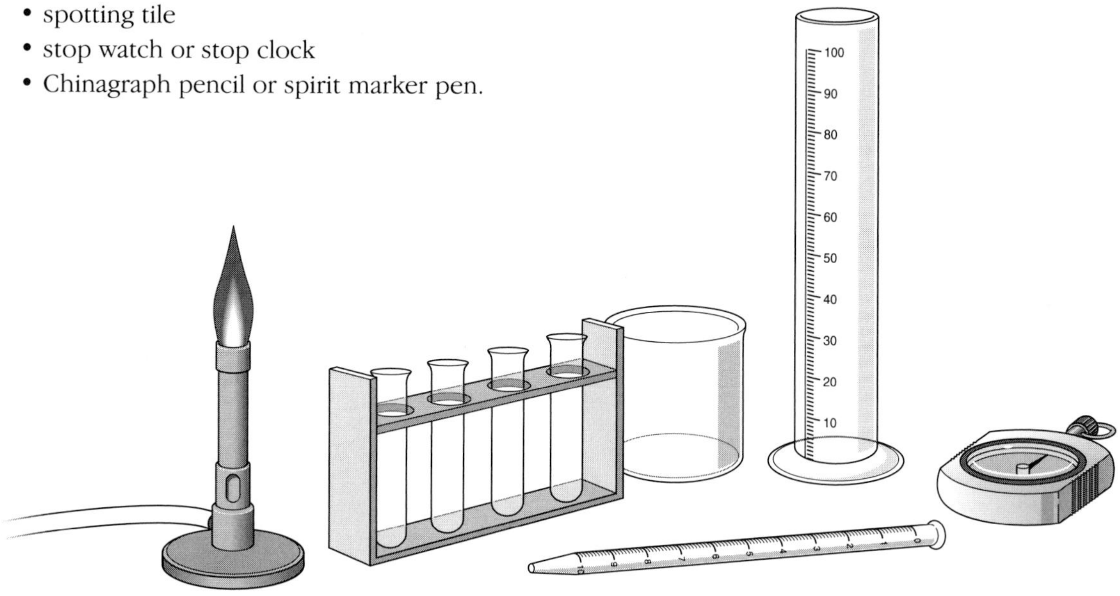

Figure 1.1 A selection of basic laboratory equipment

Test tubes and **boiling tubes** are used to carry out experiments where it is necessary, for example, to mix reagents together, such as an enzyme and substrate, and to observe any changes in the contents. A beaker can be used as a water bath, to maintain a constant temperature. The beaker should be heated carefully on a tripod with a gauze, using a Bunsen burner. Metal beakers are ideal for this purpose. Use a thermometer to monitor the temperature, which can be maintained by alternate gentle heating or addition of small pieces of ice. An electric, thermostatically controlled water bath provides a suitable alternative.

LABORATORY TECHNIQUES

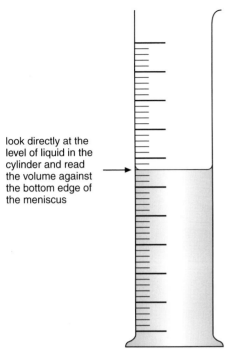

look directly at the level of liquid in the cylinder and read the volume against the bottom edge of the meniscus

Figure 1.2 When reading the volume of liquid in a measuring cylinder or a pipette, look directly at the bottom edge of the meniscus

Measuring cylinders, **graduated pipettes** and **syringes** are used for measuring volumes of liquids. Always use a pipette filler, such as a Pi pump™ when filling graduated pipettes. NEVER suck up liquids by mouth. Before using a graduated pipette, look carefully to see which way the scale is set on the pipette. Some read from zero to full volume when empty, whereas others start at full volume and read zero when empty. Also, some graduated pipettes are designed to deliver, for example, 10 cm³, when allowed to empty by gravity, leaving a small volume in the tip; others will only deliver the correct volume when completely empty. The latter type of pipette usually has 'BLOWOUT' printed at the top of the scale. When reading the volume of a liquid in a measuring cylinder or graduated pipette, you should look directly at the level of the meniscus and read the volume from the bottom of the meniscus (see Figure 1.2). Pasteur pipettes, or dropping pipettes, should be used to transfer small volumes of a liquid from one test tube to another, or from a test tube on to a spotting tile. When used correctly, a Pasteur pipette will deliver a constant drop volume, which can be useful in quantitative investigations. The Pasteur pipette should be held vertically and a drop allowed to form by exerting gentle pressure on the teat.

One of the uses of graduated pipettes is to prepare a series of dilutions, or serial dilutions, from a stock solution. Two types of serial dilutions are **doubling dilutions** and **logarithmic dilutions**. In doubling dilutions, the concentration of the stock solution decreases by $\frac{1}{2}$, $\frac{1}{4}$, $\frac{1}{8}$, $\frac{1}{16}$, $\frac{1}{32}$, etc., whereas in the logarithmic series, the concentration of the stock solution decreases by a factor of ten at each stage. One particular use of logarithmic serial dilution is to enumerate microorganisms using the pour-plate dilution method, details of which are given in the modular texts. When carrying out serial dilution, it is important to use a clean pipette at each stage, to avoid any carry-over of liquids, and to measure the volumes carefully and accurately. The principles of making doubling and logarithmic dilutions are illustrated in Figure 1.3.

Communication
Appendix V: Key Skills
Page 142

Application of Number
Appendix V: Key Skills
Page 142

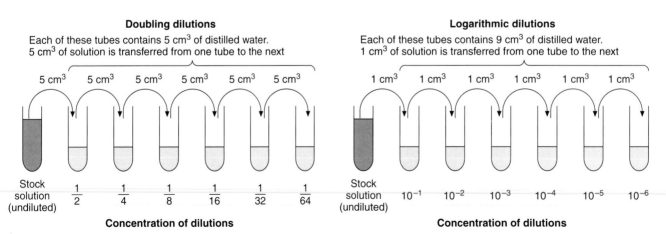

Doubling dilutions

Each of these tubes contains 5 cm³ of distilled water. 5 cm³ of solution is transferred from one tube to the next

Logarithmic dilutions

Each of these tubes contains 9 cm³ of distilled water. 1 cm³ of solution is transferred from one tube to the next

Figure 1.3 Preparing serial dilutions. The solution must be mixed thoroughly and a clean pipette used to transfer the volume to the next tube in the series

Micropipettes (also referred to as pipettors or autopipettors, Figure 1.4) are used to dispense accurately very small volumes of liquids, for example 10 mm^3. There are a number of different types of micropipettes available, most of which are relatively expensive. These include fixed-volume, which deliver a single pre-set volume, and adjustable, which can be set by the user to deliver a volume within a set range of values. Whichever type of micropipette you use, you must ensure that you fully understand the procedures for setting the volume to be dispensed and using the pipette correctly. Micropipettes are used with disposable plastic tips, which should be fitted firmly, otherwise less than the set volume will be delivered and liquid will drip from the pipette in use. Micropipettes must NEVER be used without the appropriate plastic tip.

Spotting tiles are used, for example, to test single drops of a liquid for the presence of starch, by placing drops separately in wells on the tile, then adding a drop of iodine solution. Ordinary glazed white tiles may be used as an alternative to spotting tiles.

A **stop watch** or **stop clock** will be needed to time a reaction, or to time the movement of a bubble in a capillary tube of a potometer. If these are not available, a watch or clock with a second hand can provide a suitable alternative.

It is important to label each test tube, beaker or Petri dish you use with a Chinagraph pencil or a spirit marker. Unlabelled, or inadequately labelled experiments are often the cause of anomalous results and may also be dangerous or a health hazard.

Health and safety in the laboratory

When carrying out practical activities in a laboratory, it is essential to follow a number of rules to ensure your own health and safety and that of others working around you. The following list is intended to give general guidelines for safety in the laboratory. You should note that additional guidelines will need to be followed when carrying out practicals involving microorganisms, or during field work investigations. Furthermore, your school or college should have its own safety Code of Practice, which must be closely adhered to. Several safety procedures are to minimise the risk of any unknown or harmful materials getting into your mouth. This is particularly important when dealing with harmful chemical substances or cultures of microorganisms.

- Your laboratory must have a notice telling you what to do in the event of fire. Ensure that you know how to raise the alarm, where the exit routes are, and where to assemble after leaving the building.
- Wear the appropriate protective clothing at all times – a clean laboratory coat, which must be buttoned up, and safety spectacles

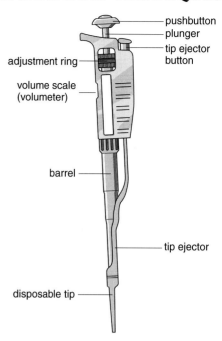

Figure 1.4 A Gilson Pipetman®, an example of an autopipettor. Autopipettors can be adjusted to deliver accurately volumes between 10 mm^3 and 1000 mm^3

Labels on figure: pushbutton, plunger, tip ejector button, adjustment ring, volume scale (volumeter), barrel, tip ejector, disposable tip if there is any risk to your eyes. Sometimes goggles or a face shield may be needed.

- Tie back long hair. This is particularly important if there are any naked flames.
- Do not eat or drink in the laboratory.
- If labels are to be used, they should be of a self-adhesive variety.
- Read the practical schedule carefully before you start, and ensure that you are clear about what you are going to do. It may be helpful to prepare a simple flow chart to show the stages in the investigation.
- Keep the bench where you are working free from clutter. Assemble the equipment and reagents you need for the investigation and have ready your laboratory notebook.
- Pay particular attention to specific hazards associated with any of the substances involved in the practical. Generally speaking, substances used in Advanced-level biology practicals are relatively harmless, but occasionally it is necessary to use substances which may be **corrosive** (such as potassium hydroxide), highly **flammable** (such as Industrial Methylated Spirit, IMS), or **harmful** (such as ethanal). You should be advised of the appropriate COSHH (Control of Substances Hazardous to Health) regulations. A risk assessment must be carried out, which includes identification of the substances or types of substances to which you are liable to be exposed and the effects of these substances on the body. This should also include suitable control measures (safety precautions) that may be needed to minimise the risk, for example use of a fume cupboard, eye protection, etc. When planning practical project work, you should always carry out a risk assessment, which must then be checked by your teacher before starting practical work.
- When using graduated or volumetric pipettes, NEVER suck up liquids, including water, by mouth. Always use a safety filler, such as a Pi pump™.
- If it is necessary to heat liquids in a test tube or a boiling tube directly in a Bunsen burner flame, hold the tube with a spring holder and point the open end of the tube away from other people. When testing for reducing sugars using Benedict's reagent, it is safer to heat the tube in a boiling water bath for 8 minutes, rather than directly using a Bunsen burner.
- Wipe up any spillages with paper towels and dispose of in a bin. Spillages of cultures of microorganisms should be treated as described in the section on safety in microbiology (page 7).
- Broken glass should be disposed of in a container reserved specifically for this purpose (a 'sharps' bin).
- When you have completed your practical work, clear away all apparatus and leave the bench clean and tidy. Do not remove your eye protection until everyone else has finished.
- If there is any accident or breakage it must be reported to the appropriate member of staff.

Additional recommendations for practical work involving microorganisms

Your attention is drawn to the following publications:

- **Control of Substances Hazardous to Health Regulations** 1994 (COSHH) [ISBN 0 7176 1308 9]. This publication includes the Approved Code of Practice and special provisions relating to biological agents. A biological agent is defined as *'any microorganism, cell culture, or human endoparasite, including any which have been genetically modified, which may cause any infection, allergy, toxicity or otherwise create a hazard to human health'*.
- **Topics in Safety** (1988) Revised second edition, published by the Association for Science Education [ISBN 0 86357 104 2]
- **The CLEAPSS (Consortium of Local Education Authorities for the Provision of Science Services) Laboratory Handbook**. Available in schools that are members of CLEAPSS.

The term **aseptic technique** is used for the correct handling procedure used in the culture of cells and microorganisms. There are two main purposes of aseptic technique, first to avoid the accidental contamination of cultures due to microorganisms or spores from external sources, and second, to prevent contamination of yourself and other students with microorganisms. In addition to the general principles of safety in laboratories, a number of other precautions must be taken for the safe handling of microorganisms.

Only those organisms in Category 1 of the Approved List of Biological Agents (categorisation 1998), published by the Advisory Committee on Dangerous Pathogens (www.open.gov.uk/hse/agents.htm) should be cultured in school laboratories. Category 1 microorganisms are those which are unlikely to cause human disease and include *Bacillus subtilis*, non-pathogenic strains of *Escherichia coli*, *Saccharomyces cerevisiae*, *Penicillium chrysogenum*, and *Chlorella pyrenoidosa*. Pure cultures of microorganisms should be obtained from recognised suppliers, such as those included in Appendix II. Microorganisms from unknown sources should not be cultured in school laboratories, as there is a risk of isolating a pathogenic species, and all cultures are treated as being potentially harmful.

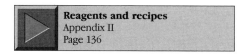

Reagents and recipes
Appendix II
Page 136

The following points are intended to be guidelines for safe handling of microorganisms and should be followed in addition to the general safety advice for working in biology laboratories. You should also adhere to any Codes of Practice produced by Education Authorities, or by Governing Bodies of schools or colleges.

- Eating, drinking, smoking, chewing, licking labels, applying make-up, chewing pens or pencils, and mouth pipetting are forbidden in any laboratory when handling microorganisms.
- Any exposed cuts or broken skin must be covered with a waterproof dressing before undertaking any practical work involving microorganisms.

LABORATORY TECHNIQUES

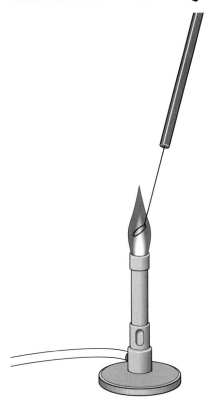

Figure 1.5 Sterilising a bacteriological loop. The loop should be held in the flame until it is red hot, then allowed to cool briefly before being used to transfer a culture aseptically. The loop must always be flamed again after use

Figure 1.6 Biohazard sign

- Before you start the practical work, wipe the surface of the bench with a suitable disinfectant.
- Bacteriological wire loops should be no more than 5 cm long and must be closed. Wire loops must be sterilised by heating the wire, held almost vertically, in a Bunsen flame until the wire is red hot (Figure 1.5) When re-sterilising the loop after use, introduce the loop slowly into the flame to prevent spattering. Allow the loop to cool for about 10 seconds, without coming into contact with a surface, before use.
- Discard jars containing fresh disinfectant should be available at each work place for disposal of contaminated items.
- Flame the neck of a bottle by passing the opening through a Bunsen flame, before pouring. Lids, caps, or cotton wool plugs should be held using the little finger of the other hand – they must not be placed on the bench. Flame the neck of the bottle again before replacing the top.
- After inoculating an agar plate, the Petri dish lid should be secured with adhesive tape. Use two pieces of tape to fasten the lid, but do not seal all the way round as this could create anaerobic conditions and encourage the growth of possible pathogenic microorganisms.
- The recommended maximum temperature for incubation of cultures is 30 °C. Cultures should not be incubated at 37 °C, as this is an ideal temperature for the growth of many pathogenic species. Agar plates should be incubated in an inverted position, that is with the agar uppermost, as this allows any condensation to collect on the lid. Do not open Petri dishes after incubation.
- All bacterial or fungal cultures must be sterilised by autoclaving at 121 °C for 15 minutes before disposal. Use the appropriate biohazard autoclavable plastic bags for this purpose, left open in the autoclave so that steam can penetrate.
- When you have finished your practical work, wipe the bench with disinfectant, wash your hands with soap and dry using disposable paper towels before leaving the laboratory.

If spillage of a culture occurs, it should be dealt with as follows:

- Disposable gloves must be worn and the broken container and/or spilled culture covered with a cloth soaked in disinfectant and left for at least 10 minutes. The materials should then be cleared away with paper towels and a dustpan, which should then be placed in a disposal bag and autoclaved.

So far, we have described some of the essential laboratory equipment and outlined safety precautions which should be taken in biology and microbiology practicals. The following investigation gives you the opportunity to put some of this theory into practice, by following the method to investigate the activity of an enzyme. This particular practical has been chosen as the materials required should be readily available.

Investigation of the activity of rennin

Introduction

The purpose of this practical exercise is to familiarise you with some laboratory procedures in the investigation of the activity of an enzyme. The practical requires you to make accurate dilutions of a solution containing an enzyme, set up a water bath to keep the enzyme and substrate at a constant temperature, and to make careful observations of the activity of the enzyme.

Communication
Appendix V:
Key Skills
Page 142

Rennin is an enzyme which is used in the manufacture of cheese. The enzyme coagulates milk proteins by converting soluble calcium caseinate particles to clumps of calcium paracaseinate, which precipitate to form the 'curd'. Traditionally, rennin is obtained from the stomachs of calves or other young mammals, but a number of rennin substitutes are now available, produced by genetically modified microorganisms. The production of chymosin (microbial rennin) is described in the modular texts.

Materials

- 50 cm^3 of a 1% rennin solution (1.0 g rennin powder per 100 cm^3 distilled water) ('Essence of Rennet', which contains rennin, is usually available from Chemists or Health Food shops). This 1% rennin solution is referred to as the 'stock solution', from which further dilutions are to be made
- 50 cm^3 of pasteurised milk
- Distilled water
- Test tubes and rack
- Graduated pipettes with safety fillers, or syringes to deliver from 1 to 5 cm^3
- Marker pen
- Beaker to use as a water bath, or a thermostatically controlled water bath
- Bunsen burner, tripod and gauze
- Thermometer
- Stop watch
- Piece of black card, about $10 \text{ cm} \times 14 \text{ cm}$

Safety note: When making up the enzyme solution, avoid inhaling the powder, which may cause an allergic reaction. The hazard of the 1% solution is very low, but avoid skin contact, or rubbing eyes with contaminated hands. Wash off any splashes.

Method

1. First prepare a series of dilutions of the rennin stock solution provided, so that you have half strength, quarter strength and one-tenth strength. This requires careful measurement of volumes of the original enzyme solution and of distilled water for dilution. To help you with the volumes required, refer to Table 1.4. Remember to label all your tubes. Notice that in the table, the final concentration of the rennin solutions are quoted in percentages with the % sign in brackets. We use brackets here, rather than a solidus, as percentage is not a unit.
2. Set up a water bath and maintain the temperature at, say, 35 °C. During the experiment, remember to monitor the temperature of your water bath and make any adjustments as necessary to maintain the temperature.
3. Place 5 cm^3 of milk in a labelled test tube, and stand this in the water bath.

LABORATORY TECHNIQUES

Application of Number
Appendix V:
Key Skills
Page 142

Table 1.4 *Preparing a series of rennin solutions*

Volume of 1% rennin stock solution / cm³	Volume of distilled water / cm³	Final concentration of rennin (%)
5.0	5.0	0.50
2.5	7.5	0.25
1.0	9.0	0.10

4. Place 5 cm³ of undiluted rennin solution (i.e. 1%) in another labelled test tube and stand this in the water bath. Leave both tubes for 10 minutes to equilibrate to the temperature of the water bath.

5. Now mix the enzyme solution and the milk together, by pouring the enzyme solution into the milk, then pouring the mixture back into the tube which contained the enzyme solution and replacing in the water bath. Immediately start the stop clock.

6. Check the contents of the tube every minute by holding the tube against a piece of black card and tilting gently. When the milk proteins begin to coagulate you will see small granules appearing in the milk.

7. Record the time taken for the first signs of coagulation of the milk proteins. It will be difficult to time the reaction to the nearest second and may be more appropriate to observe the contents of the tube every 30 seconds, until you can see signs of coagulation.

8. Repeat steps 3 to 7, using each of your dilutions of rennin.

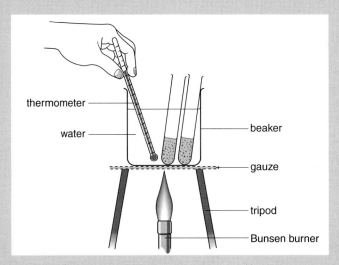

Figure 1.7 Using a water bath to maintain a constant temperature during the investigation of enzyme activity

Results and discussion

1. Record your observations in a table.

2. Write an account of your method, including precautions you took to ensure accurate results.

3. Convert the **time taken** for the milk proteins to coagulate to a relative **rate of reaction**, by calculating the reciprocal of the time taken. As an example, suppose that, using the undiluted rennin solution, signs of coagulation were first noted after 3 minutes. The relative rate of reaction will therefore be $1 \div 3 = 0.33$ min⁻¹. To make these figures easier to plot, you may wish to multiply each one by 10 or by 100.

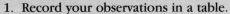

Application of Number
Appendix V:
Key Skills
Page 142

4. Plot a graph to show the relationship between the relative rate of reaction and the concentration of the enzyme.

5. Describe and explain the relationship between the relative rate of reaction and the concentration of the enzyme. Think about this relationship in terms of the availability of active sites.

Hints on the tabulation and graphical presentation of results

Results from investigations such as this should be presented in a suitable table. Each column in the table should be headed with the quantity and its SI unit, which are usually separated by a solidus (/). As an example, we would write 'Temperature / °C' or 'Mass / kg'. The units are not then repeated in the column. The same convention is used to label the axes of a graph, for example, 'Time / min'.

The first column in the table should be the **independent variable** (that is, the variable with the values chosen by the person carrying out the investigation) and the second column should be the **dependent variable** (the readings which are taken in the investigation).

Table 1.5 shows how the results should be presented for the investigation into the effect of concentration on the activity of rennin. Concentration of the enzyme is the independent variable; enzyme activity, measured in terms of the time taken for milk to clot, is the dependent variable. Note that the third column gives the relative rate of reaction, which we calculate by taking the reciprocal of the time taken for the milk to clot, that is 1 ÷ time. The activity of different batches of rennin can vary widely, so your results are likely to differ from those shown.

Table 1.5 *The effect of rennin concentration on the rate of reaction*

Concentration of rennin (%)	Time taken for milk to clot / min	Relative rate of reaction / min^{-1}
1.00	3.0	0.33
0.50	6.5	0.15
0.25	11.0	0.09
0.10	33.0	0.03

Application of Number
Appendix V:
Key Skills
Page 142

When plotting a graph, the axes should be fully labelled, using the same quantities and units given in the table of results. The independent variable should be plotted on the x (horizontal) axis and the dependent variable plotted on the y (vertical) axis. Tables and graphs should always have titles, but avoid heading a graph '*Graph to show......*' as this is not really necessary. In this case, '*The effect of rennin concentration on the rate of reaction*' is sufficient.

Plot the points clearly on the graph, using either crosses (×) or encircled dots (⊙). If you are plotting more than one set of data on a graph, use different symbols for each set and remember to include a key, or label each curve. Think carefully about how to join the points you have plotted. It may be appropriate to draw a line of best fit or a smooth curve through the points, but only if you are sure that the line correctly shows the relationship between the variables. As an example, if you plotted a graph to show the relationship between the rate of photosynthesis and light intensity, you would be justified in drawing a smooth curve through the points. However, in many cases we do not know for sure exactly what the relationship is.

LABORATORY TECHNIQUES

If you are unsure, it is safer to join successive points with straight, ruled lines. Whatever line you draw on your graph, do not extrapolate, that is, do not extend the line beyond your data points. Figure 1.8 shows a graph of the results in Table 1.5.

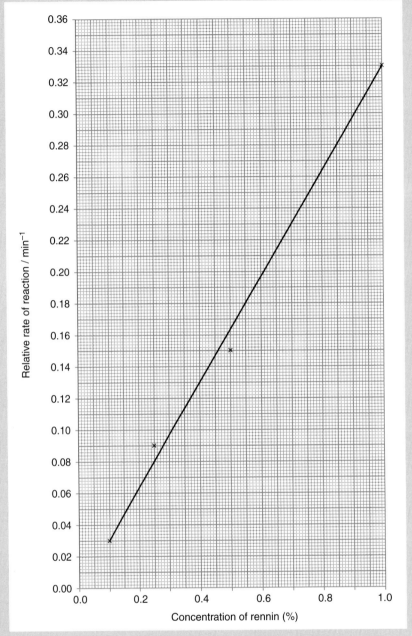

Figure 1.8 The effect of rennin concentration on the rate of reaction

Application of Number
Appendix V:
Key Skills
Page 142

Problem Solving
Appendix V:
Key Skills
Page 143

Suggestions for further work

1. Using a similar procedure, investigate the effect of temperature on the activity of rennin.
2. Compare the activity of different rennin substitutes, such as Fromase®, Rennilase®, and Chymax®.
3. Investigate the effect of the concentration of calcium ions on the activity of rennin and rennin substitutes, using 0.01 mol per dm^3 calcium chloride solution.

2 Microscopy and observation

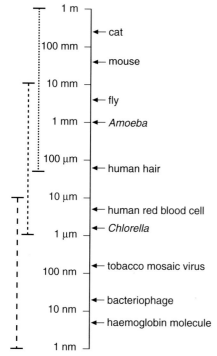

1 m
← cat
100 mm
← mouse
10 mm
← fly
1 mm ← *Amoeba*
100 µm
← human hair
10 µm
← human red blood cell
← *Chlorella*
1 µm
← tobacco mosaic virus
100 nm
← bacteriophage
10 nm
← haemoglobin molecule
1 nm

Scale is logarithmic

├········┤ visible to naked eye

├----┤ visible using light microscope

├ – ┤ visible using electron microscope

Figure 2.1 Range of size of some living organisms alongside scale

Living organisms range in size from large vertebrates, clearly visible to the naked eye, to viruses which can only be detected using the high magnifications achieved by electron microscopy. Much practical work in biology involves making and recording observations on living organisms and there are many situations where it is often desirable to use some form of magnification in order to be able to discern detail.

The amount of detail which can be seen by the human eye depends on:
- the optical properties of the lens and cornea, which are responsible for focusing the light rays from objects to form an image on the retina
- the density of the cone cells in the most sensitive area (the fovea) of the retina.

In order for two separate features of an object to be seen, their images must fall on at least two cone cells in the fovea of the retina. In other words, details in the image closer together than two neighbouring cone cells will not be detected separately and are therefore not distinguishable as separate parts of the object.

When we wish to observe the details of an object, we hold it closer to our eyes, so that the image on the retina will be larger. The normal, unaided human eye cannot focus clearly on objects closer than about 250 mm (10 inches), which is known as the **least (nearest) distance of distinct vision**.

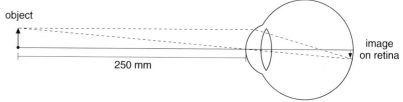

object

image on retina

250 mm

Figure 2.2 Diagram of eye focusing on small object at close range. Light from the object is refracted by the curved surfaces of the cornea and the lens, and focused on the retina. The image is real, smaller than the object and inverted

Whilst it is possible by eye to see quite small objects, such as the width of a human hair or the presence of unicellular protoctists in a culture, some form of **microscope** is needed if detailed structure is required. Three main types of microscope are used for biological observations:
- **light microscopes**
- **transmission electron microscopes** (**TEM**)
- **scanning electron microscopes** (**SEM**).

Most students will be able to use light microscopes such as hand lenses, dissecting microscopes and compound light microscopes, but not many will have the opportunity to see an electron microscope in action or to use one, although all should be familiar with the results of their use.

For the image produced by any microscope to be of use to the observer, there should be:
- sufficient total **magnification**, enabling the image of separate points to fall on separate cones on the retina
- adequate **resolution** so that the magnified detail is sufficiently sharp
- sufficient **contrast** in order that the resolved details can be distinguished from the background and each other.

The magnification of a lens produces an image which is larger than the object but, whilst it is important that the image is large enough to be seen, greater magnification does not necessarily mean that the details of the image will be clearer or more easily observable.

The better the resolution in the image, the sharper the detail will be. This is determined largely by how well the objective lens resolves detail, i.e. its resolving power. The resolving power of a given objective lens depends partly on the wavelength of light used, because objects smaller than the wavelengths of the light being used will not be seen. The ability of the lens to gather light from the object and transmit it accurately also affects its resolving power. For a compound light microscope, used with a good-quality oil immersion objective lens and light of a wavelength of 550 nm, the resolution is about 0.25 μm. In other words, it is possible for an observer to distinguish features on the specimen that are 0.25 μm apart. Where higher resolution and greater detail are required, then it is necessary to use an electron microscope, where the beam of electrons used has a much shorter wavelength than light.

Neighbouring details in the image that are similar in size and shape, but different in nature, need to be distinguished from each other, so it is important that there should be some contrast, or differences in intensity, between such features. Contrast can be improved with the use of staining techniques during the preparation of the specimen, or it can be achieved by the adjustment of the settings of the microscope during viewing.

Light microscopes

The first simple microscopes were developed in the 17th century. Anton van Leeuwenhoek (1632–1723) and Robert Hooke (1635–1703) both developed microscopes, but their approaches were different. Hooke's microscopes had two lenses, whereas van Leeuwenhoek used a single lens. The lenses used in these early microscopes had imperfections, but van Leeuwenhoek was able to achieve a magnification of ×266 and he described his observations of bacteria,

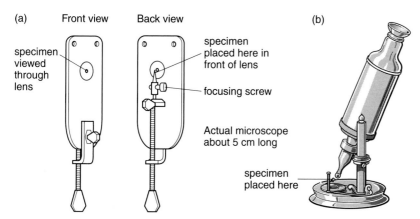

(a) Front view   Back view   (b)

specimen viewed through lens

specimen placed here in front of lens

focusing screw

Actual microscope about 5 cm long

specimen placed here

Figure 2.3 Drawings of (a) Leeuwenhoek's and (b) Hooke's microscopes

blood cells, freshwater protoctistans and the differences between the 'spring' and 'summer' wood in sections of xylem from trees, using a very simple lens system.

Light microscopes can be **simple**, consisting of a single converging lens, or **compound**, with separate objective and eyepiece lenses. Single lens microscopes range from hand lenses, or magnifying glasses, to dissecting microscopes, where the lens is supported and there is a stage on which the specimen is placed for viewing. The magnifications achieved range from ×5 to ×20.

Hand lenses in folding mounts, such as the one illustrated in Figure 2.4, are convenient for use in the field, where the ability to recognise distinguishing external features of organisms can make identification more accurate. Dissecting microscopes are also useful for viewing external features and have the added advantage of leaving both hands free so that mounted needles or forceps can be used to manipulate the specimen.

Compound microscopes have at least two lenses, or lens systems: the **objective** and the **eyepiece**. The objective lens produces a real magnified image of the specimen, which is further magnified by the eyepiece, forming a final magnified virtual image which can be seen by the observer. The structure of a typical compound light microscope is shown in Figure 2.5, together with a simplified diagram, showing the path of the light rays and how image formation occurs.

The objective lens, O, is close to the specimen, XY. Light from XY is focused by O and forms an image, X_1Y_1. The image is inverted and its size depends on the magnifying power of O. The eyepiece lens, E, magnifies X_1Y_1, forming the image X_2Y_2 seen by the observer.

The magnifying power of a lens is defined as the number of times the image is larger than the object in normal use. In typical compound microscopes, such as those used in most schools and colleges, eyepiece lenses have a magnifying power of ×10 and there are usually two objective lenses available, one giving a magnification of ×10 and

(a) ×10 in folding mount

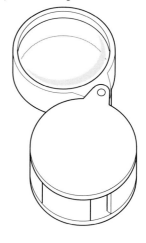

(b)

lens

glass stage

adjustment

support

Figure 2.4 Diagrams of (a) a simple hand lens and (b) a dissecting microscope or supported lens

MICROSCOPY AND OBSERVATION

(a)

(b)

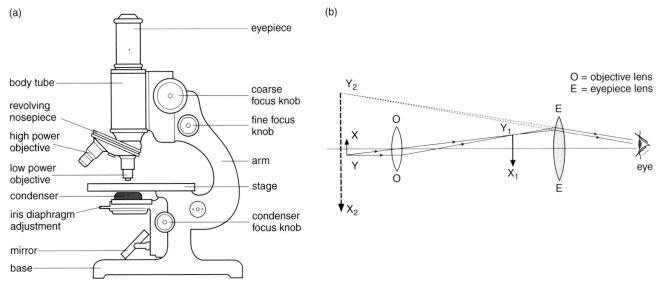

eyepiece

body tube

revolving nosepiece

high power objective

low power objective

condenser

iris diaphragm adjustment

mirror

base

coarse focus knob

fine focus knob

arm

stage

condenser focus knob

O = objective lens
E = eyepiece lens

eye

Figure 2.5 (a) A typical compound light microscope (b) Pathway of light rays in image formation

the other of ×40. The lower magnification objective lens is used for low-power observations, whereas the higher magnification enables cellular details to be observed. The total magnification achieved by such microscopes can be calculated by multiplying the magnifying power of the lenses used.

For example:

> **for low power observations,**
> eyepiece × objective $\quad$ = 10 × 10
> $\qquad\qquad\qquad\qquad\quad$ = 100

> **for high power observations,**
> eyepiece × objective $\quad$ = 10 × 40
> $\qquad\qquad\qquad\qquad\quad$ = 400

Although it is important for the student to appreciate the magnifying power available when using a compound microscope, it is often necessary to make accurate measurements of specimens. In order to do this, an eyepiece micrometer (graticule) is placed inside the eyepiece. This micrometer consists of a very fine scale and needs to be calibrated using a stage micrometer, which is another scale etched on to a microscope slide. Details of how the eyepiece micrometer is calibrated and used are given later in this chapter.

Whilst many modern compound microscopes have a built-in light source, the type illustrated here does not. This microscope has a mirror with a condenser and light from an external source is directed through the condenser and brought into focus on the specimen, situated on the stage.

Using a compound microscope

Before using a microscope to view a prepared specimen on a slide, it is necessary to adjust the mirror and the condenser so that the field of view through the instrument is brightly and evenly illuminated. It is possible to use natural daylight by placing the microscope near a window, taking care not to focus sunlight directly. It is more usual to use a separate lamp arranged so that the light falls on to the mirror. In order to achieve suitable illumination, the following steps should be followed:

- Swivel the low power objective of the microscope into the correct position for viewing by rotating the nosepiece in a clockwise direction. When the objective is correctly aligned with respect to the body tube, a slight 'click' is heard.
- Place a prepared slide on the stage of the microscope so that the specimen is immediately below the objective lens.
- Using the coarse focus adjustment knob, carefully move the objective lens so that it is about 13 mm above the surface of the slide, bringing the specimen into focus.
- Adjust the lamp and the mirror so that light shines up through the tube of the microscope and the field of view is evenly illuminated.
- Move the condenser focus knob, bringing the condenser close to the stage and then adjust until an image of the lamp can just be seen in focus.
- The brightness of the field of view can be adjusted by opening or closing the iris diaphragm situated just below the condenser.

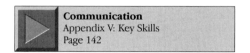

Communication
Appendix V: Key Skills
Page 142

Use of the coarse focus adjustment knob enables the specimen to be brought into focus at low power. To use the high power objective, the nosepiece should be rotated in a clockwise direction until the high power objective clicks into place directly above the specimen. At this point, it should only be necessary to use the fine adjustment (fine focus knob) in order to see the specimen clearly. Care should be taken when focusing using the high power objective, as any major downwards movement of the objective could break the slide and damage the lens. When viewing is finished, it is good practice to return to the low power objective before removing the slide from the stage of the microscope.

The highest resolution that can be achieved using a compound microscope necessitates the use of an **oil immersion objective lens**. When normal objective lenses are used, there is air between the front of the lens and the thin piece of glass (coverslip) covering the specimen on the slide, resulting in some light being reflected off the surface of the lens. When an oil immersion lens is used, a small drop of immersion oil is placed on the coverslip and the objective is carefully lowered towards the slide until contact is made with the oil. The fine focusing knob can then be used to gain a clear image of the specimen. The immersion oil has a refractive index close to that of the glass, so there is less loss of light from reflection and a reduction in the refraction of the light. In other words, more of the available light passes into the objective lens. When viewed with an oil immersion lens, there is increased resolution, the brightness of the image is increased and more detail can be seen. After use, both the lens and the slide should be cleaned carefully using lens tissue.

When using microscopes in the laboratory, there are several precautions which need to be taken to prevent damage to the instrument and to the lenses:

- use only clean slides
- keep lenses clean using special lens cleaning tissues
- avoid spillage of liquids and chemicals as the stage and the lenses should be kept dry
- support the microscope underneath when lifting or carrying it
- observe specimens under low power first, before switching to high power
- change objectives by moving the nosepiece always in a clockwise direction.

Mounting specimens for viewing

As is apparent from the description of the lens systems of the compound microscope, light must usually pass through the object being viewed in order for detail to be observed. Such microscopes are best suited to making observations on small, more or less transparent organisms or thin sections (slices) of plant and animal tissues.

All specimens should be mounted on glass microscope slides and covered with a thin piece of glass called a coverslip. Temporary mounts can be made of fresh material, but if it is desirable to keep the preparations for any length of time, it is necessary for the specimens to be specially treated and permanently mounted. All students should be familiar with the technique of making a temporary mount, but the preparation of permanent mounts is time-consuming and not relevant to A level studies, although it is of interest to appreciate how care is taken to preserve the material in as life-like a state as is possible.

Making a temporary wet mount is a simple procedure, involving the following steps:

- Using a clean, grease-free glass microscope slide, place the specimen in the centre.
- Cover the specimen with a small drop of water, or other suitable mountant, using a teat pipette.
- Using the thumb and forefinger of the left hand, hold a clean coverslip so that its bottom edge just comes into contact with the left-hand side of the drop on the microscope slide. The coverslip needs to be held at an angle of between 45 and 60°.
- Supporting the coverslip at its upper edge with a mounted needle held in the right hand, gently lower it on to the drop containing the specimen.

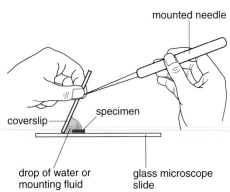

mounted needle

coverslip — specimen

drop of water or mounting fluid

glass microscope slide

Figure 2.6 Making a temporary wet mount

This method should avoid the inclusion of any air bubbles in the mount and excess fluid can be removed using a tissue or filter paper.

Description of the procedure has been given for a right-handed person: it may be easier for a left-handed person to hold the coverslip in the right hand and the mounted needle in the left.

Sometimes it is desirable to stain a specimen in order to show up particular tissues or cell components. For example, the dye, cotton blue in lactophenol, is used to show up the cytoplasm in fungal hyphae, and phloroglucinol in hydrochloric acid stains lignified cell walls red. Most chemicals used for staining have harmful effects on living tissues, so should be used with care.

If the specimen has already been mounted, a drop of the appropriate stain can be placed at one side of the coverslip and drawn through by means of a piece of filter paper or a tissue placed at the opposite side. Once the stain has permeated the specimen, a drop of water can be drawn through in a similar manner to remove excess stain, leaving the mounting liquid clear and thus making the stained parts more easily distinguishable.

Some whole organisms, such as *Daphnia*, are more easily mounted in cavity slides or ring mounts, particularly if observations are to be made on their movements under different conditions.

When permanent preparations of plant and animal tissues are made, care is taken to keep the material as life-like as possible and to avoid the introduction of any artefacts. It is often necessary to use chemicals, such as ethanol, to penetrate the material quickly and preserve, or 'fix', it so that structures are prevented from deteriorating. The material is then dehydrated and embedded in paraffin wax or epoxy resin so that very thin sections can be cut using a sharp, mounted blade called a microtome. Such sections can then be stained and mounted on microscope slides. In permanent preparations, the sections are either mounted in a clear, natural resin, such as Canada balsam, or in synthetic resins, before being covered with a coverslip. The synthetic resins have the advantage of drying more quickly and do not discolour with age. Permanent slides produced in this way are protected and can be kept indefinitely without deteriorating.

Other types of compound light microscope

Binocular microscopes have two eyepiece lenses for convenience of viewing. For correct use of such microscopes, the distance between the two eyepieces should be adjusted to the interpupillary distance of the person viewing the specimen. The interpupillary distance of an individual is the distance between the pupil of the right eye and the pupil of the left eye when looking at a fixed distant point. When the eyepieces are correctly aligned, a single circular field of vision should be seen on looking down the microscope.

A **stereoscopic** microscope is a type of binocular microscope consisting of two separate lens systems, including eyepiece and objective, one for each eye. Each lens system is inclined so that the

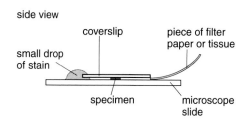

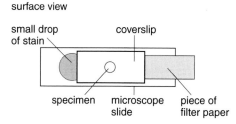

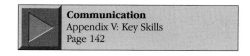

Figure 2.7 *Irrigation method of staining a temporary mount*

Communication
Appendix V: Key Skills
Page 142

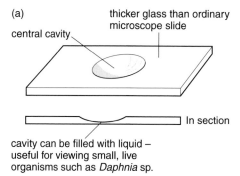

cavity can be filled with liquid – useful for viewing small, live organisms such as *Daphnia* sp.

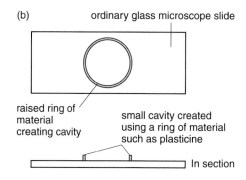

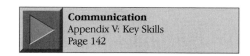

Figure 2.8 *(a) Cavity slide (b) Ring mount*

Communication
Appendix V: Key Skills
Page 142

image observed by each eye differs in the same way as normal vision does. Such microscopes, often used as dissecting microscopes, produce a three-dimensional view of specimens and are used to view larger objects not suitable for viewing with a monocular compound microscope. Typically, these microscopes allow magnifications of ×5 to ×100.

Dark field illumination is achieved by allowing light to fall on to the specimen from above at an angle. Light is prevented from passing directly through the specimen from the condenser. Structures on the specimen which reflect the light appear bright when viewed through the lens system of the microscope. Such illumination is useful for observing fine structures, such as flagella in protoctists, and when using very thin, almost transparent sections of material. Dark field illumination can be arranged quite simply by closing the iris diaphragm of the condenser on a compound microscope and using a bench lamp to illuminate the specimen from above.

Polarised and ultraviolet light sources can also be used in conjunction with the compound microscope. **Polarising microscopes** use polarised light and produce image contrast in structures such as starch grains, the cytoskeleton and spindle fibres in dividing cells, by virtue of the effect they have on the state of polarisation of the transmitted light. In **fluorescence microscopy**, the sample is illuminated with ultraviolet light. Some naturally occurring substances, such as chlorophyll, and other samples, such as cell organelles that have been stained with fluorescent dyes, will emit visible light under UV illumination and then show up as contrasting regions in the image. Both UV and fluorescence microscopy require special light sources and filters must be used to protect the eyes of the observer.

Phase-contrast microscopy gives a better image of the interior of transparent specimens than that achieved by dark field illumination. The microscope is fitted with a phase-contrast condenser containing a special glass plate, which allows only a circle of light to pass through it. There is another glass plate, called the phase plate, in the objective lens. This is a clear glass plate which has a ring-shaped slot cut into it.

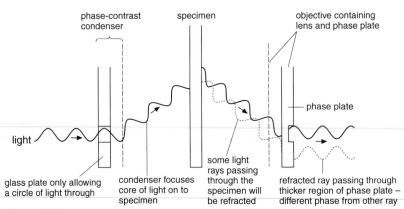

Figure 2.9 Phase-contrast microscopy

When there is no specimen on the microscope stage, light passes through the condenser and directly through the thinner part of the phase plate. If there is a specimen on the stage, some of the light rays will be refracted (their direction changed) and their phase changed. These rays will pass through a thicker region of the phase plate, increasing the contrast.

Electron microscopes

Electron microscopes use beams of electrons instead of light. A beam of electrons is produced by an electron gun consisting of:
- a tungsten filament
- a negative cathode shield
- a positively charged anode plate with a hole in the centre.

The tungsten filament is heated to a temperature above 3000 °C and this emits negatively charged electrons. Voltages of between 50 and 100 kV can be applied, causing the electrons to pass through the hole in the anode plate and then down the microscope. The density of this beam of electrons is increased by the cathode shield, which is situated between the filament and the anode plate. As the voltage in the electron gun is increased, the wavelength of the electrons is reduced and the resolution of the microscope is improved. The beam of electrons is focused on the specimen by electromagnets which form the condenser lenses.

In the **transmission electron microscope (TEM)**, the specimens are either smears or very thin sections (0.05 to 0.1 μm thick), mounted on copper grids. In order to make the features of such specimens visible, they have to be prepared by:
- fixing and dehydration in a manner similar to that used for making permanent preparations in light microscopy
- embedding in resin which is then hardened by baking
- sectioning using an ultramicrotome and a glass knife
- mounting on to a copper grid
- staining using heavy metal stains.

The fixing and staining chemicals used become attached to structures and chemicals in the cells of the material, causing the electrons in the beam to be scattered or blocked, giving rise to dark, or dense areas when the specimen is viewed on the screen.

The screen, viewed through a window at the bottom of the microscope tube, is fluorescent, giving a greenish-grey image which can be observed using low-power binoculars. Electron micrographs are prepared by focusing the image by adjustment of the electromagnetic lenses and allowing the beam of electrons to fall on to photographic plates, which can be developed and printed. The dark areas represent regions of the specimen which have taken up the heavy metal stains, thus preventing the electrons from passing through. Light areas indicate regions of the specimen through which the electrons are able to pass.

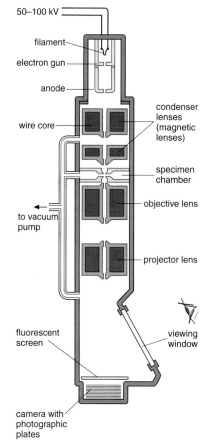

Figure 2.10 Section through a transmission electron microscope (TEM)

MICROSCOPY AND OBSERVATION

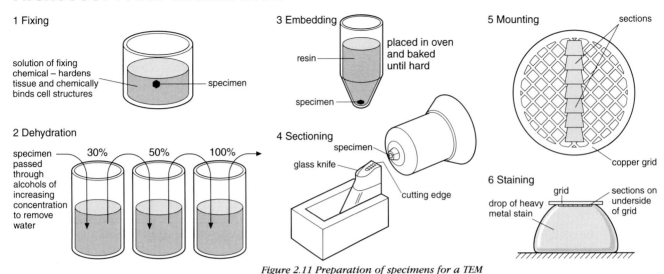

Figure 2.11 Preparation of specimens for a TEM

1 Fixing

solution of fixing chemical – hardens tissue and chemically binds cell structures — specimen

2 Dehydration

specimen passed through alcohols of increasing concentration to remove water — 30% 50% 100%

3 Embedding

resin — placed in oven and baked until hard

specimen

4 Sectioning

specimen

glass knife

cutting edge

5 Mounting

sections

copper grid

6 Staining

drop of heavy metal stain — grid — sections on underside of grid

---

Communication
Appendix V: Key Skills
Page 142

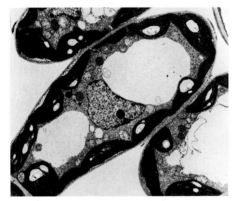

Figure 2.12 Transmission electronmicrograph of a leaf palisade cell.

Figure 2.13 A freeze-fracture transmission electronmicrograph of part of the nuclear envelope of a liver cell showing nuclear pores (×23200)

The technique of **freeze-fracturing**, or **freeze-etching**, eliminates the need for chemical fixation and embedding of specimens. In the preparation of specimens using this technique, the biological material is:

- frozen in liquid nitrogen at a temperature of –210 °C and mounted in a vacuum chamber
- fractured along a line of weakness, often the cell membranes, using a razor blade
- evaporated to remove the ice at the exposed surface (etched).

A layer of carbon is then deposited on the surface, forming a replica, which is then shadowed using heavy metals. The specimen is thawed and the replica floated off and mounted for examination. This technique is used in the preparation of specimens viewed using a scanning electron microscope.

Image formation using a **scanning electron microscope (SEM)** is achieved in a different way from that in the transmission electron microscope. Specimens, which are not usually sectioned, are placed in the microscope at an angle to a fine beam of primary electrons, generated from an electron gun and focused by electromagnetic lenses. The primary beam is scanned stepwise across the specimen, interacting with it at each point in the area covered. When the primary electrons collide with the specimen, secondary electrons, together with X-rays and light, are emitted. The secondary electrons are attracted to a positively charged collector, which accelerates them, producing light in a scintillator and then an electric current by means of a photomultiplier. The electric current is used to alter the intensity of a cathode-ray beam, in correspondence with each point on the sample. An image is built up on a fluorescent screen, in much the same way as the picture is built up in a television set. The brightest parts of the image will correspond to those parts of the specimen which produce most secondary electrons. The images appear to be three-dimensional as all parts are in focus.

The SEM is simpler to use than the TEM because the preparation of the specimens is less complicated. However, each sample is usually coated with a thin layer of gold, which is necessary to prevent it charging up electrically under the primary electron beam, thus spoiling the image. Some biological material, such as organisms with rigid exoskeletons, shells and pollen grains, do not need to be treated chemically, and the technique of freeze-etching can be used on more delicate material. A wide range of magnification, from ×10 to ×10 000, is possible, but the level of resolution is not as high as can be achieved with the TEM. The resolving power is determined mainly by the cross-section of the primary electron beam.

Biological drawings

The purpose of a biological drawing is to make an accurate record of the observed features of a specimen – simple line drawings can often show structures more clearly than photographs. The ability to make good drawings requires certain skills which can be acquired with patience and practice. The most informative drawings are not necessarily the most 'artistic', and it is customary to avoid shading, as this can often obscure the scientific detail.

It is relevant to attempt to distinguish between a diagram and a drawing, although there are situations in which the distinction may not be clear. A **drawing** is an accurate record of your observations of a particular biological specimen. When making your drawing, you should only draw those features which can be seen clearly. You should not include any features which you might expect to see or that you think ought to be there. A **diagram** is a more stylised representation of a structure and usually includes all the essential features known to be associated with the specimen, whether visible or not.

In order to illustrate and clarify the distinction between drawings and diagrams, we can compare the drawing of a transverse section (TS) through a leaf with a diagram of the same structure (Figure 2.15). Several obvious differences should be apparent. On the diagram, the structure is shown to be symmetrical, that is both halves either side of the midrib are identical. The same number of veins of the same size are shown, at the same positions along the lamina, and there is an even distribution of stomata along the lower epidermis. The cuticle, upper epidermis and lower epidermis are shown as layers of even width, although it is customary to draw them in correct proportion to the thickness of the other layers – the palisade and the spongy mesophyll. In the drawing, made from observations of a particular leaf section, the distribution of veins would be more random, as would the distribution of the stomata. Some of the veins might show the vascular tissue in longitudinal, as well as transverse, section, depending on how and where the leaf had been sectioned in the preparation of the slide.

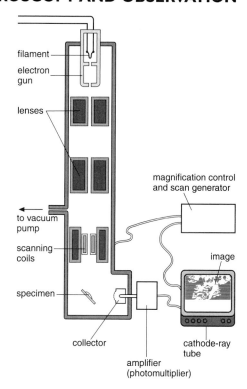

Communication
Appendix V: Key Skills
Page 142

*Figure 2.14 (a) Section through a scanning electron microscope (SEM) (b) SEM micrograph. A Scanning electronmicrograph of a grain of pollen from the Hollyhock (*Althaea rosa*). Magnification ×202*

(a)

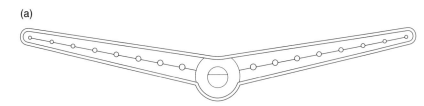

(b)

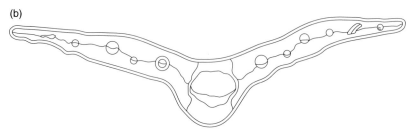

Figure 2.15 (a) Diagram and (b) biological drawing of a transverse section (TS) through a dicotyledonous leaf

All biological drawings and diagrams should:
- be of an appropriate size so that essential features can be seen clearly
- have the correct proportions, e.g. size of appendages in relation to body size in arthropods, correct relative widths of tissues in sections of plant organs and cell wall thicknesses in relation to the size of the lumen in drawings of lignified plant cells
- have clear outlines drawn with a sharp pencil (usually HB to 2H)
- have a title which includes all the relevant information
- have the essential features labelled clearly and accurately, using straight, ruled labelling lines which do not cross each other
- have a scale to give some indication of the actual size of the original specimen.

Most drawings and diagrams that form part of A level coursework are better drawn in pencil. Any mistakes can be rectified easily using an eraser. It is also better to use pencil for labels and labelling lines for the same reason. Labels should be neat and legible.

In many cases, it is desirable to annotate diagrams and drawings. **Annotations** are short, explanatory comments on the biological significance or functions of structures, written alongside or immediately beneath the labels. Care should be taken to ensure that such comments are *brief*, so that drawings are not obscured by mini-essays written alongside each label. Reference to Figure 2.17 gives some indication of the level of annotation appropriate to the leaf sections shown.

When drawing whole, large organisms or structures, without using a microscope, it is customary to indicate the scale in terms of magnification. A drawing of a section through an onion bulb, for example, could be the same size as the original (×1), half the original

MICROSCOPY AND OBSERVATION

size ($\times\frac{1}{2}$) or twice the original size ($\times2$). Reference to scales and magnification for microscope drawings is made in the next section of this chapter.

Microscope drawings

When making microscope drawings, it is convenient to place the drawing paper to the right of the microscope if you are right-handed. Keeping both eyes open, it should be possible, with practice, to see both the specimen and the drawing paper at the same time. The specimen is viewed using the left eye and the right eye can see the drawing paper. Even if you find this difficult, the positions of the paper and the microscope ensure that only small movements of the head are necessary when making observations and drawing. If you are left-handed, then it may be more convenient to place the drawing paper to the left of the microscope and use the right eye for making the observations.

The size of a specimen or structure drawn from microscope observations is measured using an **eyepiece graticule**. This graticule consists of a glass disc with a scale etched on to it. The scale is usually 10 mm long divided into 100 divisions. The glass disc is inserted into the eyepiece of the microscope, so that when a specimen is observed, the graticule is seen in the field of view. The eyepiece graticule can be calibrated by placing a slide with another scale etched upon it on the stage of the microscope. This slide is called a **stage micrometer** and has the length of its scale marked on it. The two scales can be aligned so that one is superimposed on the other. The total length of the eyepiece scale can be measured against the scale on the stage micrometer and the value of each small division calculated in μm. This calibration must be done separately for each objective lens on a microscope. Once an eyepiece graticule has been fitted and calibrated for use with a particular microscope, it can be left in place in the eyepiece. It is a good idea to write the values of each division for each objective on a small label which can be attached to the microscope, thus avoiding the necessity of re-calibrating the eyepiece each time it is used.

Once the eyepiece graticule has been calibrated, it is possible to measure a particular feature of the specimen being observed, such as the width of a vascular bundle or the diameter of a nucleus. A small scale bar can then be added to the drawing, indicating the actual size of the specimen. Although it is helpful to indicate the magnification achieved by the microscope lenses, this will not give an accurate indication of the true size of the specimen, so it is essential that the scale is included.

You may be required to produce both low- and high-power microscope drawings as part of your teacher-assessed coursework. Low-power drawings are usually made using the ×10 objective lens and such drawings should show the distribution of tissues only. They are

(a)

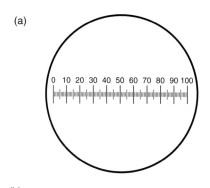

(b)

eyepiece
graticule scale

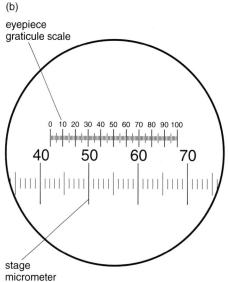

stage
micrometer

Figure 2.16 (a) Eyepiece graticule
(b) Calibration

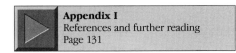

Appendix I
References and further reading
Page 131

not expected to include details of cells or cell structure. Suitable tissues for such low-power plans include transverse sections through plant organs (leaves, stems, roots) and animal organs (ileum, artery, vein). High-power drawings are made using the ×40 objective lens and should consist of only a small number of cells. The cells should be of a reasonable size and show such internal structures as can be seen. Plant cells are more suitable for such drawings as they have rigid cell walls and their outlines are more readily distinguishable than those of most animal cells. In such high-power drawings, it is important to get the proportions right and only to draw what can be observed. Suitable material for such drawings includes palisade, mesophyll or epidermal cells, vascular tissues, stomata from plant tissues, stages in mitosis and meiosis and columnar epithelia from the ileum.

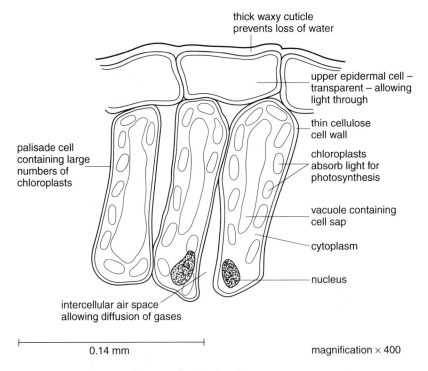

Figure 2.17 High-power drawing of palisade cells

Communication
Appendix V: Key Skills
Page 142

3 Presentation: using data and writing up

The results of any biological experiment should be recorded as the investigation is taking place (the raw data) and then presented in a suitable format that can be understood and used to support the hypothesis being tested. In this chapter, we look at the different ways in which data can be presented within the context of reports of laboratory and fieldwork investigations. In addition, it is relevant to understand how the reports of longer experiments, individual studies and projects may differ from that of a straightforward laboratory investigation. The criteria for such reports are set out in your syllabus and you should be familiar with the quantity and extent of the investigations you need to submit as part of your teacher-assessed coursework.

Laboratory investigations

Written reports of laboratory investigations usually consist of:
- a **title**, setting out the purpose of the investigation or stating the **hypothesis** under investigation
- a description of the **method** used
- a record of the **results**, which should include the raw data (the original observations, readings or measurements made), together with graphs or other means of showing the trends and patterns
- the **conclusions**, summarising the results, identifying trends and patterns, evaluating the experiment, including accounting for anomalies and errors, and commenting on the biological significance of the results.

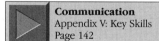

Communication
Appendix V: Key Skills
Page 142

It is customary, and often helpful, to include some background information of the biological principles involved and this can be given as an introduction to the investigation. This helps to put the investigation into its biological context and to link the practical exercise with the study of the syllabus topic. Students often find it helpful to formulate a testable hypothesis for their laboratory investigations, so such an introduction could give the opportunity to explain how the hypothesis has been derived and enable some predictions of the outcome of the investigation. For example, in all syllabuses, there is a section on the factors affecting enzyme activity, which usually follows a consideration of enzymes as organic catalysts. Practical work associated with these sections requires investigations into the effects of temperature, pH, enzyme concentration and substrate concentration on enzyme activity. From the theoretical knowledge gained from a study of these syllabus areas, it is possible to formulate an hypothesis, design an experiment and predict the outcome.

PRESENTATION: USING DATA AND WRITING UP

Let us consider the effect of temperature on the activity of the enzyme amylase in starch breakdown. We know that:

- amylase will catalyse the hydrolysis of starch to maltose
- an increase in temperature will increase the rate of an enzyme-catalysed reaction because it will increase the movement of the reacting molecules and increase the number of collisions between enzyme and substrate
- high temperatures can affect the enzyme molecules by causing a distortion of the active site.

This knowledge, together with a suitable test to detect the presence of starch, enables us to suggest an hypothesis and design the experiment. We can select a range of temperatures, suitable quantities of enzyme and substrate and the means whereby we can determine whether the starch has been hydrolysed. Thus it can be seen that there is a close association between the practical investigation and the theoretical study of the topic.

Although accounts of **methods** do not always contribute to the marks awarded for the teacher-assessed coursework, it is good practice to write your own account of any investigation you carry out. It helps to clarify the experimental procedure and to give you practice in including all the relevant details, so that when you write up methods for longer investigations and your individual study you will find it much easier to remember what needs to be included. In addition, some questions on the theory papers may require you to design an experiment or to state precautions taken when setting up apparatus. Such questions expect a detailed knowledge of experimental methods, particularly of experiments which are specified in the syllabus.

Accounts of methods are usually written in continuous prose, i.e. in complete sentences, rather than as numbered points. The instructions for laboratory experiments are usually given as numbered points or steps, but your account should be more informative, giving reasons for, or explaining special precautions you took to ensure the accuracy or reliability of your measurements. It is also customary to use the past tense, for example 'Ten leaves were taken and measured .....', rather than instructions such as 'Take ten leaves and measure ....'. Opinions vary as to whether it is good practice to use 'We took ten leaves ....' or 'I took ten leaves ....'. In class experiments, the former is perfectly acceptable: it can then be made clear if you were individually responsible for part of the procedure. The use of 'we' in the report of an individual study is not acceptable, for obvious reasons!

All quantities used and measurements taken should be clearly stated, using the appropriate SI units. The use of 'about' should be avoided, as in 'We took about 5 g of liver tissue ...'. If the quantity of liver tissue needs to be weighed accurately, then this should be stated, but if the mass is not critical, perhaps the term 'approximately' should be used instead of 'about'. Similarly, it is important to avoid the use of 'amount'. 'We used the same amount of amylase each time' does not indicate whether mass or volume was used.

It is important to explain the reasons for certain experimental procedures. If the instructions for the experiment require the test tubes to be kept covered or to be shaken gently, then it is of interest, and often important, to know why. Statements such as 'The test tubes were kept covered to exclude the air' and 'The tubes were shaken gently to mix the contents thoroughly' help to make the procedure clear and contribute to the accuracy and reliability.

In most biological experiments, it is customary and desirable that there should be some kind of control. For example, in certain enzyme experiments it is usual to include one set of apparatus without the enzyme or to use boiled (denatured) enzyme. In this way, the results of the experiment can be attributed to the effect of the enzyme and not to any other factor. The use of controls in any experiment should always be described and explained in the account of the method.

All **results**, including original observations and readings, should be recorded as accurately as possible. Quantities such as volumes and times need to be stated precisely and the appropriate SI units used. The most convenient way of recording results is in the form of a table, where the headings for each of the columns should indicate what observations or measurements have been made and the nature of the units used. It should be possible to determine exactly how the experiment has been carried out from the information given in the headings of a table of results. It is worth emphasising that where an account of the methods used has not been included in a piece of teacher-assessed coursework, the headings on the results table are the only indication of what measurements or observations have been made.

It is desirable to give some thought to the arrangement of the data in tables, so that the results are clear to an observer and so that the data are conveniently organised for subsequent graph plotting. If several repeat readings have been taken, these should be recorded, together with a calculation of the mean value. Where possible, one table should include all the relevant information. Some advice on the recording of results and the construction of a table is given in the practical on the investigation of the activity of rennin in Chapter 1 page 10.

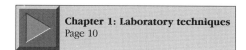

Chapter 1: Laboratory techniques
Page 10

The majority of the laboratory investigations generate quantitative data (numerical results) which can be plotted as a graph, histogram or bar chart, so that the trends or patterns in the data show up clearly. The nature of the data collected governs the choice of graph by which it can be displayed. It is not always relevant or desirable to draw a line graph and Table 3.1 over the page summarises the main methods used to display the results of experiments.

Communication
Appendix V: Key Skills
Page 142

Application of Number
Appendix V: Key Skills
Page 142

Temperature /°C	Time taken for disappearance of starch (mins)				Rate of reaction ($\frac{1}{t} \times 100$)
	1st reading	2nd reading	3rd reading	Mean	
5	40.5	50	51.5	47.3	2.11
15	20	25	26	23.6˙	4.23
25	10.5	14	13.5	12.6˙	7.90
35	5	7	6.5	6.16	16.22
45	2	3.5	4.5	3.33˙	30.03
55	10.5	14.0	15.5	13.33˙	7.50
*100	blue–black colour remains	blue–black colour remains	blue–black colour remains	/	/

A test tube containing 10 cm³ of 0.5% amylase solution mixed with 10 cm³ of 1% starch solution was incubated at each temperature and tested at 30 second intervals for the presence of starch using iodine solution.
The time taken for the blue-black colour of the starch–iodine complex to disappear was recorded.

*The control experiment: the enzyme will be denatured at this temperature.

Figure 3.1 A typical results table

Table 3.1 *Main methods of displaying experimental results*

Communication
Appendix V: Key Skills
Page 142

Type of display	Description of use
line graph	used when the relationship between two variables can be represented as a continuum, e.g. the effect of temperature on the activity of amylase (illustrated in Figure 3.4)
bar chart	shows the frequency distributions of a discrete variable, e.g. energy conversion in domesticated animals (Figure 3.2a)
histogram	shows the frequency distribution of continuous variables, e.g. individual milk yield per cow (Figure 3.2b)
scattergraph	used to show the relationship between individual data values for two interdependent variables, e.g. intake of sodium and systolic blood pressure (Figure 3.2c)
pie chart	illustrates the data as portions of a whole, e.g. composition of a soil sample (Figure 3.2d)
pictograph	pictorial representation of data, e.g. zonation of brown seaweeds on a rocky shore (Figure 3.2e)

(a) Energy conversion in domesticated animals

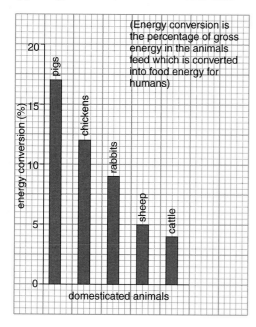

(Energy conversion is the percentage of gross energy in the animals feed which is converted into food energy for humans)

(b) Frequency distribution of individual milk yield per cow in dm³

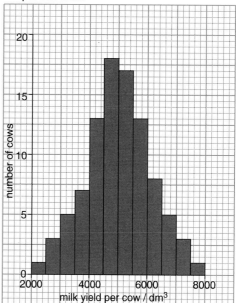

(c) Intake of sodium and systolic blood pressure in developed and developing countries

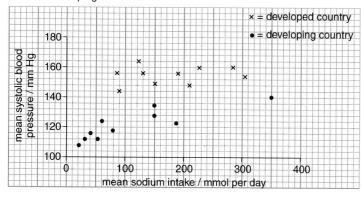

Communication
Appendix V: Key Skills
Page 142

(e) Zonation of brown seaweeds on a rocky shore

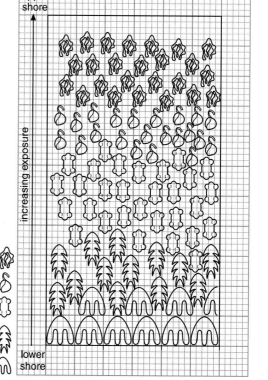

(d) To show composition of a soil sample

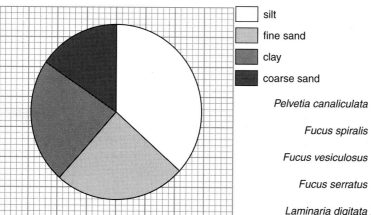

Pelvetia canaliculata

Fucus spiralis

Fucus vesiculosus

Fucus serratus

Laminaria digitata

Figure 3.2 Different ways of displaying experimental results (a) bar chart (b) histogram (c) scattergraph (d) pie chart (e) pictograph

Application of Number
Appendix V: Key Skills
Page 142

PRESENTATION: USING DATA AND WRITING UP

Any graphs, bar charts or histograms are best plotted on graph, or squared, paper and each should have:

- a title explaining the content
- correctly orientated axes, i.e. the axes the right way round
- correctly labelled axes with appropriate SI units
- a suitable numbered scale on each axis
- a key to identify the curves if more than one set of data are plotted.

In most experiments, where one variable is determined by the other, the horizontal x axis (abscissa) is usually used for the independent variable (e.g. the treatment, such as temperature, light intensity, pH) and the vertical y axis (ordinate) for the dependent variable (e.g. the response). Where neither variable is determined by the other or where the variables are interdependent, the axes may be orientated either way round.

Scales should be chosen so that:

- the graph fits on to the paper and is large enough to be seen easily
- all the relevant points can be plotted accurately
- the points are easily read and intermediate values can be determined if necessary.

The points should be plotted accurately using a × or •, surrounded by a hollow symbol such as ○ or △. All lines are best drawn in pencil, so that errors can be remedied. The line on a graph is referred to as a curve, whether it is straight or not. It should either be a smooth curve or a series of straight, ruled lines joining successive points. When the points are joined by straight lines, this indicates that it is not known how the values between the recorded points could vary. It is usual to draw smooth curves if there is good reason to believe that intermediate values would fall on a curve. If there is any doubt about whether to draw a series of straight lines or a smooth curve, then the former should be chosen. In theory papers, where students are required to plot a given set of data, it is expected that successive points are joined by straight, ruled lines.

Where the mean of several replicates is used, it is possible to calculate the standard error for each mean value. This can be shown on the graph as a vertical bar for each value and could be appropriate where class results have been pooled.

Extrapolation, or extension, of the curve beyond the range of your observations is usually unwise and can not often be justified. When plotting and drawing curves from data supplied, only those values given should be plotted as points. Students often make the error of extrapolating curves to 0, especially if the data relates to time or temperature.

In the experiment being considered earlier (the effect of temperature on the activity of amylase), it is possible to time the disappearance of

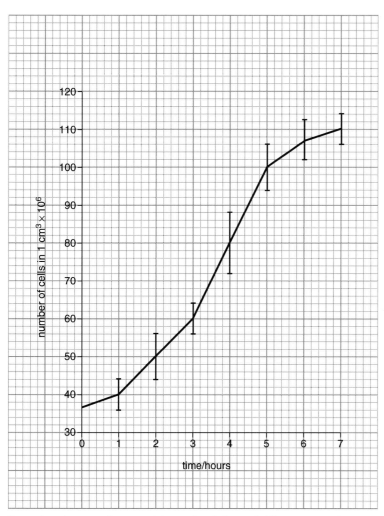

Several random samples were taken at hourly intervals. The means and standard deviation for each sample were calculated and from these data the standard error (or standard deviation from the mean) was calculated. The vertical bars represent 95 per cent confidence limits.

Figure 3.3 Growth curve for a yeast culture where standard error has been calculated and confidence limits shown by vertical bars at each plotted value

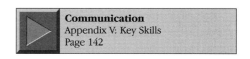

Communication
Appendix V: Key Skills
Page 142

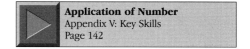

Application of Number
Appendix V: Key Skills
Page 142

starch, from mixtures of starch and amylase, at the different temperatures chosen. The results table (Figure 3.1) includes the temperatures used and the time for the disappearance of the starch, together with the results of the control used. If the readings had been repeated at the different temperatures, these should be recorded and a mean time calculated. The most suitable way of showing the trend in this case, is by means of a line graph. The temperature is the independent variable and should be on the x axis, with the times on the y axis. Depending on the temperatures chosen, the graph will resemble that shown in Figure 3.4(a). It is possible to see that as the temperature is increased, so the time taken for the starch to disappear decreases, i.e. the activity of the enzyme increases, up to a certain temperature. After that, the time increases until there is no longer any breakdown of the starch. It is possible to use the data collected to work out the rate of reaction ($1/t$, where t is the time taken for the disappearance of the starch at a given temperature) and then to plot rate of reaction against temperature, as shown in Figure 3.4(b). The second graph expresses the results in a different way and enables the conclusions to be expressed more generally in terms of rate of reaction. Visually, the trends are more obvious; it is easier to comment on the optimum temperature for the reaction and the results of this experiment can be directly compared with rates of reaction under other conditions, such as differences in pH or enzyme concentration. Often, a little thought given to the presentation of the data, perhaps involving a simple calculation, results in a more appropriate representation of the results.

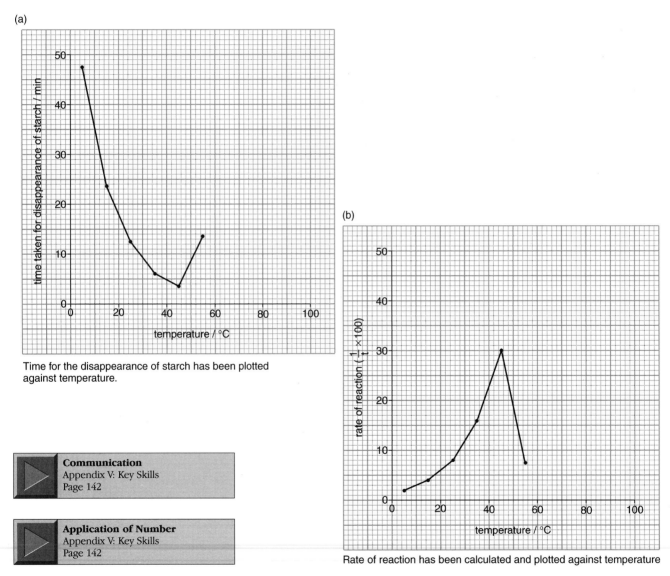

(a)

Time for the disappearance of starch has been plotted against temperature.

(b)

Rate of reaction has been calculated and plotted against temperature

Communication
Appendix V: Key Skills
Page 142

Application of Number
Appendix V: Key Skills
Page 142

Figure 3.4 Graphs showing (a) effect of temperature on the breakdown of starch by amylase and (b) how the rate of reaction of amylase varies with temperature

Bar charts are used when one of the variables is not numerical. In a determination of the vitamin C content of different foods, we would construct blocks for each food on the x axis, leaving a space between each block in a similar manner to that shown in Figure 3.2(a). The blocks can be arranged in any order, but usually the food with the highest content is placed at the left hand side, nearest the y axis. In histograms, drawn when plotting frequency distributions with continuous data, the blocks should touch (Figure 3.2(b)).

Pie charts are normally drawn with the sectors in rank order (the largest first), starting at 12 o'clock and proceeding in a clockwise direction. If a comparison between two pie charts is made, then the same sequence is used for the second pie chart as was used for the first. The area of each pie chart can be made proportional to the size of each sample (Figure 3.3).

Laboratory investigations need **conclusions**, which should include:
- a short description of the trends and patterns shown by the results
- an awareness of the limitations of the methods used
- an indication of whether or not the original hypothesis was accepted, justified by the results
- some consideration of the biological significance of the results.

The description of the trends and patterns shown by the results does not need to include reference to every measurement or observation. It should be a summary. If there are strange results that do not fit into the general pattern (anomalous), then it is reasonable to try to account for these or at least draw attention to them. In many cases, these odd results could be attributed to limitations of the technique used.

When it comes to discussing limitations of the methods used, it is easy to blame poor apparatus ('With better apparatus . . . . .') or shortage of time ('If I had had more time, I would have repeated the experiment/taken more readings . . . . .'). It is unwise to dwell on such things, which are either beyond your control or which should have been taken into account when planning the experiment in the first place. Limitations such as difficulty in detecting colour changes, measuring volumes accurately, or detecting end points may have had an effect on the accuracy or reliability of results and are worthy of comment. It would be relevant, where there was difficulty in detecting a colour change, to suggest that the use of a colorimeter could have been a more accurate technique.

The investigation should be put into its biological context by giving consideration to the biological significance of the results. It is not difficult, in the case of the effect of temperature on the rate of enzyme activity, to explain that higher temperatures increase the kinetic energy of the enzyme and substrate molecules, resulting in a greater number of collisions and thus a faster rate of reaction. It is relevant to bring in a discussion of the Q_{10} effect over a certain range of temperatures and then to relate the decrease in rate to the nature of protein molecules and their denaturation at high temperatures. Some discussion of the effect of temperature on the rate of enzyme reactions in different organisms could also be relevant. For all investigations, it should be possible to show that the results have some biological significance. Even if some of the biological background and significance of the investigation has been given in an introduction, it should be repeated here in the conclusion to reinforce the results.

Sometimes it is relevant to suggest further investigations or possible extension of the investigation carried out. For example, if a wide range of temperatures or pH values had been chosen for the original investigation, repeating the experiments using a narrower range or testing at more frequent intervals could be of value, particularly if an optimum temperature or pH value was sought.

Longer investigations, individual studies and projects

In teacher-assessed coursework, there are marks awarded for **planning** in both longer investigations and individual studies or projects. It is usually expected that a written plan is prepared by the student and submitted to the teacher or supervisor for approval. It should also be submitted with the completed investigation. The plan should include:
- a clearly stated, testable hypothesis which has been formulated by the student
- an indication that the student has some knowledge and understanding of the biological principles involved
- an understanding of the variables involved and reasoned decisions about which variables should be controlled
- a description of how control of the chosen variables is to be achieved
- the basic steps of the method
- an indication of the techniques to be used, e.g. methods of sampling
- a list of the apparatus and materials needed.

The plan is not a substitute for an account of the methods used and should not be written as though it has been carried out, i.e. the past tense should not be used.

The methods' accounts should be similar in format to that already described for laboratory investigations. Depending on the nature of the investigation, it is often desirable to carry out a 'pilot' study to try out the experiment on a small scale, before attempting the main experiments. In the light of the results from such a study, it may be necessary to make some modifications or alterations to the original procedure outlined in the plan. Any such modifications need to be described and reasons for the changes explained in the method. Diagrams of apparatus are useful and often help to clarify details of the method. If special apparatus has been used, then a diagram, perhaps even a photograph, of the apparatus in use is particularly helpful.

The criteria for the results section are the same as for the laboratory investigations and have been described earlier in this chapter. In longer investigations, it is a requirement that a suitable simple statistical test is used to analyse the results obtained. The steps of the chosen test are usually shown in the results section, but the significance of the values obtained should be assessed in the discussion.

Discussions include the same criteria suggested for the conclusions of the laboratory investigations. In addition, some comment is expected on:

- the significance of the results of the statistical analysis
- the acceptance or rejection of the stated hypothesis in the light of the results or conclusions
- anomalous or unusual observations, included in an evaluation of the experimental investigation.

It may be recommended that the form of the report of an individual study or project should be similar in style to that used in papers submitted for publication in scientific journals. In such papers, it is usual to include:

- an abstract, which is a brief summary of the investigation, including reference to the hypothesis, methods, and results obtained, finishing with a summary of the conclusions
- an introduction, explaining the background to the investigation and including a statement of the hypothesis being tested
- references to previous experiments or similar investigations.

Abstracts are quite difficult to write as they need to be concise, but yet contain all the essential information about the investigation. A paper submitted to *The Journal of Biological Education* is shown in Figure 3.5 on pages 38 and 39, and includes an example of an abstract. Note the use of key words.

In the introduction, it is usual for the student to express some personal interest in the topic, as well as outlining the biological background and the hypothesis. Often, the choice of the topic is an opportunity to extend some of the laboratory investigations or field studies that have already been carried out. In addition, the studies provide opportunities for students to show initiative and originality in the design of their experiments.

It is usual to quote published references to previous work, similar experiments or techniques used, in the introduction and then to list each reference systematically at the end of the report as shown in Figure 3.5. For each reference, the author's name is given first, followed by the title of the paper or book and the date of publication.

The influence of coins on the growth of duckweed

Shogo Kawakami, Takahito Oda, and Rika Ban

The influences of a British one-pence coin and a Japanese ten-yen coin on the growth of duckweed were studied. These coins inhibited the growth of duckweed

Introduction

Copper metal has many uses today. However, copper ions are injurious to living things. For example, it is well known in Japan that copper ions inhibit the growth of plants, as has been shown at the Ashio copper mine. Furthermore, it is also well known that heavy metals, such as mercury, lead, and cadmium, can harm animals.

For the purpose of teaching science classes about the effect of metals on living things, there are few suitable ways to demonstrate this to students. So, we used a British one-pence coin and a Japanese ten-yen coin instead of copper, because they are made mainly of copper and are easily available in the UK and Japan respectively. We used duckweed as an indicator plant. Duckweed grows throughout Japan i.e. in rice fields, ponds, and slow brooks, etc. from spring to late

Abstract

It is well known that copper inhibits the growth of plants, but there are few good materials to demonstrate this fact to students. We used a British one-pence and a Japanese ten-yen coin instead of copper, because they are made mainly of copper. Duckweed serves as an indicator plant, for it could easily be collected and its frond number would increase over a short period, i.e. one or two weeks. The growth could be evaluated by counting the number of fronds. Both coins inhibited the growth of duckweed. *Spirodela* died in a solution containing a penny after 10 days' culture, and after nine days with a ten-yen coin. The growth curve of *Lemna* is very similar to *Spirodela*. From these results, the coin and duckweed investigations were considered to be suitable materials for use in environmental education.
Key words: Coin, Duckweed, Environmental education, Influence of metal ions.

autumn. Species of duckweed are equally common in Britain.

Nuffield Biology (1966) was probably the first to use duckweed (*Lemna minor*) in a biology textbook. The objective was to observe the growth of the plant, and this seems to be a pioneer investigation using *Lemna*. Miura and Hirahara (1979) and Okuma (1980) have reported that *Spirodela* and *Lemna* could be used as new science teaching materials in various ways, because duckweed is smaller than other plants, and easier to collect and use. Moreover, they have a high rate of growth and are sensitive to their environment.

Okuma (1980) proposed the *Lemna* test, by which water pollution by heavy metals can easily be measured by the growth of *Lemna*. Nasu and Kugimoto (1981) reported how *Lemna* was affected by heavy metals that were the main causes of Minamata disease (caused by mercury poisoning), and Itaiitai disease (caused by cadmium). Duckweed has been used as a teaching material for pollution in a science textbook (Toda and Iwahashi, 1992) for 5th grade students in Japanese elementary schools. It has also been used in review exercises in another textbook (Mizuno, 1992). *Lemna* is also used as an indicator of copper in a biology textbook for lower secondary school students (Toda, 1993).

As mentioned above, duckweed is widely used in environmental education as an indicator of water pollution. Since *Lemna* is smaller than other duckweeds, it is the plant most often used.

Spirodela is larger than *Lemna*, but *Spirodela* has not been studied. So, in our study, *Spirodela* was used together with *Lemna*. As coins are very popular among students, a British one-pence coin and a Japanese ten-yen coin, both consisting mainly of copper, were used to investigate the influence of metal ions on the growth of duckweed.

Communication
Appendix V: Key Skills
Page 142

Influence of coins on duckweed   Kawakami, Oda, and Ban

Materials and methods

The species used in this study were as follows:
Spirodela polyrhiza Schleiden;
Lemna paucicostata Hegelmaier.

Both species are easily collected in rice fields, reservoirs, ponds etc. throughout Japan from April to November. The frond size of *Spirodela* is about 10 mm and that of *Lemna* about 5 mm.

The solution for culturing was Murashige and Skoog (MS solution), whose components are given in table 1. Plastic containers 150 mm in diameter, and 92 mm high were used for cultivation. The volume of the solution was 400 cm³. Three kinds of culture condition (a-c) were used:

(a) MS solution, as a control;
(b) MS solution containing a British one-pence piece;
(c) MS solution containing a Japanese ten-yen piece.

The composition of the British one-pence and the Japanese ten-yen coins is given in table 2.

Three or four individual duckweed plants either *Spirodela* or *Lemna*, with a total of 10 fronds, were used for each investigation. Three containers were prepared for each cultural condition, and were left under a window-sill. The number of fronds was measured each day at 1500 h. When the amount of solution decreased, due to evaporation, distilled water was added to maintain the 400 cm³ of solution. Growth was determined by measuring the number of fronds according to Miura and Hirahara (1979). Thus, when a young frond of *Lemna* became 2 mm wide, it was counted as one increase in frond number. In *Spirodela*, a young frond of 3 mm wide was counted as one unit of growth.

Table 1   Composition of MS solution (in 1 dm³)

Chemical	Quantity in mg
NH₄NO₃	817
KNO₃	943
CaCl₂·2H₂O	218
MgSO₄·7H₂O	183
KH₂PO₄	84
H₃BO₃	3
MnSO₄·4-5H₂O	12
ZnSO₄·7H₂O	5
KI	0.4
Na₂MₙO₄·2H₂O	0.1
CuSO₄·5H₂O	0.01
CoCl₂·6H₂O	0.01
Na₂—EDTA	19
FeSO₄·7H₂O	14

Table 2   The composition of the coins

Coins	Mass in g	Copper %	Zinc %	Tin %
One-pence piece	3.55	97	2.5	0.5
Ten-yen piece	4.975	95	4	1

Note: Since the writing of this paper, the one-pence piece now comprises copper-plated steel.

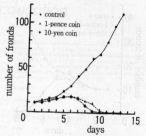

Figure 1   Change in the number of *Spirodela* over time. *Spirodela* in the control solution increased the number of fronds everyday. After 13 days, the number had reached 111. On the other hand, *Spirodela* in the solution with the penny and with the ten-yen coins slightly increased the frond number after five to six days, and then decreased in number. They had all died in the penny solution after 10 days, and in the ten-yen solution after nine days.

When more than two-thirds of a frond lost its green colour, it was considered to have died, and the number of fronds was counted as minus one. The number of fronds was determined by averaging the number of duckweed plants in each of the three containers.

The periods of cultivation for each species were as follows:
Spirodela, 13 days (from June 27th to July 9th, 1994);
Lemna, 8 days (from August 8th to 15th, 1994).

Results and discussion

The number of fronds of *Spirodela* is shown in figure 1 and that of *Lemna* in figure 2. *Spirodela* in the control solution increased its number of fronds each day. After 13 days, the number increased to 111.

On the other hand, *Spirodela* in the solution with the one-pence and ten-yen coins increased its frond number slightly for five or six days, but thereafter decreased in number. In the penny solution, the plants all died after 10 days, and in the ten-yen solution after nine days. Figure 3 shows the *Spirodela* growing vigorously in the control solution. Fronds of the *Spirodela* fully covered the surface of

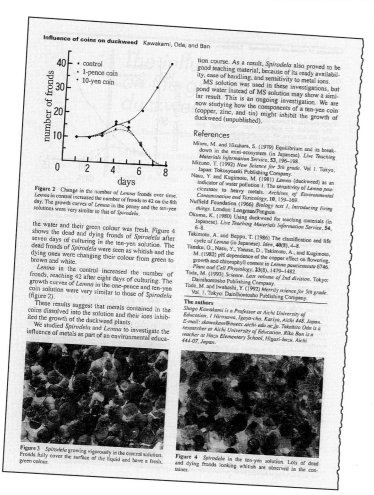

Influence of coins on duckweed Kawakami, Oda, and Ban

Figure 2 Change in the number of *Lemna* fronds over time. *Lemna* in control increased the number of fronds to 42 on the 8th day. The growth curves of *Lemna* in the penny and the ten-yen solutions were very similar to that of *Spirodela*.

the water and their green colour was fresh. Figure 4 shows the dead and dying fronds of *Spirodela* after seven days of culturing in the ten-yen solution. The dead fronds of *Spirodela* were seen as whitish and the dying ones were changing their colour from green to brown and white.

Lemna in the control increased the number of fronds, reaching 42 after eight days of culturing. The growth curves of *Lemna* in the one-pence and ten-yen coin solution were very similar to those of *Spirodela* (figure 2).

These results suggest that metals contained in the coins dissolved into the solution and their ions inhibited the growth of the duckweed plants.

We studied *Spirodela* and *Lemna* to investigate the influence of metals as part of an environmental educa-

tion course. As a result, *Spirodela* also proved to be good teaching material, because of its ready availability, ease of handling, and sensitivity to metal ions.

MS solution was used in these investigations, but pond water instead of MS solution may show a similar result. This is an ongoing investigation. We are now studying how the components of a ten-yen coin (copper, zinc, and tin) might inhibit the growth of duckweed (unpublished).

References

Miura, M. and Hirahara, S. (1979) Equilibrium and its breakdown in the mini-ecosystem (in Japanese). *Live Teaching Materials Information Service*, **53**, 196–198.

Mizuno, T. (1992) *New Science for 5th grade*. Vol 1. Tokyo, Japan: Tokosyoseki Publishing Company.

Nasu, Y. and Kugimoto, M. (1981) *Lemna* (duckweed) as an indicator of water pollution I. The sensitivity of *Lemna paucicostata* to heavy metals. *Archives of Environmental Contamination and Toxicology*, **10**, 159–169.

Nuffield Foundation (1966) *Biology text 1, Introducing living things*. London: Longman/Penguin.

Okuma, K. (1980) Using duckweed for teaching materials (in Japanese). *Live Teaching Materials Information Service*, **54**, 6–8.

Takimoto, A. and Beppu, T. (1986) The classification and life cycle of *Lemna* (in Japanese). *Iden*, **40**(8), 4–8.

Tanaku, O., Nasu, Y., Yanase, D., Takimoto, A., and Kugimoto, M. (1982) pH dependence of the copper effect on flowering, growth and chlorophyll content in *Lemna paucicostata* 6746. *Plant and Cell Physiology*, **23**(8), 1479–1482.

Toda, M. (1993) *Science. Last volume of 2nd division*. Tokyo: Dainihontosho Publishing Company.

Toda, M. and Iwahashi, Y. (1992) *Merrily science for 5th grade*. Vol 1. Tokyo: Dainihontosho Publishing Company.

The authors

Shogo Kawakami is a Professor at Aichi University of Education, 1 Hirosawa, Igaya-cho, Kariya, Aichi 448, Japan. E-mail: skawakam@auecc.aichi-edu.ac.jp. Takahito Oda is a researcher at Aichi University of Education. Rika Ban is a teacher at Hazu Elementary School, Higasi-hazu, Aichi 444-07, Japan.

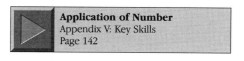

Figure 3 *Spirodela* growing vigorously in the control solution. Fronds fully cover the surface of the liquid and have a fresh, green colour.

Figure 4 *Spirodela* in the ten-yen solution. Lots of dead and dying fronds looking whitish are observed in the container.

Figure 3.5 A paper from the Journal of Biological Education

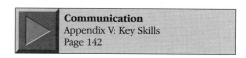

Communication
Appendix V: Key Skills
Page 142

Application of Number
Appendix V: Key Skills
Page 142

The presentation of any report, whether it is of a laboratory investigation, a longer experiment or an individual study, needs to be legible and intelligible, so care is needed with handwriting, with spelling and with grammar. Many students use word processors, which make the reports easier to read, but it is always worth carrying out a separate check on the spelling and the grammar to reduce errors. The inclusion of computer-generated graphs and diagrams in teacher-assessed coursework has increased recently and the development of students' skills in the use of computers in this way is to be encouraged. It should be pointed out, however, that some computer-generated graphs do not always include all the necessary information and students should take care to choose the most appropriate method of presenting their data. Clarity and scientific accuracy should not be sacrificed for three-dimensional columns, shading or the use of colour.

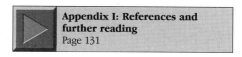

Appendix I: References and further reading
Page 131

It would be useful for students to read accounts of investigations and experiments and reference to such accounts in *School Science Review* and the *Journal of Biological Education* would be valuable.

Quantitative techniques in biology

In this chapter, we look at a number of techniques which can be used in laboratory practicals that involve making accurate measurements. The principles of these techniques can be applied to many different situations which you may encounter in, for example, individual investigations or experiments you yourself have chosen and planned. Practical details are given for cell counting, using a colorimeter and a potometer, and a bioassay technique to investigate the effect of a plant growth substance. We also outline some of the possible uses of datalogging in biological investigations, in which a computer can be used for data collection and analysis.

Counting cells using a haemocytometer

Introduction

A haemocytometer consists of a special glass slide with an accurately ruled, etched grid of precise dimensions. Originally developed for counting blood cells, hence the name, the haemocytometer can also be used for counting microorganisms in a liquid medium. It is particularly suitable for counting yeast or *Chlorella* cells, as these are readily visible and non-motile, but not suitable for bacteria. Unless special staining techniques are used, it is not possible to distinguish between living and dead cells, therefore this method of counting, known as a **direct count**, gives the total number of cells including both living (or viable) and dead (non-viable) cells. There are several different types of haemocytometers, one which is frequently used is known as the **Improved Neubauer**. This has two counting grids, each of which consists of a central area measuring 1 mm × 1 mm, divided into 25 large squares. Each large square is edged by triple-ruled lines and consists of 16 small squares. There are therefore **25 × 16 = 400 small squares** in the counting grid.

When the coverslip is correctly positioned over the counting grid, the depth of the counting chamber is 0.1 mm, and the volume over one small square is therefore $1/4000$ mm^3. In practice, we usually count the number of cells present in five large squares, that is, 80 small squares, so to calculate the total number of cells present per mm^3, the following formula is used

$$\textbf{Number of cells per mm}^3 = \frac{\textbf{N}}{\textbf{80}} \times \textbf{4000}$$

where **N** is the number of cells counted in **80** small squares.

Application of Number
Appendix V:
Key Skills
Page 142

To use the haemocytometer accurately, it is essential to set it up and fill the counting chamber carefully, otherwise gross errors will be introduced.

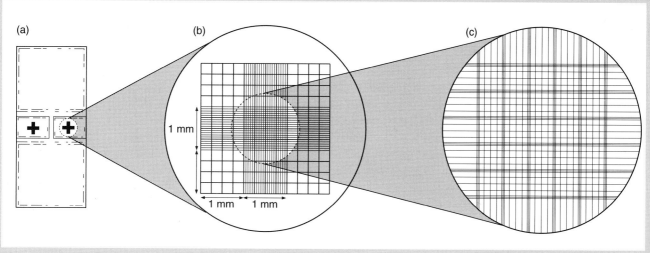

Figure 4.1 The Improved Neubauer haemocytometer, viewed at increasing magnifications (a) ×0.5, (b) ×10, (c) ×35

Materials

- Improved Neubauer haemocytometer and coverslip
- IMS and tissues to clean the haemocytometer
- Broth culture of suitable organism to count
- 1 cm^3 syringe with needle
- Microscope

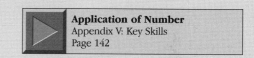

Application of Number
Appendix V: Key Skills
Page 142

Safety note: Unless a single-celled alga is used, aseptic technique with *Saccharomyces* species, especially *S. pombe*, is recommended. After use, the counting chamber should be placed in disinfectant.

Method

1 Place the haemocytometer on a flat surface and thoroughly clean the slide and coverslip using alcohol.

2 Slide the coverslip into position using a firm, downward pressure. When correctly positioned, a rainbow pattern (Newton's rings) should be visible along the two edges of the coverslip where it is supported by the slide. Note: if you are using an ordinary thin coverslip, do not press downwards as this can bend the coverslip downwards and decrease the volume of the counting chamber.

3 Thoroughly mix the cell culture to ensure a homogeneous suspension and, using the syringe, carefully inject a sample of the culture under the coverslip. The culture must exactly fill the silvered part of the counting chamber, it MUST NOT overflow into the grooves on either side. If it does, the counting chamber must be cleaned and refilled.

4 Leave the haemocytometer for at least 5 minutes to allow the cells to settle onto the grid, then, using a low light intensity, carefully focus under the low power of the microscope to locate the grid. When the grid is in focus, increase the magnification to ×400.

5 Count the number of cells present in five large squares (80 small squares), using the pattern shown in Figure 4.3. Some cells will lie on the boundaries between large squares, that is, touching the triple lines. To ensure a consistent counting method, count only those cells which touch the central line on the north and west sides of the square. Those cells touching the central line on the south and east sides should be ignored. You might find it helpful to use a hand tally counter (Figure 4.2).

Communication
Appendix V:
Key Skills
Page 142

QUANTITATIVE TECHNIQUES IN BIOLOGY

Figure 4.2 A hand tally counter. The count increases by one each time the button is pressed. The counter is reset to zero by turning the knob at the side

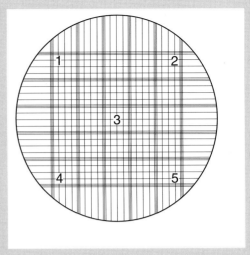

Figure 4.3 Count the total number of cells in these five, triple-lined squares

6 If there are too many cells to count, an accurate dilution, such as 1 in 100, should be made and your final count should then be multiplied by the dilution factor.

If you wish to count small invertebrates, such as freshwater or marine zooplankton, where the organisms are typically less than 1 mm in length, it may be appropriate to use a **Sedgwick–Rafter** counting chamber. This consists of a slide, usually made of plastic, with a central area measuring 50 mm × 20 mm. The depth of the chamber is 1 mm, therefore the volume, when filled, is 1000 mm^3, (or 1 cm^3). To facilitate counting, the chamber is ruled with a grid, dividing it into 1000 small squares. If you wish to count small invertebrates and do not have available a counting chamber, you can improvise using a small transparent plastic box, placed on 1 mm squared graph paper. The lids of coverslip boxes are ideal for this purpose.

An introduction to colorimetry

A colorimeter is an instrument that measures the amount of light which either passes through, or is absorbed by, a coloured solution. Some colorimeters have two scales:

- **absorbance**, an exponential (logarithmic) scale from zero to infinity
- **transmittance**, a linear scale from zero to 100, giving the percentage transmittance.

The absorbance scale is normally used for practical purposes, as there is a direct relationship between the absorbance of a coloured solution, and the concentration of the coloured substance. This relationship is summarised by the **Beer–Lambert Law**:

$$\text{absorbance } (A) = \varepsilon l [C]$$

where ε is a constant, known as the absorptivity, or absorption coefficient
l is the length of the absorbing solution
$[C]$ is the concentration of the coloured substance.

Application of Number
Appendix V: Key Skills
Page 142

Figure 4.4 shows the principle of a colorimeter. The light source is usually a tungsten filament bulb, the rays from which pass through a coloured **filter**, then through a glass or plastic sample tube, known as a **cuvette**, holding the solution. The light then passes to a **photocell**, which produces an electrical signal which is proportional to the intensity of light reaching the photocell. This signal is amplified and displayed on a **meter**, which may be either a galvanometer, or a digital display. In some colorimeters, the filter is placed between the cuvette and the photocell, rather than between the light source and the cuvette as shown in Figure 4.4.

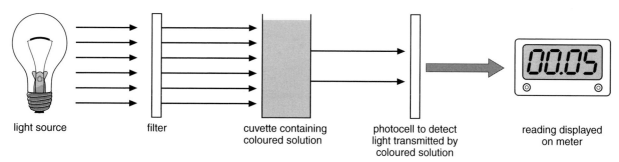

light source   filter   cuvette containing coloured solution   photocell to detect light transmitted by coloured solution   reading displayed on meter

Figure 4.4 Principle of a colorimeter

Colorimeters can be used to determine the concentration of a coloured substance in solution. Some substances, such as chlorophyll, haemoglobin and food dyes, are strongly coloured, but with some other substances, a colour is produced by adding an appropriate reagent. The concentration of starch in a solution, for example, can be determined by adding iodine solution, and the intensity of the resulting blue colour then measured colorimetrically.

Determination of the concentration of a substance requires the use of a **calibration curve**. This is prepared by plotting a graph of the absorbance of a range of standard solutions against their concentrations. The concentration of the test solution is then found by reading a value from the calibration curve. If the absorbance of the test solution is off the scale, or higher than the maximum value on your calibration curve, an appropriate dilution of the test solution must be made. An example of a calibration curve is shown in Figure 4.5.

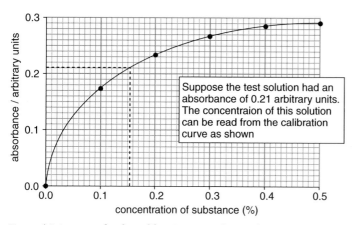

Suppose the test solution had an absorbance of 0.21 arbitrary units. The concentraion of this solution can be read from the calibration curve as shown

Figure 4.5 An example of a calibration curve for a colorimeter

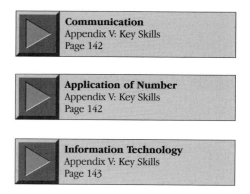

Communication
Appendix V: Key Skills
Page 142

Application of Number
Appendix V: Key Skills
Page 142

Information Technology
Appendix V: Key Skills
Page 143

QUANTITATIVE TECHNIQUES IN BIOLOGY

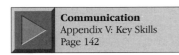

Communication
Appendix V: Key Skills
Page 142

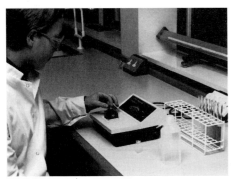

Figure 4.6 A colorimeter. The cuvette, containing a coloured solution, is placed in the instrument and the absorbance read off the scale

Guidelines for the use of a colorimeter

- Switch on the instrument and allow it to warm up for at least 5 minutes.
- Select an appropriate filter for the colour of your solutions. A complementary coloured filter should be used. For example, a blue solution will absorb red light, so a red filter should be used, whereas a blue filter should be used with a red solution.
- Prepare a range of standard solutions, including a blank (which could be distilled water), for your calibration curve.
- Ensure that the cuvette is clean and avoid touching the optical surfaces. Use the same cuvette for all readings, rinsing between each solution. Wipe the outside of the cuvette with a tissue to make sure that it is dry before placing in the colorimeter.
- Set zero absorbance using the blank, then read and record the absorbance of each of your standard solutions. Check the zero reading with the blank frequently.
- Read and record the absorbance of the unknown solution. If this value is off the scale of the instrument, or higher than the absorbance of the most concentrated standard solution, an appropriate dilution must be made.
- Plot a calibration curve for your standard solutions, as shown in Figure 4.5. Draw a smooth curve through the points, which will not necessarily form a straight line.
- Read off the concentration of the unknown solution from the calibration curve. If a dilution has been made, remember to multiply this value by the dilution factor.

You could practise using a colorimeter and preparing a calibration curve with food colouring. Prepare a series of dilutions as shown in Table 4.1 and record the absorbance of each solution, using an appropriate filter. You could develop this method to quantify the concentration of colours used as additives in, for example, bottled drinks.

Table 4.1 *Suggested dilutions of food dye for a colorimetric investigation. The original colouring may need initially to be diluted so that the absorbance is on the scale. Use this as the stock solution to prepare further dilutions*

Volume of food dye / cm³	Volume of distilled water / cm³	Concentration of solution (%)
10.0	0.0	100 (undiluted)
8.0	2.0	80
6.0	4.0	60
4.0	6.0	40
2.0	8.0	20
0.0	10.0	0 (blank)

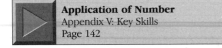

Application of Number
Appendix V: Key Skills
Page 142

The first two of the following practical exercises illustrate two uses of a colorimeter. The first investigates enzyme activity in germinating cereal grains, the second investigates the effect of temperature on osmosis in plant tissues.

Using a colorimeter to follow the course of an enzyme-catalysed reaction

Introduction

In this practical, an enzyme extract is prepared from germinating barley grains, then the activity of this extract is determined by investigating its effect on starch solution. Germinating barley grains contain a mixture of α-amylase and β-amylase, which hydrolyse the stored, insoluble starch into soluble products, including maltose. When iodine solution is added to a solution containing starch, a blue colour is produced, the intensity of which is related to the concentration of the starch. We can therefore investigate the breakdown of starch by following changes in the intensity in the blue coloration, using a colorimeter.

There are two main parts to this practical: firstly, preparation of the enzyme extract, and secondly, investigation of the enzyme activity.

Preparation of the enzyme extract

Materials

- 8 g of dry barley grains
- 0.1% sodium chlorite(I) solution. As an alternative, use 1.0% domestic bleach solution
- 250 cm^3 beaker with cover
- Sterile water
- Small plastic tray, approximately 120 cm × 170 cm (trays in which some fruit and vegetables are sold are ideal for this purpose)
- Filter paper or blotting paper
- Cling film
- Mortar and pestle
- Muslin
- Centrifuge and tubes
- Sample bottle for enzyme extract

Method

1. Place 8 g of dry barley grains in a beaker and cover with 1 per cent bleach solution. Leave for 3 minutes to surface sterilise, then pour off the solution. Rinse the grains twice with sterile water.
2. Cover the grains with sterile water and leave at room temperature for 24 hours.
3. Pour off the water, then place the grains in a thin layer on wet filter paper in a plastic tray. Cover with cling film to prevent drying out and leave for a further 24 hours at room temperature.
4. The barley grains should now have begun to germinate and roots should be visible. Grind the grains thoroughly in a mortar with a small volume of distilled water. Transfer the ground-up material to a beaker and add more distilled water so that a total of 100 cm^3 of distilled water is added to each original 8 g of dry grains.
5. Filter the extract through several layers of muslin into another beaker. Squeeze the muslin so that most of the liquid is removed.
6. Pour the extract into centrifuge tubes and, ensuring that the centrifuge is correctly balanced, spin at $1000 \times g$ for 5 minutes.
7. Carefully pour off the clear supernatant into a labelled bottle and discard the residue at the bottom of the tube. This supernatant is the enzyme extract, which is to be used in the second part of this practical. If necessary, store the extract in a refrigerator at 4 °C until ready for use.

QUANTITATIVE TECHNIQUES IN BIOLOGY

This procedure for the preparation of the enzyme extract is illustrated in Figure 4.7.

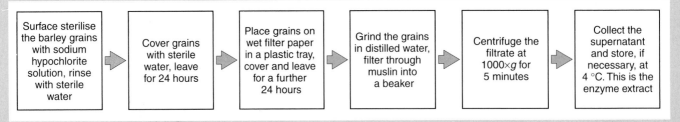

Figure 4.7 *Flow diagram for the preparation of an enzyme extract from germinating barley grains*

Communication
Appendix V:
Key Skills
Page 142

Information technology
Appendix V:
Key Skills
Page 143

Investigating enzyme activity using a colorimeter

Materials

- Colorimeter and cuvettes
- Red filter for colorimeter
- Test tubes and rack
- 250 cm³ beaker
- Water bath at 20 °C
- Syringes or graduated pipettes
- Stop clock or stop watch
- Marker pen
- Standard iodine solution
- 0.5% starch solution, prepared with soluble starch
- Barley grain enzyme extract

WEAR EYE PROTECTION

Safety note: Eye protection is advised when dispensing iodine solution.

Method

Preparation of calibration curve

1 Into each of five test tubes, pipette 5.0 cm³ of distilled water and 0.25 cm³ of standard iodine solution. Mix thoroughly.
2 Prepare a series of dilutions of the 0.5 per cent starch solution:
   - half strength (0.25 per cent)
   - quarter strength (0.125 per cent)
   - one-eighth strength (0.0625 per cent)
   See Chapter 1, Figure 1.3 for information on making doubling dilutions. Ensure that all your tubes are correctly labelled.
3 To the first tube containing the dilute iodine solution, add 0.25 cm³ of distilled water and mix well. Pour this into a cuvette and use this to set zero absorbance on the colorimeter scale.
4 To the second tube containing the dilute iodine solution, add 0.25 cm³ of the one-eighth strength starch solution. Mix thoroughly, pour into a cuvette and read the absorbance.

5 Repeat step 4 with the quarter strength and the half strength starch solutions. Lastly, add 0.25 cm³ of 0.5 per cent starch solution to the remaining tube of dilute iodine solution, mix, and record the absorbance.

6 Record your results in a suitable table, such as Table 4.2.

Table 4.2 *Absorbance of a range of concentrations of starch–iodine solutions*

Concentration of starch solution (%)	Absorbance (red filter) / arbitrary units
0.0 (blank)	
0.0625	
0.125	
0.25	
0.50	

Communication
Appendix V:
Key Skills
Page 142

7 Use your results to plot a calibration curve with absorbance on the vertical axis and concentration of starch on the horizontal axis.

Investigation of enzyme activity

1 Measure 30 cm³ of 0.5 per cent starch solution into a beaker and stand in a water bath at 20 °C.

2 Pipette 10 cm³ of the enzyme extract into a test tube and stand this in the water bath.

3 Leave both the starch solution and the enzyme extract for 5 minutes to equilibrate to the temperature of the water bath.

4 Pipette 5.0 cm³ of distilled water into a cuvette and add 0.25 cm³ of standard iodine solution. Mix well.

5 When you are ready to begin the experiment, pour the 10 cm³ of enzyme extract into the beaker of starch solution, leaving the beaker in the water bath. Mix thoroughly and immediately start a stop clock.

6 After 1 minute, remove one 0.25 cm³ sample from the enzyme–starch mixture and add to the cuvette containing iodine solution. Mix by inverting the cuvette and measure the absorbance in the colorimeter. Record both the time and the absorbance.

7 Discard the contents of the cuvette, rinse with distilled water, then replace with iodine solution as in step 4.

8 Take further 0.25 cm³ samples of the enzyme–starch mixture, add to the iodine solution and record the absorbance at suitable time intervals, such as 2, 5, 10, 15 and 20 minutes from the start of the experiment.

9 Remember to check zero periodically during the experiment, using the blank prepared for the calibration curve.

Application of
Number
Appendix V:
Key Skills
Page 142

Results and discussion

1 Tabulate your results, showing colorimeter readings (absorbance) and times for which the enzyme extract and starch substrate have been incubated.

2 Use your calibration curve to convert colorimeter readings to concentration of starch.

3 Plot a graph to show the relationship between starch concentration (vertical axis) and time (horizontal axis).

4 Describe and explain the shape of your graph.

5 What are the sources of errors and inaccuracies in this experiment? How could it be improved? You may find it helpful to read the advice in Chapter 3 on writing reports of laboratory investigations.

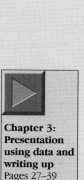

Chapter 3:
Presentation
using data and
writing up
Pages 27–39

Suggestions for further work

1   Compare the amylase activity of different types of cereal grains, such as wheat, barley, oats and maize.

2   Investigate amylase activity in seeds such as peas and beans. It is interesting to note that in some species, there is no relationship between the activity of a particular enzyme and the concentration of its substrate stored in the seed. As an example, soya bean seeds have a relatively high β-amylase activity, but contain little starch.

3   Investigate changes in amylase activity in germinating barley grains, by measuring amylase activity in samples of grains which have been allowed to germinate, after soaking, for 2, 4, 6, 8, 10 and 12 days. Plot graphs to show the percentage of grains which have germinated (use the emergence of radicles as a criterion for germination) and changes in amylase activity, against time.

4   Use a colorimeter to compare the chlorophyll content of leaves from different species of plants, or to investigate differences in chlorophyll content of sun and shade leaves from the same plant. You can extract the chlorophyll by cutting out discs from leaves, using a cork borer. The leaf discs are immersed in boiling water for 1 minute, then transferred to a test tube containing 10 cm^3 of Industrial Methylated Spirit (IMS). This tube is then placed in a water bath at 80 °C and left for a few minutes to extract the chlorophyll. Allow the extract to cool, then add IMS as necessary to return the volume to 10 cm^3. Record the absorbance of the extract in a colorimeter, using a red filter.

Safety note: Industrial Methylated Spirit is HIGHLY FLAMMABLE. Under no circumstances must there be any exposed flames nearby when heating Industrial Methylated Spirit in a water bath.

FLAMMABLE
industrial
methylated
spirit

Using a colorimeter to investigate the uptake of water by plant tissues

Introduction

In this experiment, the rate of uptake of water by plant tissue is investigated by immersing cylinders of potato tissue in a solution of blue dextran. Blue dextran has a very high relative molecular mass and has practically no osmotic effect. As the cells take up water from the solution, the concentration of blue dextran will increase and, consequently, the absorbance of the solution will increase.

Materials

- Blue dextran solution, containing 0.1 g per 100 cm^3 of distilled water. Blue dextran is available from Sigma Aldrich (see Appendix II)
- Graduated pipette or syringe
- 250 cm^3 of 0.4 mol dm^{-3} sucrose solution in a beaker
- Large potato
- Boiling tube with stopper and rack
- Beaker to use as a water bath
- Thermometer
- Cork borer, 8 to 10 mm in diameter
- Single-edged razor blade or scalpel
- Ruler

Appendix II:
Reagents and
recipes
Page 136

- Colorimeter and cuvettes
- Red filter for colorimeter

Method

1 Use a cork borer to cut out cylinders of potato, then cut each into slices exactly 5 mm long. You will need 30 pieces for each experiment. Take care with the razor blade or scalpel.
2 Immerse all of the pieces of potato in 0.4 mol dm^{-3} sucrose solution, leave for 1 hour.
3 Rinse away the sucrose solution with several changes of tap water.
4 Transfer the potato cylinders to a boiling tube and add 25 cm^3 of blue dextran solution.
5 Immediately remove a sample of the blue dextran solution, place in a cuvette and use to set zero absorbance in the colorimeter.
6 Place a stopper in the boiling tube and leave in a water bath at 25 °C.
7 Remove further samples of the blue dextran at 20 minute intervals, record the absorbance, then return the blue dextran to the boiling tube.

Application of Number
Appendix V:
Key Skills
Page 142

Results and discussion

1 Record your results in a table.
2 Plot a graph to show changes in absorbance (vertical axis) against time (horizontal axis).
3 Explain why the potato was initially immersed in 0.4 mol dm^{-3} sucrose solution.
4 Discuss your results fully.

Suggestions for further work

1 Investigate the effect of temperature on the **rate** of uptake of water.
2 Compare the rates of uptake of water by different types of storage roots or tubers.

Problem Solving
Appendix V:
Key Skills
Page 143

Using a potometer to investigate transpiration

Introduction

A **potometer** is an instrument which, strictly speaking, measures the **uptake** of water by a leafy shoot. However, of the volume of water taken up by a plant, only a very small percentage is used by the plant in processes such as photosynthesis, hydrolysis reactions and maintaining turgor of cells. Almost all of the water which is taken up is lost by the process of transpiration, in which water evaporates from cells into intercellular spaces, then water vapour diffuses out of the plant. The process of **transpiration** is described in detail in *Systems and their Maintenance*.

There are many different designs of potometer, but they generally work on the same principle, that is, that water is taken up by a suitable leafy shoot, connected to the apparatus. As water is taken up, a small air bubble is drawn along a horizontal capillary tube, so that the rate of movement of the bubble corresponds to the rate of water uptake by the shoot. One type of potometer, known as Ganong's potometer, is illustrated in Figure 4.8.

Method

There are number of precautions which need to be taken when using a potometer to ensure reliable results.

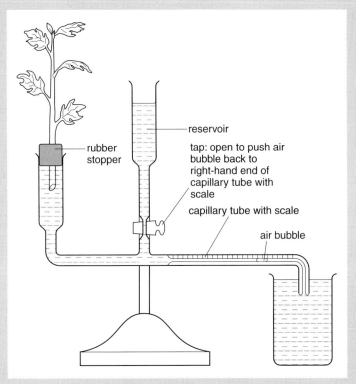

Figure 4.8 A potometer set up to measure the uptake of water by a leafy shoot

Communi-cation
Appendix V:
Key Skills
Page 142

1 Use a leafy shoot with a round, woody stem, such as laurel (*Prunus laurocerasus*).
2 As soon as the shoot is cut off, the cut end should be placed in a suitable container of water, such as a bucket. In the laboratory, a second cut is made, under water, to remove about 5 cm from the end of the shoot. These precautions are to prevent air locks in the xylem.
3 The potometer should be assembled in a sink full of water. After the shoot is fitted through the hole in the rubber bung, the last 3 cm of bark should be removed. This prevents any sap from the phloem from blocking the xylem.
4 When the potometer has been assembled, the bent end of the capillary tube should remain in water, by placing in a small beaker of water, as shown in Figure 4.8.
5 To introduce a bubble into the capillary tube, the tube is lifted out of the water in the beaker, blotted with a paper towel, then replaced into the water when an air bubble has entered the end of the tube. The air bubble should be between 3 and 6 mm long.
6 Do not use Vaseline on the potometer in the hope that this will make a water-tight seal!
7 When the potometer is set up and the air bubble is moving at a steady rate, record the movement of the bubble along the scale, at suitable time intervals.
8 In potometers with a reservoir, the bubble can be returned to the beginning of the scale by carefully opening the tap to allow water to flow out of the reservoir.
9 Compare rates of water uptake in still air and in moving air, by allowing an electric fan to blow air onto the shoot.

Results and discussion

1 Tabulate your results, showing the times and position of the bubble along the scale.
2 Plot a graph to show the position of the bubble (vertical axis) against time (horizontal axis).

3 If your graph is nearly a straight line, what does this indicate about the **rate** of water uptake?

4 If you know the radius of the capillary tube, you can calculate the **volume** of water taken up, using the formula below.

Application of Number
Appendix V: Key Skills
Page 142

$$\text{volume } = \pi r^2 d$$

where $\pi = 3.142$,
 r = the radius of the capillary tube,
 d = the distance moved by the bubble.

5 When you have completed the measurements, determine the total leaf surface area. Your results can then be expressed in the form of volume of water taken up per unit leaf surface area, per unit time.

6 List the factors which affect transpiration and, consequently, the rate of uptake of water by a leafy shoot.

Figure 4.9 A student using a potometer to investigate factors which affect transpiration. Note the stop clock, used to time the movement of the bubble along the graduated capillary tube

An introduction to bioassay

A **bioassay** is a technique for determining the concentration of a substance by measuring its effect on living tissue or living organisms. Bioassays can be used to detect very low concentrations of a substance, which may be difficult to detect by means of conventional chemical analysis. Two uses of bioassay include the determination of concentrations of plant growth substances such as indole-3-acetic acid (IAA, or auxin) and gibberellic acid, and antibiotics. One assay for gibberellic acid, for example, in which the effect of gibberellic acid on the growth of lettuce seedling hypocotyls is measured, is sensitive to about 4×10^{-3} μg of gibberellic acid.

A microbiological assay is a technique to determine the concentration of a chemical substance by its effect on the growth of a microorganism. In one type of microbiological assay, known as an agar diffusion assay, nutrient agar is inoculated with a suitable test organism, and the active substance is allowed to diffuse from a solution in a reservoir into the agar. After incubation, a zone is formed around the reservoir. If an antibiotic is used, a clear zone of inhibition is formed, the diameter of which is proportional to the concentration of the antibiotic. This forms the quantitative basis for a microbiological assay. Figure 4.10 illustrates the principle of a diffusion assay and shows how the zone diameter is measured. This technique can be carried out using relatively simple equipment and used to investigate the antibacterial properties of a number of different substances, including antibiotics, antiseptics and disinfectants, and natural plant extracts.

In practice, a Petri dish can be used for an assay. Nutrient agar is melted, then allowed to cool to between 50 °C and 55 °C, and inoculated with a suspension of the test organism. One commonly used assay organism is

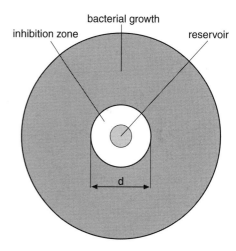

Figure 4.10 Outward diffusion of an antibacterial substance from a reservoir into a layer of inoculated agar medium in a Petri dish produces a clear, circular zone of inhibition. The zone diameter is shown as d

Communication
Appendix V: Key Skills
Page 142

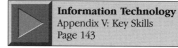

Information Technology
Appendix V: Key Skills
Page 143

QUANTITATIVE TECHNIQUES IN BIOLOGY

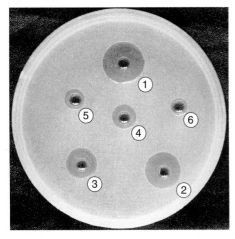

Figure 4.11 An agar diffusion assay for the antibiotic penicillin. Six reservoirs, numbered 1 to 6, have been cut in the agar. Each reservoir contains the same volume of antibiotic solution, 1 is the most concentrated, 6 the least

Bacillus subtilis, which can be added to the nutrient agar in the form of a spore suspension. The medium is then poured into a sterile Petri dish and allowed to set. Reservoirs are cut in the agar using a sterile cork borer, and the cylindrical plug of agar carefully removed, leaving a well in the agar. The plugs of agar are easily removed using a wooden applicator stick, snapped to produce a tapered end. Once removed, the plugs are disposed of into a disinfectant solution. Dilute solutions of the test substance are placed in the wells, then left for 1 to 2 hours at room temperature, or in a refrigerator, to allow the substance to diffuse into the agar. The dishes are then incubated overnight at a suitable temperature for the test organism. As an alternative to cutting wells in the agar, small, circular filter paper discs may be used.

Figure 4.11 shows the result of such an assay for the antibiotic penicillin, using the test organism *Bacillus subtilis*. Reservoir 1 contains the highest concentration of penicillin, reservoir 6 contains the lowest. Notice that as the concentration of the antibiotic increases, the diameter of the inhibition zone increases. Using solutions of known concentrations, a **dose-response curve** can be plotted, from which it is possible to determine the concentration of an unknown solution of the same substance, provided it is within the range of standards. In practice, a graph of mean zone diameter is plotted against the logarithm of the concentration; this results in a straight line, or a line showing a slight curve.

WEAR EYE PROTECTION

FLAMMABLE ethanol

TOXIC some plant growth substances

Wheat coleoptile bioassay for indole-3-acetic acid (IAA)

Materials

- Wheat grains
- Vermiculite (obtainable from Garden Centres)
- Plastic trays
- Petri dishes with lids
- Single-edged razor blades
- Ruler
- 4% sucrose solution
- Distilled water
- Volumetric flasks
- Graduated pipettes
- Measuring cylinders
- Stock indole-3-acetic acid (IAA) solution. Prepare 1 dm^3 of stock solution by dissolving 200 mg of IAA in 2 cm^3 of absolute ethanol. Add 900 cm^3 of distilled water and heat at 80 °C for 5 minutes to evaporate the ethanol. Cool, then make up to 1.0 dm^3 with distilled water. Store this solution in a refrigerator at 4 °C.

Safety note: Some plant growth substances may be toxic. Handle the solid substances or concentrated stock solutions with care. It is recommended that plastic gloves and eye protection should be worn. Any spills should be cleaned up immediately, first removing any solid material, then washing the area with plenty of water.

Method

1 Soak wheat grains in water at room temperature for 2 hours, then place in moist vermiculite. Leave in darkness at 25 °C for about 3 days, or until the coleoptiles are 2 cm long.

2 Prepare a range of standard solutions of IAA in 2 per cent sucrose solution, as shown in Table 3.3. Ensure that your flasks are carefully labelled.

Table 4.3 *Preparation of IAA solutions for wheat coleoptile bioassay*

IAA concentration / parts per million (ppm)	Method
100	Add 100 cm^3 of 4% sucrose solution to 100 cm^3 of stock IAA solution
1.0	Take 10 cm^3 of stock IAA and make up to 1 dm^3 with distilled water. To 100 cm^3 of this solution add 100 cm^3 of 4% sucrose solution
10^{-3}	Take 1.0 cm^3 of the 1.0 ppm solution and make up to 1 dm^3 with distilled water. To 100 cm^3 of this solution add 100 cm^3 of 4% sucrose solution
10^{-5}	Take 10 cm^3 of the 10^{-3} ppm solution and make up to 1 dm^3 with distilled water. To 100 cm^3 of this solution add 100 cm^3 of 2% sucrose solution
0 (control sucrose solution)	Add 100 cm^3 of distilled water to 100 cm^3 of 4% sucrose solution

Communi-cation
Appendix V:
Key Skills
Page 142

Application of Number
Appendix V:
Key Skills
Page 142

3 Measure 30 cm^3 of each solution into separate, labelled Petri dishes. Cover each with a lid.

4 Cut the coleoptiles into 1 cm long sections, using a single-edged razor blade. The last 0.3 cm of the coleoptiles should be cut off and discarded. If possible, cut the coleoptiles in a dark room illuminated with a green safe light, or at least in as dark a place as possible.

5 Place five coleoptile sections into each of the Petri dishes, replace the lids, then incubate them in the dark at 25 °C for 48 hours.

6 After 48 hours, remove the coleoptile sections and measure accurately the length of each.

Results and discussion

1 Tabulate your results, showing the **change** in lengths of the coleoptiles in each solution. Collect class results.

2 Calculate the mean change in length for each treatment.

3 Plot a graph showing the mean change in length (vertical axis) against the concentration of IAA (horizontal axis). You will find it more convenient to space the different concentrations of auxin equally on the axis.

4 Discuss your results fully, mentioning possible sources of error.

Suggestions for further work

1 You will probably find that there are variations in the changes in lengths of the coleoptiles in each solution. A measure of the reliability of the means can be obtained by calculating the **standard deviation** in each solution. Using the class results, calculate the standard deviations, as described in Chapter 7.

2 Investigate the effect of the IAA solutions on radicles.

Investigations: statistics and planning
Chapter 7
Page 102

Datalogging in biological investigations

The term **datalogging** is used to describe the monitoring of an experiment by electronic means. This usually involves an electronic **transducer**, such as a temperature probe or light sensor, which produces a low-voltage signal. For example, a light sensor will detect changes in light intensity and produce a voltage which is related to light intensity. The electrical signal can be detected by a computer and converted to a suitable reading. Appropriate software will organise and display the data in a graphical form. One of the advantages of datalogging is that it allows relatively long-term monitoring of experiments, both in the field and in the laboratory. Changes in light intensity, for example, can be recorded electronically over a period of several days, or plant growth measured and recorded automatically, as illustrated in Figure 4.12.

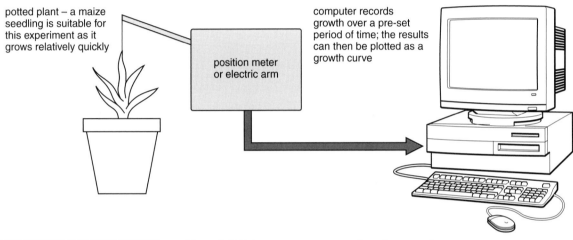

potted plant – a maize seedling is suitable for this experiment as it grows relatively quickly

position meter or electric arm

computer records growth over a pre-set period of time; the results can then be plotted as a growth curve

Figure 4.12 Using a computer to monitor plant growth

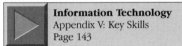

Information Technology
Appendix V: Key Skills
Page 143

A wide range of sensors is available, which make it possible to record changes in variables, including:

- air pressure
- conductivity
- relative humidity
- infra-red irradiance
- light
- dissolved oxygen
- pH
- position
- pressure
- sound
- temperature
- ultraviolet.

Some of the experiments already described in this chapter can be adapted to use with datalogging equipment, for example, the hydrolysis of starch by barley grain amylase extract. This can be followed by adding iodine solution to the starch–amylase mixture and using a light sensor to detect changes in the absorbance of the solution. In this way, the light sensor acts as a colorimeter and the results can be displayed graphically, showing changes in absorbance against time. It is also possible to record several variables over the same period of time, so that changes in turbidity, pH, temperature and dissolved oxygen could be measured during a batch fermentation.

Many practicals in biology are suitable for datalogging, such as those outlined below.

- investigating factors affecting enzyme activity. Minced potato can be used as a source of catalase and a simple experiment used to investigate factors affecting catalase activity. Figure 4.13 shows the apparatus which can be used to measure oxygen production, using an electronic manometer, or pressure sensor
- measuring oxygen production in photosynthesis using an oxygen sensor
- monitoring changes in temperature, light intensity, pH, dissolved oxygen, BOD, humidity, etc., in fieldwork investigations
- investigating factors affecting transpiration using an electronic balance or electronic potometer
- investigating lung volumes and pulse rate using an electronic stethograph and pulse meter
- measuring plant growth using a position sensor or electronic arm
- measuring temperature changes in a compost heap using a temperature probe
- monitoring animal behaviour using an infra-red probe
- using Videologging™ (available from Philip Harris) it is possible to combine datalogging with time-lapse capture of video images.

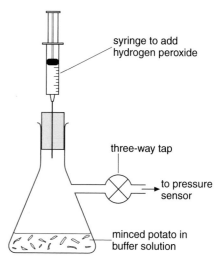

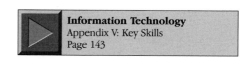

Figure 4.13 Investigating catalase activity using a pressure sensor

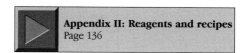

Information Technology
Appendix V: Key Skills
Page 143

Appendix II: Reagents and recipes
Page 136

5 More advanced tools and techniques

Practicals with an eye on the future

The practicals described in this chapter begin to push the frontiers out beyond the laboratory and fieldwork investigations which traditionally have formed part of an A level Biology course. Some are quite simple, but others simulate, on a small scale, more complex operations which may be used in research, in industry or in diagnostic procedures in medical or forensic science. This introduction to the techniques should enhance your understanding of the theory of some topics in the syllabus, and perhaps prepare you for further study at a higher level.

The accounts are presented in a way that will introduce you to possible practical work, and explain the background to the procedures. In some cases, specialised apparatus, such as that used for gel electrophoresis or manipulation with DNA, is available in kit form from certain suppliers. Relevant addresses are given in Appendix II. Accompanying these kits are detailed practical instructions for the materials required and how the procedures are carried out. These details are not repeated in this chapter, but full references are provided for their source, including how to access the information from websites on the Internet. With some practicals, there may be limited scope at this level for further or individual investigations, but, nevertheless, you may gain some useful understanding and experience from handling DNA, from simulating a massive industrial fermentation or using an immunological assay which represents an important technique in diagnostic procedures. Overall, this selection of practicals should help you look forward into the 21st century, and see how applications of biology and biological techniques are playing an increasingly important part in contemporary society.

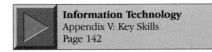

Information Technology
Appendix V: Key Skills
Page 142

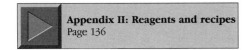

Appendix II: Reagents and recipes
Page 136

Doing things with DNA

DNA has become a household word, with daily newspaper reports of how analysis of DNA samples has provided evidence for use in paternity cases, in identifying rape suspects or tracing the ancestors of groups of humans. There are accounts of development of genetically modified organisms (GMOs) giving us improved crops or producing enzymes or pharmaceuticals to order, and hopes are raised with the potential for gene therapy by repairing faulty genes. There is, however, a noticeable gulf in understanding between the scientists who are the practitioners, working with DNA, and many amongst the general public and even GCSE and A level students who are following syllabuses which expect some study of events relating to DNA.

Practical work with DNA is still limited at A level, but the exercises described here should give you a useful introduction to the tools and techniques used by research scientists, and give you greater understanding and insight into the public debates about handling and modifying DNA. As with any practical work, consideration must be given to safety aspects and strict regulations apply to work with DNA in schools and colleges. References to appropriate safety information are given in Appendix II and safety information is also provided with the specialised kits that are available for work with DNA. You should, however, be aware that some of the practical protocols described on websites, particularly those in the USA, are forbidden in schools and colleges within the European Union, unless the national laws that govern genetic modification have been complied with. Within the EU, it is forbidden to transfer genetic material between species without special permission from the relevant authorities, and without strict health and safety guidelines being adhered to. Self-cloning experiments (see page 65) can be carried out but the genetically modified organisms cannot be released into the environment.

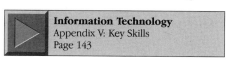

Information Technology
Appendix V: Key Skills
Page 143

Extraction and isolation of DNA

Relatively simple methods can be used for isolation of DNA, and protocols are available describing its extraction from plant material, such as onions, kiwi fruit, cress and dried peas. These preparations are fairly crude, but nevertheless illustrate the principles involved, and the DNA which has been extracted by these methods can be used for some further studies. Starting with whole cells, other cell components are progressively removed until DNA is isolated from within the nucleus. These crude extractions also include mitochondrial DNA and chloroplast DNA.

Summary of steps in the procedure:
- break up tissue mechanically – using grinder and/or blender
- degrade membranes using detergents – first the cell membrane, then the nuclear membrane (and membranes of other organelles)
- separate and remove cell fragments – filtering through filter paper and/or muslin, followed (usually) by centrifuging
- degrade proteins (which remain with the DNA) – using protease enzymes
- precipitate the DNA in ethanol (DNA is insoluble in ethanol)
- store the isolated DNA – reasonably stable when frozen, or it can be re-suspended in buffer solution.

Communication
Appendix V: Key Skills
Page 142

There is sometimes an additional step using RNase to remove RNA and use of protease enzymes may not always be necessary. The extracted DNA can be pulled out on a glass rod or centrifuged into a pellet.

Quantitative estimates of DNA are routinely carried out in research laboratories by determining its absorbance of UV light. Simpler semi-quantitative methods can be devised, based on the density of colour developed with certain stains for DNA (such as methylene blue),

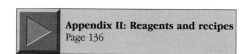

Appendix II: Reagents and recipes
Page 136

using a set of standards made up from known quantities of DNA. 'Dip' sticks are available with certain DNA extraction kits. Quantitative gels can be run, in which a small sample of known volume from the DNA extract is run on a gel alongside known amounts of DNA. After staining, the band size and intensity can be compared with the known samples to make a quantitative estimate of the DNA in the original sample. At A level, investigations could, for example, be carried out into the effect of different detergents, using different source materials or determining the effect of temperature on extraction of DNA.

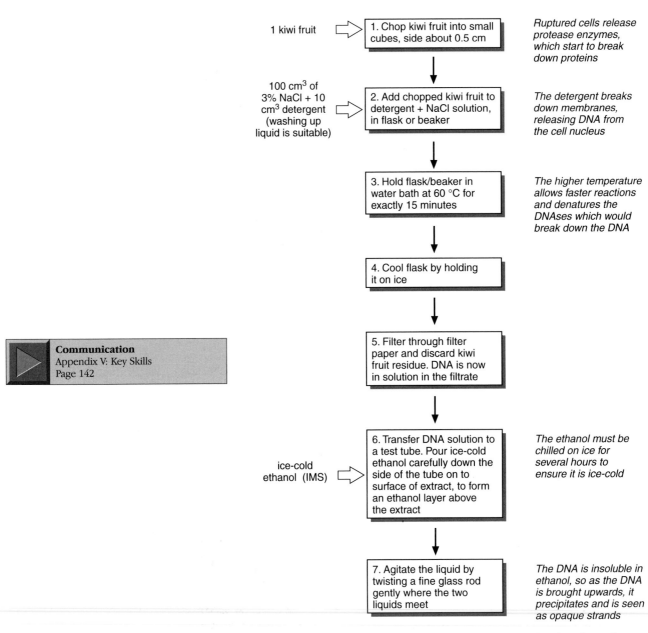

Figure 5.1 Outline of practical details for isolation of DNA from kiwi fruit – kiwi fruits provide a good source for this simple method of extraction, with enough protease enzymes to eliminate the need for treatment with proteases

Communication
Appendix V: Key Skills
Page 142

Cutting up DNA and separating the fragments

A sample of DNA can be 'cut up' or digested using enzymes known as **restriction endonucleases**, and the resulting fragments can then be separated by **gel electrophoresis**. The patterns of bands produced are analysed and this can be an important first stage in trying to match one sample of DNA with another or in recognising similarities between DNA from different sources.

Restriction endonucleases have become a very important tool for molecular biologists. They are produced by microorganisms and many have now been isolated. Their natural function is probably to be a defence against entry of foreign nucleic acids, say from invading bacteriophages. Thus they 'restrict' invasion of the host cell – hence the term restriction enzymes. The names given to these enzymes are derived from the source organism: the first letter of the microbe's genus is combined with the first two letters of the specific name to give the enzyme name (written in italics). Thus the restriction enzyme *Eco* comes from the bacterium *Escherichia coli*, *Bam* comes from *Bacillus amyloliquefaciens* and *Hin* comes from *Haemophilus influenzae*. Roman numerals after the name are used when there are different enzymes from the same species or strain. Restriction enzymes act by cutting or cleaving between the nucleotide bases of the DNA sequence. Some, known as **exonucleases**, cut bases only from the *end* of the DNA molecule, whereas **endonucleases** cut between bases *within* the DNA molecule. It is the endonucleases that are the more useful in molecular biology techniques. There are different types of endonucleases. Some are fairly general in where they cleave the DNA, whereas **type II endonucleases** are the most useful because they are quite specific in their cleavage sites. *Eco* RI, for example, recognises the base sequence G/AATTC and cuts at the position of the slash, and, in a similar way, *Hin* dIII recognises and cuts the base sequence A/AGCTT, *Xba* recognises and cuts the base sequence T/CTAGA and *Bcl* recognises and cuts the base sequence T/GATCA.

Communication
Appendix V: Key Skills
Page 142

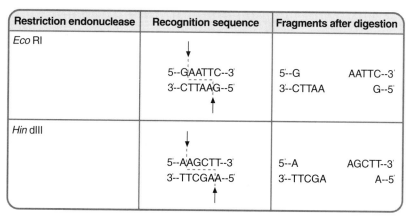

Restriction endonuclease	Recognition sequence	Fragments after digestion
Eco RI	5'--GAATTC--3' 3'--CTTAAG--5'	5'--G AATTC--3' 3'--CTTAA G--5'
Hin dIII	5'--AAGCTT--3' 3'--TTCGAA--5'	5'--A AGCTT--3' 3'--TTCGA A--5'

Figure 5.2 Recognition sites for the restriction enzymes Eco *RI and* Hind *III. Each restriction enzyme recognises a particular sequence of bases in the DNA molecule and cleavage is the result of hydrolysis of the phosphodiester backbone. The recognition sites are indicated by the arrows. Both* Eco *RI and* Hin *dIII give fragments with sticky ends*

MORE ADVANCED TOOLS AND TECHNIQUES

Gel electrophoresis provides a means of separating the digested fragments of DNA. The technique depends on the movement of charged molecules in an applied electrical field. The gel is used as the support medium and is contained in an electrical cell or tank. The direction of movement depends on the charge of the molecule and the relative rate of movement is determined by the size, with the smallest moving furthest in a given time. The DNA digest is loaded into small wells cut in the surface of the gel, which is flooded with a suitable buffer. The DNA fragments are negatively charged, so move towards the positive pole (anode). By using different restriction enzymes on the same DNA sample, a pattern of fragments is obtained which can, in some cases, be compared with known samples. Alternatively, the pattern may reveal particular or unique sequences of bases within the DNA molecule.

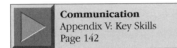

Communication
Appendix V: Key Skills
Page 142

Summary of steps in the procedure:
* prepare solution of DNA sample
* add restriction enzymes to cut DNA at specific sites
* incubate DNA–enzyme mixture
* load the DNA digest into wells on agarose gel (flooded with buffer) for electrophoresis
* apply electric current to run gel electrophoresis – smaller fragments move faster, thus spreading the fragments, allowing separation
* stain the DNA in the gel so that the bands of the separated DNA fragments become visible
* compare the pattern of the bands – with each other, or with known sample
* record the pattern (e.g. by photograph or drawing, as staining will fade).

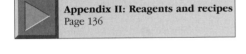

Appendix II: Reagents and recipes
Page 136

If a 'loading' dye is added to the DNA mixture, it helps you to see what you are doing. The mixture (including the DNA) sinks to the bottom of the wells and then runs ahead of the DNA bands so you can check on the movement through the tank. The principle of electrophoresis can be demonstrated using dyes alone, without any extracted DNA sample.

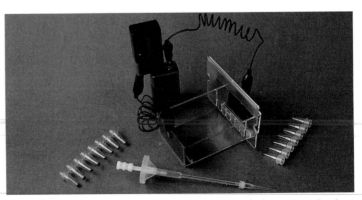

Figure 5.3 A small-scale electrophoresis tank, suitable for use at A level

Looking at the results of a DNA digest

Lambda (λ) phage provides a convenient source of DNA for use of restriction enzymes followed by separation of the DNA fragments obtained. Lambda (λ) DNA consists of 48 502 base pairs. The whole of its DNA has been sequenced, which means we know the order of the bases in the DNA strand. Different restriction enzymes recognise specific base sequences and so cut the DNA into particular fragments, each containing a known number of bases. Thus, for example, *Eco* RI cuts the DNA into six fragments, with base pair lengths of 21 226, 4878, 5643, 7421, 5804 and 3530. *Bam* HI cuts the DNA into six fragments (with different base pair lengths), *Hin* dIII cuts it into eight fragments, *Xba* I into two fragments and *Bcl* I cuts it into nine fragments. These restriction maps are summarised in Figure 5.4. From this information, you can make certain predictions and work out, for the restriction enzymes used:

- which fragments will travel the furthest on the agarose gel
- the relative positions of the different fragments which would be obtained with each restriction enzyme.

Figure 5.5 shows typical results of DNA bands obtained from a restriction enzyme digest. Because the size of the bands obtained from digests with λ DNA are now well established, they can be used as markers for comparison with other samples of DNA to obtain an estimate of the sizes of their fragments.

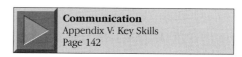

Communication
Appendix V: Key Skills
Page 142

Communication
Appendix V: Key Skills
Page 142

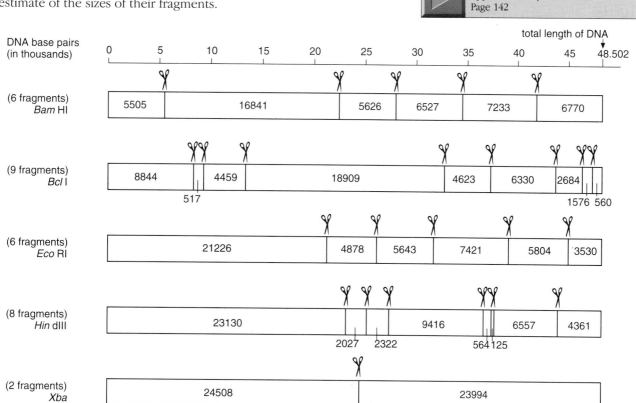

*Figure 5.4 Restriction map showing fragments obtained from digests of λ DNA. λ DNA **has a total of 48 502 base pairs and the maps show** **the fragments obtained with different restriction enzymes (**Bam HI, Bcl I, Eco RI, Hin dIII, and Xba I**). The scissors (✂) mark the precise** **positions of the cuts for each enzyme and the numbers on the strands indicate the number of base pairs in each fragment**

MORE ADVANCED TOOLS AND TECHNIQUES

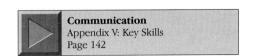

Communication
Appendix V: Key Skills
Page 142

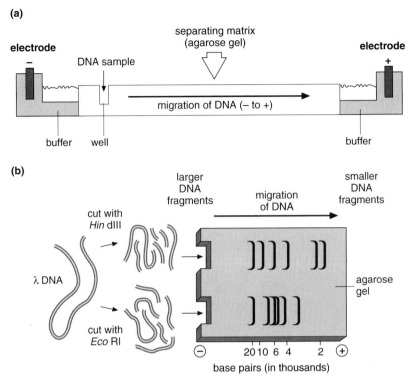

Figure 5.5 Relative positions of DNA bands on a gel after electrophoresis (a) side view of an electrophoresis tank, showing essential features and direction of migration of fragments (b) separation of bands from digestion of λ DNA with two restriction endonucleases. Smaller fragments move further than larger fragments in a given time, and uncut DNA, with no restriction enzyme treatment, would move only a short distance from the well. The positions of the bands can be revealed by staining, or by use of a suitable dye which makes them visible under UV light

You can, in some respects, compare the technique of gel electrophoresis with that of chromatography (column and paper). Both can be used to separate and then identify or compare the patterns of molecules. In each case, think about what acts as the solid medium, what causes the movement of the molecules through the system and how the molecules being analysed can be identified or compared.

Communication
Appendix V: Key Skills
Page 142

Amplifying DNA – the polymerase chain reaction (PCR)

Detective work may have to depend on only minute quantities of material for use as clues in an investigation. The mystery to be solved may be concerned with forensic analysis, DNA fingerprinting, comparative evolutionary studies, pre-natal detection of genetic abnormalities or diagnosis of disease. The material might be a single hair, a drop of blood, just one cell, viruses in clinical samples, or a fragment of ancient DNA from mammoths preserved in ice, extinct plants or mummified human remains. The PCR provides an *in vitro* means of amplifying (copying many times) a specific section from a sample of DNA, thus increasing the amount of material which can then be used for further investigation. The PCR copies are available in just a few hours, whereas making copies through the technique of gene cloning in bacteria would take several days.

The target length of DNA to be copied is selected using **primers**. These are short lengths of about 20 to 30 nucleotides which are artificially synthesised. The primer nucleotide sequence precisely complements the nucleotide sequence which lies at each end of the target DNA. Two primers are used – one is complementary to the target strand and the other primer is complementary to the opposite (complementary) strand of the DNA. The PCR reaction mixture contains the sample of DNA, an excess of appropriate primers, a **DNA polymerase enzyme**, the four **(deoxy)nucleotide phosphates** (dCTP, dATP, dGTP, dTTP – to build the new DNA) and **buffer**. The PCR cycle involves heating the reaction mixture to separate the strands of DNA, allowing the mixture to cool so that the primers anneal (join) to their respective strands, heating again to allow a fresh DNA strand to be synthesised extending from the primer position, then further heating to separate these newly formed strands of DNA. The exact temperatures used depend upon the base sequence and the length of the primers. The cycle is repeated many times, and each time the number of copies of the target length of DNA is doubled.

Summary of steps in the procedure:
- heat the sample of DNA to 95 °C for about 20 seconds – the hydrogen bonds between the strands break, so the complementary strands of the DNA separate and the DNA is **denatured** into single strands
- cool to between 55 °C and 60 °C for 20 seconds – this allows the primers to anneal (join at the hydrogen bonds) to the complementary portion of the DNA. Using an excess of primers ensures that some bind with the DNA rather than the original strands joining again
- heat to 72 °C for 30 seconds – the DNA polymerase binds at the end of the primer, enabling free nucleotides to build a complementary strand along the exposed portion of the DNA thus **extending** the primers and restoring the double strand of DNA
- repeat the cycle 20 or more times – each time the target length of DNA which is copied becomes the template for the next cycle.

Communication
Appendix V: Key Skills
Page 142

When first described in 1985, the PCR technique was carried out manually and was a rather lengthy process. The reaction mixtures had to be transferred manually through the series of water baths and fresh polymerase enzyme was added at each new cycle. The procedures were repeated for each cycle, 20 or 30 times. Development of automated PCR machines has allowed much more widespread use of this technique for amplifying DNA, and its application in a variety of fields outside the research laboratory. Further developments of simpler, smaller scale machines means it is probable that PCR machines will become available for use with A level practical work in

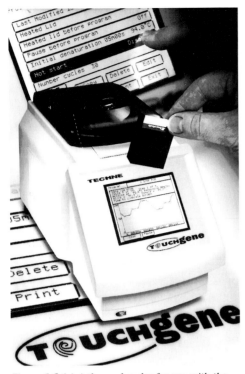

the near future, though the process can be carried out manually (but is tedious). The technique requires a polymerase enzyme which is active at the high temperatures involved in the cycle. A useful source of a heat-stable DNA polymerase has been from the bacterium *Thermus aquaticus*, which is stable beyond 95 °C. This is known as *Taq* polymerase. As with any DNA work, it is important to avoid contamination of the target sample with DNA from people handling the material.

The sequence of events in the polymerase chain reaction is summarised in Figure 5.6. You can see that in four cycles, a single length of the target DNA produces 16 copies. Work out how many copies would be produced in 20 cycles – see if it exceeds 1 million! You will begin to appreciate that the PCR is a powerful tool to use in generating enough DNA to do further analysis. Looking for a single gene has been described as 'searching for a needle in a haystack'. Using the PCR has now been dubbed 'making a haystack out of needles'. The PCR is also referred to as a means of carrying out 'molecular cloning'.

Figure 5.6 (a) A thermal cycler for use with the PCR process. The programme for the cycle is controlled by the disk being inserted and the graphical display shows the stage of the cycle and the sample temperature; b) temperature changes during each PCR cycle; (c) a summary of the PCR process, showing how the DNA doubles at each cycle

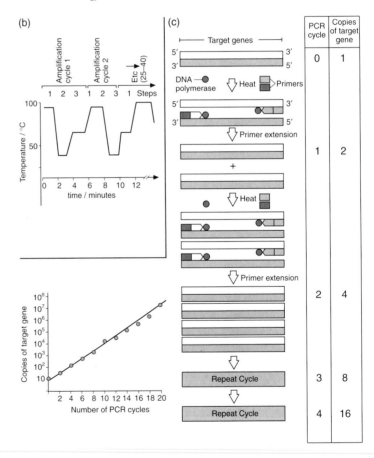

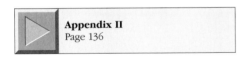

Appendix II
Page 136

Communication
Appendix V: Key Skills
Page 142

Information Technology
Appendix V: Key Skills
Page 143

Transformations with DNA – an introduction to recombinant gene technology

Transformations with DNA provide a way of introducing new genes into a cell or organism. The term **transformation** is used to describe the uptake and expression of DNA by a living cell or organism. Transformation occurs naturally in some bacteria but is now used extensively as an artificial means of getting a desired length of DNA (a gene) into a new host cell – in other words, a tool for producing genetically modified organisms. Different methods have been devised to introduce the DNA into the cell, including purely physical methods, such as microinjection of the DNA directly into the nucleus. Here, we give an introduction to transformation using plasmids as the vector, as this method is now possible to do with A level work.

The principle of transformation can be illustrated with the bacterium *Escherichia coli*. The strain that is used (*E. coli* K-12) is descended from one that was isolated from the human gut in the 1920s, but over the countless bacterial generations since then the original strain has become so debilitated that it cannot thrive outside the laboratory. The strain has 'lost' certain genes so that it can no longer inhabit the human gut.

Communication
Appendix V: Key Skills
Page 142

Plasmids are rings of DNA, separate from the bacterial chromosome, which are found in many bacteria. Plasmids provide a useful means of transferring DNA between microorganisms. In the example given above, the plasmid pUC 18 carries the genes for ampicillin resistance and for synthesis of β-galactosidase. pUC 18 can be used to 'transform' *E. coli* bacteria lacking these genes.

Relatively few bacterial species are known to be able to take up DNA naturally. However, certain treatments can make these cells 'competent' and able to be transformed. Treatment with calcium chloride is one such treatment, though the mechanism of action is not fully understood. Any procedures involving transformations should be carried out aseptically, using safe microbiological techniques and in line with relevant legal regulations (see page 57).

Summary of steps in the procedure:
- prepare 'competent' cells of *E. coli*, by treatment with calcium chloride – this makes holes in the cell membrane
- mix the suspension of competent *E. coli* cells with the plasmid DNA
- incubate the mixture on ice followed by a heat shock – the shock promotes uptake of the DNA and it is at this stage that the transformation takes place
- add broth containing nutrients – this allows the cells to grow and develop expression of the genes carried by the plasmid
- plate out the cell culture on to agar plates which have been set up to detect whether transformation has occurred

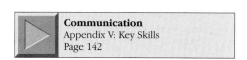

Communication
Appendix V: Key Skills
Page 142

- incubate the plates to allow growth of bacterial colonies and examine to detect those which have been transformed.

A control set of tubes, using the original strain of *E. coli* but without adding the plasmid, can be run alongside the reaction tubes for comparison. In the example referred to above, for the final stage, two sets of agar plates would be prepared – one containing the antibiotic ampicillin and the other containing X-gal, a substance (related to lactose) which gives a blue colour when broken down by β-galactosidase. The original *E. coli* cells are not able to grow in the presence of ampicillin, nor can they break down lactose (or X-gal). Cells that have been transformed will grow on the plates containing ampicillin and will give blue-coloured colonies due to the breakdown of X-gal. Even though a relatively small number of cells are likely to have been transformed, there should be enough to illustrate the success of this method for genetic modification of bacterial cells. Other transformations include colour reactions which assist in the detection of transformed colonies. A particularly attractive example is the incorporation of a green fluorescent protein gene (GFP) from the jellyfish *Aequorea victoria* into *E. coli*, though special permission is required to do such work in schools within the European Union.

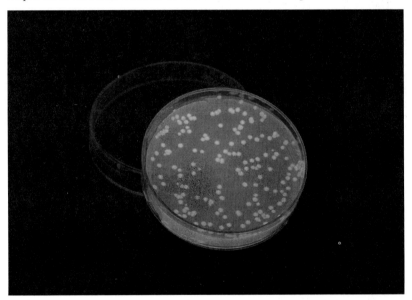

Figure 5.7 A transformation that glows! The gene for GFP (green fluorescent protein) came originally from bioluminescent jellyfish. The gene has now been incorporated into a plasmid and can be used in transformation experiments with bacteria. Cells which have taken up the GFP glow (fluoresce) in UV light when grown on agar containing the sugar actinose.

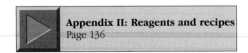

Appendix II: Reagents and recipes
Page 136

Bioreactors in the laboratory

As the name implies, the term **bioreactor** refers to a vessel in which biological reactions take place. Frequently, bioreactors are associated with activities of microorganisms and their fermentation reactions, which may be exploited for their products. We can also use the term to include vessels used for enzyme reactions, such as columns containing immobilised enzymes, and for a range of biosensors.

Fermenters as bioreactors

Fermenters can range from quite simple containers, such as a test tube or a 1-litre (dm^3) plastic lemonade bottle, to huge industrial fermenters, with a capacity up to 200 000 dm^3. With increased size inevitably the equipment becomes more complex, usually to ensure there is control over the conditions within the fermenter and the facility to add or remove materials during the fermentation reaction. On a laboratory scale, a useful size would be from about 500 cm^3 up to 2 dm^3, examples of which are shown in Figure 5.8. Such fermenters can give an insight into the operation of large-scale industrial fermenters, such as would be used for production of antibiotics, for brewing beer or manufacture of yoghurt.

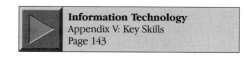

(a) (b) (c)

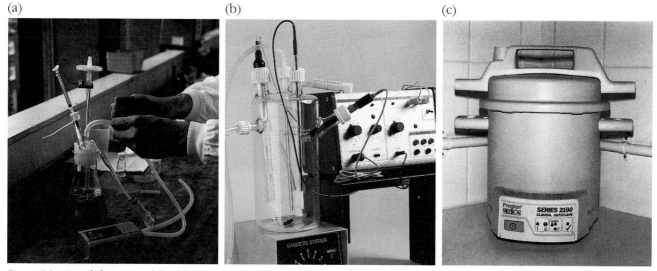

Figure 5.8 (a) and (b) two models of fermenter, suitable for use in the laboratory at A level (c) A small autoclave sterilises using steam under pressure at 126 °C for 11 minutes.

We can use the model shown in Figure 5.8(a) to illustrate the principles of working with a fermenter and the procedures to be undertaken when setting up investigations involving fermentations with microorganisms.

Summary of steps in the procedure:
- sterilise all equipment and culture media
- assemble the bioreactor, including syringes and three-way taps
- set up system for agitation and aeration
- allow for inputs
- control variables, such as temperature or pH
- monitor progress of reaction or growth of population
- collect or harvest products
- dispose of waste at end of fermentation.

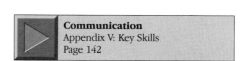

Sterilisation of equipment and culture media is carried out by high-temperature steam, in an autoclave or in a pressure cooker. In the laboratory, this is usually carried out at 120 °C, for 15 minutes, though the time required depends on the size of the flask and the nature of the materials. Care should be taken to ensure the vents from the container are correctly adjusted (open or sealed) during the sterilisation procedure. Sterilisation is intended to kill all microorganisms and their spores. **Aseptic technique** should then be used at all stages when transferring media and cultures. Similarly, at the end of the fermentation, equipment and remaining cultures and media should be sterilised before disposal.

When assembling the apparatus, **syringes** are used for adding materials, or for removing samples during the fermentation. **Three-way taps** facilitate the direction of flow of materials and also isolate the contents of the flask and of the syringes. The syringes and three-way taps are generally supplied in aseptic packages. If aeration is required, incoming air passes through a filter to ensure that it is sterile and passes through a second filter when leaving the vessel to prevent contamination of the atmosphere. A simple pump, such as that used in an aquarium, maintains circulation of the air, thus providing **aeration**. The contents can be kept **stirred** by means of a magnetic stirrer.

It may be necessary to add ingredients while the fermentation or reaction is in progress. These materials could include more nutrient, inoculum, acids or alkalis, or, at the start, anti-foam liquids may be advisable. It is likely that heat will be generated by the reaction which may necessitate cooling of the fermenter and its contents. The **temperature** can be checked by reading the thermometer, or recorded continuously with a temperature probe linked to a computer. Changes in **pH** which occur during the reaction can be monitored by use of a pH probe attached to a pH meter, or by extracting samples and titrating against acid or alkali as appropriate. If adjustments need to be made to the pH, this can be done by adding acid or alkali through the syringe.

Growth of a microorganism can be determined by removing samples and either making a direct count of cells with a **haemocytometer** (see page 40), or estimating the turbidity with a **colorimeter** (see page 42). Another way of monitoring the rate of metabolic activity (representing rate of growth of the population) is to measure the gas (carbon dioxide) which is evolved.

In the laboratory, you may be interested in monitoring the progress of a fermentation, or perhaps comparing activity of different cultures or using different conditions at a particular time. In industrial fermentations, however, the aim is to harvest an end-product and to recover this from the mass of materials that have accumulated in the bioreactor during the fermentation. This is known as **downstream processing**. In large-scale fermentations, depending on the nature of the desired product, various methods are used to recover the material, including precipitation, centrifugation, distillation, drying, chromatography or electrophoresis. In the laboratory (or in the home) you can use a simple wine fermentation as an example to illustrate the

Figure 5.9 This 'bubble logger', placed here on the tube of a fermentation lock, contains a sensor which is activated when a bubble passes. A light flashes and the counter adds one for each bubble. You could record the bubbles registered at specified intervals over a period of time or, alternatively, link the bubble logger to a data logger or computer for continuous recording

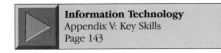

Information Technology
Appendix V: Key Skills
Page 143

principles of downstream processing. As the fermentation nears completion, the fermentation activity ceases. At this stage, bubbles no longer rise to the surface or pass through the airlock. The liquid gradually clears and a residue (mainly dead yeast cells) sinks to the bottom. The wine can then be siphoned off from the residue. This may be done more than once, until a sparkling clear liquid is obtained, though sometimes enzymes, such as pectinases or amylases, may be used to help clarify the wine.

The apparatus in Figure 5.10 shows a laboratory simulation of a **chemostat**, which enables continuous culture of microorganisms by allowing fresh medium to be added during the fermentation. The additional medium provides more nutrients, and also dilutes the existing culture solution, thereby encouraging further growth of the population. You could use available laboratory equipment to adapt the fermenters described above to provide a continuous culture fermenter.

Appendix II: Reagents and recipes
Page 136

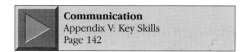

Communication
Appendix V: Key Skills
Page 142

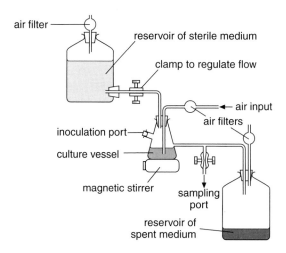

Figure 5.10 Chemostat for continuous culture set up in the laboratory

Outline of suggestions for investigations with fermentations

Yeast and different sugars

You can use a simple fermenter, or those described earlier, to compare the ability of yeast (*Saccharomyces cerevisiae*) to ferment sugars such as glucose, fructose, galactose, sucrose, lactose, maltose and raffinose. Inorganic nutrient is supplied as ammonium phosphate and ammonium sulphate (which can be obtained as yeast nutrient as sold for home-made wine making). A simple fermenter is fitted with an airlock which contains water to which universal indicator can be added. You would set up a series of flasks, each with the same concentration of a different sugar solution, the same mass of yeast and the same quantity of nutrient. The flasks can be placed in an incubator (at between 20 and 25 °C) to encourage the fermentation. You could do a pilot run (best with glucose as the substrate) to get an idea of a suitable time over which the fermentation can be monitored.

MORE ADVANCED TOOLS AND TECHNIQUES

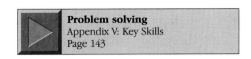

Problem solving
Appendix V: Key Skills
Page 143

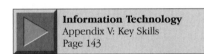

Chapter 4: Quantitative techniques
Page 40-42

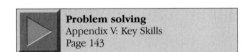

Information Technology
Appendix V: Key Skills
Page 143

Problem solving
Appendix V: Key Skills
Page 143

There are different ways of comparing the rate of fermentation:

- devise a means of counting the bubbles of carbon dioxide given off, at different time intervals after the start – this could be done, say, by recording the number of bubbles passing through the airlock in one minute
- note the time at which the indicator in the airlock changes colour
- extract a sample from the flask (say after 24 hours) and titrate this against a solution of alkali to determine the changes in acidity in the solution during the fermentation. A few drops of phenolphthalein would be used as an indicator and a comparison made of the volume of alkali required to neutralise the acid
- extract samples at the start and over a period of time and estimate the number of cells in the population, using a haemocytometer or other counting method (see Chapter 4).

Changes of pH during fermentations of sauerkraut, silage or yoghurt

A simple simulation of making sauerkraut from cabbage or silage from grass can be undertaken in the laboratory. In each case, the material (cabbage or grass) is chopped, placed in a container such as a beaker, weighted down and covered closely. Salt is added in the sauerkraut fermentation and this helps to draw water out of the cells. Microbes which occur naturally on the living material ferment the sugars present in the cells to lactic acid, resulting in a lowering of the pH. This change can be monitored by using a pH probe or by titration at intervals. Continuous records of the pH changes could be achieved by linking the pH probe to a computer. You could then devise investigations to compare the fermentation rate using material harvested at different times, after storage (for cabbage), or with different degrees of chopping the original material or at different temperatures over a period of time.

Rapid-cycling brassicas – or experiments with 'fast plants'

Rapid-cycling brassicas ('fast plants', or specially selected strains of *Brassica rapa*) are a welcome addition to plant material which is available for experimental work at A level. With a life cycle completed in just 5 weeks, these plants require only limited space in the laboratory for growth, and allow you to undertake small-scale individual investigations using whole plants within a reasonable time scale. A range of investigations can be undertaken relating, for example, to genetics and inheritance patterns, artificial selection, control of growth (in relation to light or plant growth substances), studies on photosynthesis, transpiration or nutrition, or an introduction to methods of tissue culture.

These plants originated from some research work carried out in the early 1970s, by Dr Paul Williams at the University of Wisconsin–Madison in the USA. His interest was to find varieties of plants with a short life-cycle and which could then be used to give results more quickly in a breeding programme concerned with disease resistance in crop plants. He had access to a wide range of wild and cultivated brassicas (cabbage family) from different parts of the world and by artificial selection produced some brassicas which consistently had very short life cycles. Table 5.1 shows a range of rapid-cycling brassicas, including *B. rapa* which has found particular use for experimental work with plants in schools and colleges.

Table 5.1 *Growth characteristics of some rapid-cycling brassicas*

Growth characteristic	*Brassica* species					
	*B. rapa**	*B. nigra*	*B. oleracea*	*B. juncea*	*B. carinata*	*B. napus*
Mean days to first flowering	14	20	30	19	26	25
Height at first flowering / cm	13	27	23	30	42	35
Seeds per plant	78	69	18	107	67	76
Days per cycle	36	40	60	39	56	55
Cycles per year	10	9	6	9	6	6

* *B. rapa* is also known as *B. campestris*.

The plants are grown under continuous light in a suitable growth medium to which nutrients are added in a convenient form, such as slow-release fertiliser pellets. Any suitable small container, such as polystyrene blocks or discarded black film containers, can be used. The small size of the container probably restricts root growth and encourages flowering by stressing the plant. The containers and their wicks stand on capillary matting which dips into a reservoir of water. Figure 5.12 shows a typical unit for growing rapid-cycling brassicas on a laboratory bench. Controlled pollination can be carried out, using a 'bee-stick' to mimic natural pollination processes, or by deliberate self-pollination. A number of mutant forms are available, thus allowing genetic breeding experiments to be completed in a relatively short time.

Figure 5.11 Growing rapid-cycling brassicas on the laboratory bench showing a typical light bank

Figure 5.12 Investigations with rapid cycling Brassica rapa. *Normal height wild type in the centre, with a mutant rosette form on the right. On the left, the plant shows the effect of GA (gibberellic acid) on the mutant rosette form. What sort of progeny (rosette or normal) would you get if you crossed the treated rosette plants among themselves?*

MORE ADVANCED TOOLS AND TECHNIQUES

Table 5.2 *Rapid-cycling brassicas lend themselves to investigations which can be used for individual projects or as class investigations. This table outlines a few situations with suggested hypotheses which could be investigated in relation to the biological observations given*

Observation	How would you test these hypotheses?
1. It is well known that, if you subject plants to stress, their vegetative growth may be restricted but they may flower more rapidly.	→ that the use of containers with a very small soil volume restricts vegetative growth → that the use of containers with a very small soil volume promotes more rapid flowering
2. When seedlings are exposed to uneven illumination, they respond by bending towards the strongest light source. This is known as positive phototropism. The stimulus could be detected in a number of different parts of the seedling, such as the cotyledons, apical meristem, hypocotyl, etc.	→ that the stimulus of uneven illumination is detected in the cotyledons of (say) 4-day-old rapid-cycling brassica seedlings → that the stimulus . . . is detected in the apical meristem . . . → that the stimulus . . . is detected in the hypocotyl . . .
3. If you examine a population of rapid-cycling brassica plants of identical age, you will notice some clear differences between individual plants. For example, some will be more hairy than others.	→ that hairiness is a heritable trait in rapid-cycling brassicas
4. Various mutant rapid-cycling brassicas are available. In one, known as *rosette*, the internodes are very short giving the plant a flat rosette-type habit. In other respects, the plant is normal in appearance. The leaves, for example, are the normal dark green colour. In another mutant, known as *yellow-green*, the leaves and stem are a pale yellow-green colour, but the plant is normal in other respects, such as height.	→ that the *rosette* character is under the control of a single Mendelian recessive pair of alleles and that normal (tall) is therefore dominant to rosette → that the *yellow-green* character is under the control of a single Mendelian recessive pair of alleles and that normal (dark-green) leaf and stem colour is therefore dominant to yellow-green → that the pairs of alleles for *rosette* and for *yellow-green* are not linked and therefore that they obey Mendel's Second Law

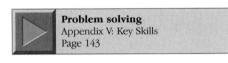

Problem solving
Appendix V: Key Skills
Page 143

Appendix II
Page 136

Development of equipment for the growth of these plants, together with ideas for experimental work that could be undertaken, has been carried out by Science and Plants for Schools (SAPS). See Appendix II for information and references giving full practical details for work with rapid-cycling brassicas, together with a kit containing equipment and necessary materials plus supplies of seeds.

Plant tissue culture

Techniques for growing or culturing plant cells *in vitro* are now well established, with important applications in research and in the horticultural industry. The principles for culturing isolated cells are essentially similar to those used for growing microorganisms – the cells are grown in a medium, usually agar, supplemented with a carbon source and inorganic nutrients. Plant growth substances are also included in the medium at different stages, to encourage growth of shoots, or of roots as required. As with microbial cultures, it is essential to work under sterile conditions as far as possible to reduce contamination from microorganisms, such as bacteria and fungi including yeasts, some of which are found naturally in plant tissues. Failures in attempts to grow cultures are often because of these

contaminants, because they tend to grow much faster than the plant tissue. Plant tissue cultures can be stored at low temperatures, then grown on at normal temperatures when required.

For A level practical work with tissue culture, a range of plant material has been used, such as cauliflower curds, poplar twigs and *Brassica* seedlings, though with varying success. The main difficulties encountered arise from contamination and the need to maintain sterile conditions when working with the plant tissues at early stages. The availability of improved methods of sterilising the material and use of rapidly growing species ('fast plants') which then help to minimise the problems associated with contamination, has increased the success rate within a reasonable time scale. This, in turn, reduces the need for elaborate equipment and brings the technique into the scope of project work at A level. The summary below outlines the steps taken in standard procedures for tissue culture, including those used on a commercial scale, but suitable protocols for A level work are given in references quoted in Appendix II.

Appendix II: Reagents and recipes
Page 136

Summary of steps in the procedure:
- select suitable plant material (ensure the plant is healthy)
- disinfect or surface sterilise the material, then wash in sterile distilled water
- cut out (excise) small portions of tissue, known as **explants** – often cut from inside a bud or apical meristem
- work as far as possible in sterile conditions
- transfer explant to culture dish containing agar and nutrient (generally sucrose, mineral salts and vitamins)
- incubate culture (usually between 15 °C and 30 °C) to allow some cell division and growth of undifferentiated tissue known as a callus (in some cases, e.g. growth of pollen grains direct to embryos, there is no callus stage)
- transfer to medium containing plant growth substances to initiate shoots
- subculture, as required, at intervals of a few weeks (usually 4 to 8)
- store until needed, usually between 5 °C and 8 °C
- transfer to medium containing plant growth substances to induce rooting of the shoots
- transfer young plants to grow on in soil
- acclimatise young growing plants in glasshouse or similar – high humidity is needed in early stages.

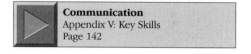

Communication
Appendix V: Key Skills
Page 142

The term **micropropagation** is used to describe propagation of whole plants by tissue culture. Micropropagation allows production of large numbers of genetically identical plants (clones) in a short time, and can be achieved from just one or very few original stock plants. In the horticultural industry, use of micropropagation enables close control over stocks, both as a means of determining the variety selected and to adjust the growth of the plants to coincide precisely with market requirements. For A level work, details of protocols for

tissue culture with cauliflower curds, poplar twigs and fast plants, together with ideas for experimental work that could be undertaken are given in Appendix II.

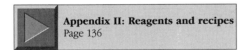
Problem solving
Appendix V: Key Skills
Page 143

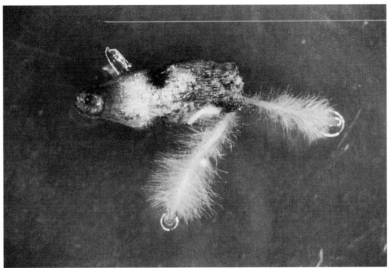

Figure 5.13 Tissue culture with rapid-cycling Brassica rapa. *Explants can be taken from different parts of the germinating seedling, illustrating the extent of 'totipotency' in plant cells. Here an explant from the mid-hypocotyl region is shown developing roots. The agar medium contained sucrose. MS (Murashige & Skoog) salts, and IAA (indole acetic acid). Investigations can be carried out using different parts of the seedling or with variations in the medium used*

Enzyme-linked immunosorbent assay (ELISA)

Enzyme-**L**inked **I**mmuno**S**orbent **A**ssay, or ELISA for short, is an immunological technique which exploits the **antigen–antibody** reaction, giving an analytical tool that is both highly specific and extremely sensitive in detecting small amounts of a molecule. Each antibody binds specifically to only one antigen, with the recognition often limited to a single species. The antigen to be detected is usually a protein or polysaccharide, originating from, for example, pathogenic microorganisms, tumour cells, a hormone, a plant growth substance or other living material. In the ELISA assay, the presence of the antigen is revealed by a colour reaction, due to the linking of an enzyme with an antibody, thus providing a highly sensitive technique.

Appendix II: Reagents and recipes
Page 136

The required antibodies for a particular antigen are produced as **monoclonal antibodies** by standard techniques. This involves injecting an animal with the antigen, then removing antibody-secreting cells from the spleen and fusing the lymphocytes from these with myelomas to produce hybridomas. While the lymphocytes have a limited life span, they can be made 'immortal' by this fusion with myeloma cells (abnormal cells which are capable of indefinite growth) and are thus clones of the original cell. The cell lines produced are tested and those which recognise specific antigens are grown on. Hybridomas which retain the ability to produce the antibody are grown using cell-culture techniques, to provide a supply of the specific antibody. Large quantities of a specific antibody can thus be obtained. Antibodies can be raised against a large number of different organisms.

Many large molecules, such as proteins, glycoproteins and some complex carbohydrates, show the property of 'sticking' to certain plastics. This means that the molecules are held on a fixed surface, enabling a series of reactions to take place at the surface. In the ELISA technique described below, the antigen to be detected is allowed to bind on the surface of a plastic plate containing wells which hold the liquid containing the substances to be assayed. The specific antibody is introduced to the well and incubated for an appropriate period of time. If the specific antigen is present, the antibody will bind to it and also be held on the surface of the well. Solutions are then washed out and a second antibody linked to an enzyme is added. The enzyme is chosen so that it gives a colour reaction with a particular substrate. After incubation, these solutions are again washed out thoroughly. If the original antigen is present, the antibodies plus enzyme will be retained and appropriate substrate added to allow the colour to develop. A positive colour reaction indicates presence of the original antigen. The intensity of the colour which develops is proportional to the amount of enzyme held, so colorimetric or other techniques can be used to make a quantitative estimate of the material being assayed.

Summary of steps in the procedure:

- collect sample(s) of material to be assayed and suspend in buffer
- filter (e.g. through muslin) to remove debris
- transfer a few drops of each suspension to microwells or other container with suitable plastic surface
- leave for a period of time to allow antigens to become attached to inner surface of well
- pour off suspension of buffer containing antigens (from original sample) from the wells
- wash out wells several times with buffer (with added detergent), to remove excess uncombined antigens – a range of antigens is likely to remain attached to the surface of the wells
- add first antibody – specific for antigen to be detected
- leave for a period of time to allow antibody to become attached to antigen (which is held on surface of well)
- wash out wells several times with buffer and detergent, to remove excess antibody
- add second antibody combined with enzyme
- leave for a period of time to allow antibody to bind with first antibody (already attached)
- add appropriate substrate for the enzyme and allow colour to develop
- compare colour with standard chart or make quantitative estimate using colorimeter or equivalent.

Communication
Appendix V: Key Skills
Page 142

MORE ADVANCED TOOLS AND TECHNIQUES

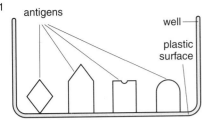

1

A number of different antigens bind to the surface of the plastic. The antigens are large molecules, such as proteins, glycoproteins and carbohydrates.

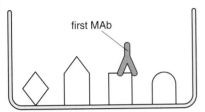

2

The first (monoclonal) antibody (MAb) recognises only its specific antigen and binds to it.

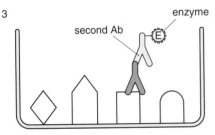

3

The second antibody with attached enzyme (E) then binds to the first (monoclonal) antibody.

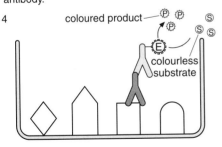

4

The enzyme allows conversion of a colourless substrate (S) to a coloured product (P).

Figure 5.14 Stages in the ELISA procedures

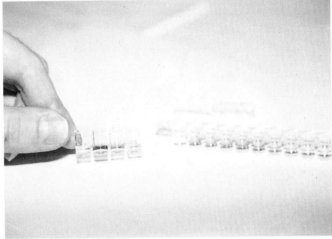

Figure 5.15 (a) A strip of microwells being used in the ELISA procedure for detection of Botrytis *infection (b) Comparing the result with a set of standard solutions. The intensity of coloration (blue) gives a quantitative measure of the original antigen*

reaction to develop, kits are available which enable a response to be obtained, which is both specific and sensitive, in a much shorter time, and so become feasible for A-level investigations. As an example, a kit has been developed for detection of the pathogenic fungus *Botrytis cinerea* (see Appendix II), and this could be used to monitor *Botrytis* infection in fruits, vegetables or flowers (such as strawberries, grapes, flower petals), say after harvest and during storage.

See Appendix II for protocols for ELISA, as developed by SAPS (Dr Mary MacDonald) and Dr Molly Dewey (Department of Plant Sciences, University of Oxford).

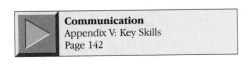

Communication
Appendix V: Key Skills
Page 142

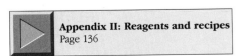

Appendix II: Reagents and recipes
Page 136

Field work techniques

Ecosystems are complex associations of plants, animals and microorganisms, which interact with each other and with their non-living environment. The organisms within the ecosystem make up the **biotic** component and their distribution is influenced by each other and by physical and chemical factors, the **abiotic** component.

An understanding of the associations between organisms and their environment is an important part of any course in Biology and it is desirable that field studies in the form of practical investigations of the distribution of plants and animals in at least one habitat, together with the influence of the abiotic factors, should be undertaken.

A number of different methods of investigating and analysing the distribution of organisms, varying from simple descriptive, qualitative techniques to more complex quantitative measurements, may be used. In this chapter, a range of techniques is considered, including methods of sampling and estimations of the distribution and abundance of organisms. In addition, the methods of measuring environmental factors are described.

Sampling

The purpose of sampling is to obtain a series of **independent estimates** of the variables you are measuring. For example, you might want to look at the percentage cover of moss on the trunk of oak trees, or the number of shrimps in a freshwater stream. Clearly, you cannot take measurements from all of the trees in the wood, or count all of the shrimps in the stream. Therefore, you will need to take a **sample** of the population from the site you are studying. Generally, some form of **random sampling** is the best way to select a sample that is **unbiased**.

Random sampling

Random co-ordinates can be used to locate sampling positions in a habitat, such as an area of moorland or a meadow. Mark out a **sampling area** using tape measures and select random coordinates from a **table of random numbers**:
- mark out the area (Figure 6.1) using 20 m tape-measures
- look at the first column of random numbers (Table 6.1); work your way systematically down the column and select the first number less than 20 (14), which gives the *x*-coordinate
- the next number less than 20 (10) gives the *y*-coordinate
- the 2nd quadrat would then be (12 and 7) and so on; carrying on down the table until you have sampled the number of quadrats you need.

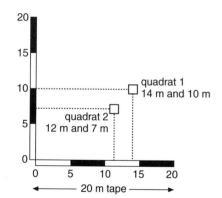

Figure 6.1 Random co-ordinates being used to locate quadrats within a 20 m × 20 m sampling area

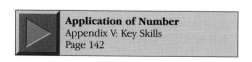

Application of Number
Appendix V: Key Skills
Page 142

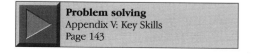

Problem solving
Appendix V: Key Skills
Page 143

FIELD WORK TECHNIQUES

Table 6.1 *Table of random numbers showing the selection of random co-ordinates and random paces*

34	29	12	21	74	12	48	50	93	88	6	9	7	29	82
80	37	65	7	51	53	35	14	99	30	57	37	98	42	49
70	12	71	31	62	72	89	65	49	19	40	26	91	57	39
14	49	87	23	78	67	26	35	61	81	21	2	23	76	71
67	48	28	43	69	80	58	38	43	19	64	12	23	88	17
89	64	72	39	88	8	98	70	74	6	23	29	88	76	13
92	7	78	68	65	29	73	38	28	4	16	47	59	91	29
10	76	34	56	6	27	42	83	77	83	39	7	76	79	34
72	18	57	36	95	14	38	5	51	34	41	39	99	73	15
27	89	20	13	70	90	80	58	31	4	4	80	92	69	58
97	49	91	71	15	41	73	86	53	37	94	35	21	33	68
32	94	66	45	78	9	49	36	3	94	53	36	98	36	86
54	87	45	52	68	45	31	81	42	57	4	53	89	56	44
80	85	4	50	92	7	38	91	34	77	67	6	69	39	7
35	7	48	96	26	60	81	74	21	53	44	8	84	80	70

Communication
Appendix V: Key Skills
Page 142

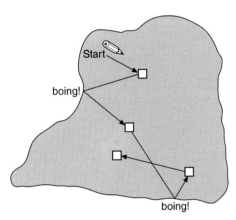

Figure 6.2 A random walking method being used to locate quadrats within an irregular sampling area. Each quadrat is positioned after walking a random number of paces (from a table of random numbers) in a random direction (determined by the spin of a pencil)

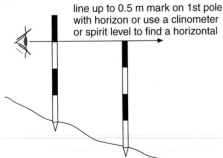

2 m range pole divided into 0.5 m sections

line up to 0.5 m mark on 1st pole with horizon or use a clinometer or spirit level to find a horizontal

by lining up the top of the 2nd range pole with the imaginary line drawn from the 0.5 m mark on the 1st range pole and the horizon, you can select a site 0.5 m vertically below the first

Figure 6.3 Sampling down a slope

A **random walking** method (Figure 6.2) might be more suitable for a small or less regular area, or if you wish to take samples from the entire area. Suppose you wanted to look at 25 quadrats in an area:

- from a table of random numbers (Table 6.1) choose any block of numbers (the 2nd down in the 2nd column will do)
- select a **random direction** by spinning a pencil and then walk for the required number of paces, which in this example is eight
- once that has been sampled take the next number down (29), spin the pencil again and walk for 29 paces in that direction
- after 16 paces you hit the boundary and bounce off so that your angle of reflection equals your angle of incidence
- at 29 paces do the next quadrat and continue through the block until all 25 quadrats have been done.

If your investigation involves a **population** of trees, or other discrete objects, you could number all the individuals which meet your sampling criteria; they may need to be of a certain specified size, age or sex. You can then use the random numbers to pick a set to be measured from the population.

Systematic sampling

Occasionally a purely random approach will not work. If, for example, you wanted to correlate the number of stoneflies with flow rate, then a series of random sites along a stream might happen to give all slow or all fast sites. In this case a more **systematic** approach might be better.

Systematic sampling is appropriate if you are looking at changes across a habitat such as the **zonation** of plants and animals down a rocky shore or **successional changes** across a dune system. Sampling needs to be carried out along some form of **transect**:

- at fixed horizontal or vertical distances (Figure 6.3)

- or according to fixed morphological features (on ridges and in hollows on a dune system)
- or at fixed intervals of some other variable such as flow rate.

If you think of a transect as being a line across a habitat, then because most sampling will be carried out using some form of quadrat, transects generally take the form of a belt of certain width crossing the habitat. Transects (Figure 6.4) can be
- continuous – every possible position along the transect is examined
- interrupted – samples are taken at intervals with gaps in between.

On large sites, such as extensive dune systems, transects can extend for hundreds of metres. You could end up with far too many sampling sites if you sampled at fixed intervals of, for example, 10 metres. It would be better to sample at fixed morphological features such as on top of every dune ridge and in each hollow (Figure 6.5).

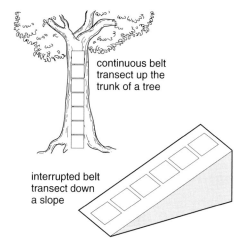

Figure 6.4 Continuous and interrupted belt transects

Communication
Appendix V: Key Skills
Page 142

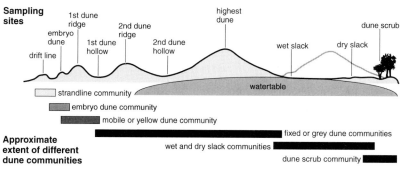

Figure 6.5 Sampling at fixed morphological intervals (ridges, hollows, etc.) on sand dunes

A random sampling method can lead to problems if you are trying to **correlate** two variables. For example, a student was looking at the relationship between water velocity and the number of flat mayflies (*Ecdyonurus* sp.) in a stream and used a random sampling method where a tape-measure was placed alongside the stream and sampling distances selected using a random number table. By chance, most of the sampling positions were in slow-flowing areas of the stream (Figure 6.6(a)) with only one sample at a much higher velocity. It would have been better to use a systematic approach. The first step would be to identify the slowest and fastest sections, measure their velocities and then select sampling sites at intermediate velocities (Figure 6.6(b)).

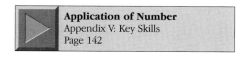

Application of Number
Appendix V: Key Skills
Page 142

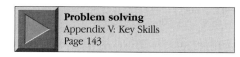

Problem solving
Appendix V: Key Skills
Page 143

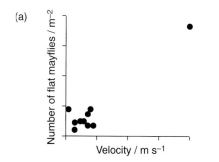

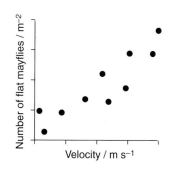

Figure 6.6 (a) Random sampling can give a clumped distribution of velocities sampled; (b) a systematic approach can give a more even distribution of velocities sampled

FIELD WORK TECHNIQUES

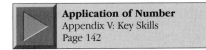

Application of Number
Appendix V: Key Skills
Page 142

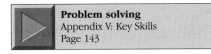

Problem solving
Appendix V: Key Skills
Page 143

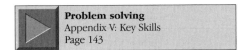

Problem solving
Appendix V: Key Skills
Page 143

Describing vegetation

Whole area descriptions – species lists and ACFOR scales

The most basic description of the vegetation within a habitat is a list of those species which are present. As you walk through a site you can compile a list of species you find. This is probably more efficient than spending time examining quadrats. An obvious limitation of a simple species list is the lack of any **estimate of abundance**. A quick estimate can be made by giving each species a subjective rating of abundance: **A**bundant, **C**ommon, **F**requent, **O**ccasional, **R**are. This is known as the **ACFOR** scale and has certain limitations:

- it is unlikely that two people would ever score the same set of plants identically
- there is no definition of how common a plant has to be to earn a particular rating
- the ratings given to species may depend on their conspicuousness rather than their abundance.

Quadrat-based estimates

Apart from the very basic methods outlined above, most vegetation sampling will need some form of quadrat. A quadrat can be defined as a frame used to mark out a unit of habitat. Conventionally, quadrats are square frames covering an area of 0.25 m² or 1 m², but they can be of any size and can also be circular, rectangular or even three-dimensional. Various methods of determining quadrat size exist, but they are of little use practically. Most ecologists adjust the quadrat size based on experience and the size and scale of the vegetation being studied. As a guideline try these:

- a quadrat covering an area of 0.25 m² (0.5 m × 0.5 m) for most low-growing vegetation
- a larger quadrat of 1 m² (1 m × 1 m) on seashores and when looking at larger plants such as tree saplings
- a 0.01 m² (100 mm × 100 mm) quadrat for lichens and mosses on tree trunks or gravestones.

Table 6.2 *The Domin scale*

Cover	Domin Value
91%–100%	10
76%–90%	9
51%–75%	8
34%–50%	7
26%–33%	6
11%–25%	5
4%–10%	4
<4% many individuals	3
<4% several individuals	2
<4% few individuals	1

Subjective estimates of cover

A simple, subjective estimate of **percentage cover** will sometimes be a sufficiently good measure of the relative abundance of species present within a quadrat. For example, a quick estimate of percentage cover would be sufficient if you wanted a description of the differences in vegetation in two habitats as a back-up to the main enquiry, which was a quantitative comparison of various animal species in the habitats. Subjective estimates will always be prone to observer error because no two people will necessarily estimate covers identically.

By defining bands of percentage cover and allocating each a score, then it becomes more likely that people would agree on where each species should be on the abundance scale. The **Domin scale** (Table 6.2) defines 10 percentage cover bands and can add consistency to your estimates of cover. It is, for example, relatively easy to distinguish between a species that covers between 34 and 50 per cent of the area

(7 on the Domin scale) and one covering 26 to 33 per cent of the area (6 on the Domin scale).

Table 6.3 *Crapp scales of abundance for rocky shore work*

Score	Lichens	Seaweeds	Barnacles	Limpets and periwinkles	Dog whelks
Ex	>80% cover	>90% cover	>5 cm⁻²	>200 m⁻²	>100 m⁻²
S	50–80% cover	60–90% cover	3–5 cm⁻²	100–200 m⁻²	50–100 m⁻²
A	20–50% cover	30–60% cover	1–3 cm⁻²	50–100 m⁻²	20–50 m⁻²
C	1–20% cover	5–30% cover	<1 cm apart	20–50 m⁻²	11–20 m⁻²
F	large patches	<5% cover	<10 cm apart	5–20 m⁻²	5–10 m⁻²
O	small patches	scattered plants	1–100 m⁻²	1–5 m⁻²	1–4 m⁻²
R	just present	1–2 plants only	<1 m⁻²	<1 m⁻²	<1 m⁻²

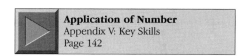

The **Crapp scale** (Table 6.3) is a similar scale devised for lichens and seaweeds on rocky shores and is named after a member of the Irish Fisheries Board rather than after its effectiveness. Estimates of the percentage cover of lichens and seaweeds are made within a 1 m² quadrat. For completeness, abundance scales for rocky shore animals are also shown in Table 6.3.

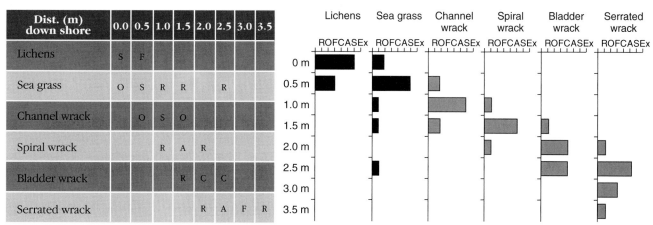

Figure 6.7 The distribution of some rocky shore plants. Conversion for plotting bar charts: Rare = 1, Occasional = 2, Frequent = 3, Common = 4, Abundant = 5, Super abundant = 6, Extremely abundant = 7

ACFOR and Crapp scales can be converted into numerical values which then can be used in bar charts to show distribution patterns (Figure 6.7). These subjective scales are suitable for simple descriptive work and enable the abundance of quite different organisms to be directly compared. They are, however, of limited use for the statistical comparison of sites or most other investigative work.

Objective estimates of abundance

Subjective estimates of percentage cover, either within an area as a whole or within individual quadrats, are prone to observer errors. A group of 25 students looking at Figure 6.8(a) produced estimates ranging from 20 per cent to 40 per cent cover. When using quadrats

FIELD WORK TECHNIQUES

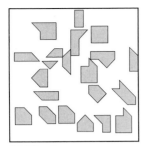

(a) What is your 'guesstimate' of the % cover of this species?

(b) Using 25 large random quadrats estimate the percentage frequency of this strange species as:

% Frequency

$$= \frac{\text{no. of quadrats containing plant}}{\text{total no. of quadrats examined}} \times 100$$

$$= \frac{24}{25}$$

$$= 96\%$$

(c) By using 50 smaller quadrats, the % frequency drops to 48% [out of the 50 quadrats only 24 contain the plant (shown in bold) making 48%]. As the size of quadrats gets smaller, so we would expect the % frequency to fall further. The lower limit is fixed by the actual percentage cover of species.

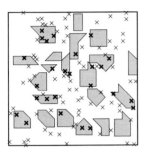

(d) We can estimate the % cover by using a point sampling method. The crosses represent the locations of 100 point quadrats. The plant is present at 26 of these (again shown in bold) so our estimate of percentage cover is 26%.

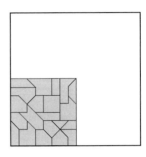

(e) *Sortosquarus regulatus* is a very convenient species to study as it can easily, and without being harmed, be moved and all the individuals fit into a nice regular square shape. If you actually measure the percentage of the area covered by this square, it is 25%. So point sampling has given a reasonably good estimate of the percentage cover.

Figure 6.8 The distributions of Sortosquarus regulatus

we have a number of alternative, **objective estimates of abundance**:

- percentage frequency
- percentage cover
- local frequency
- density
- biomass.

Percentage frequency

Percentage frequency is defined as the percentage probability of a plant occurring within a quadrat. To determine percentage frequency you need to record presence and absence data. You have to decide what constitutes presence – it could be:

- only plants rooted within the quadrat
- any plant which is in, touches or overhangs the quadrat
- only plants which are in or touch the top and right sides of the frame.

In Figure 6.8(b), 25 quadrats are positioned randomly in the area. As one of them does not contain the plant, the estimate of percentage frequency is 96 per cent. Clearly, much less than 96 per cent of the area is covered by the plant. Frequency depends very much on the size of quadrats used. In Figure 6.8(c), 50 smaller quadrats give an estimate of 48 per cent frequency. As the size of the quadrat decreases, the estimated percentage frequency also decreases (Figure 6.9). Because of the relationship between quadrat size and frequency it is hard to interpret what frequency values actually mean.

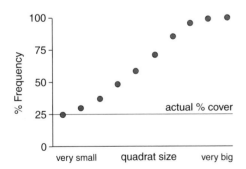

Figure 6.9 The relationship between quadrat size, % frequency and % cover

Percentage cover

Percentage cover can be estimated using a point sampling method. In Figure 6.9 we saw that as the size of the quadrat decreased, the estimated percentage frequency also decreased. In theory, a quadrat the size of a point should give the best estimate of percentage cover. This is the theoretical basis of **point quadrat sampling**. Providing you look at a large number of points, this method can give some very good results (Figures 6.8(d) and 6.8(e)). Ideally the points should be randomly distributed with respect to the plants, but for practical reasons points are usually located using some form of gridded quadrat (Figure 6.10) for low-growing plants or a point frame (Figure 6.11) in taller vegetation.

Figure 6.10 A gridded quadrat

Local frequency

A limitation of using a point sampling method to estimate cover is that, unless a large number of points are examined, rare species can be missed altogether (Figure 6.12). If available time is limited then it might be better to use a gridded quadrat (usually 100 squares per quadrat) to estimate **local frequency**, which is defined as the number of squares in which a species is found. This gives an idea of abundance for all species present within the quadrat. Since the values of frequency and local frequency depend on quadrat and grid size, it is essential for these to be stated in any description of methods used.

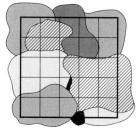

Applicaton of Number
Appendix V: Key Skills
Page 142

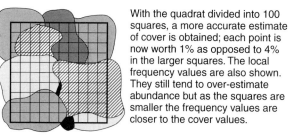

Figure 6.11 Point frame being used to estimate the cover of vegetation

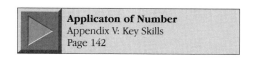

With the quadrat sub-divided into 25 squares and using the top right hand corners as locations for point samples, the touches estimate % cover. One species has not been recorded at all. By looking at presence / absence for each species we can work out % frequency (as it is for a single quadrat we call it **local frequency**). The figures are very large compared with the cover values but all species have a value.

With the quadrat divided into 100 squares, a more accurate estimate of cover is obtained; each point is now worth 1% as opposed to 4% in the larger squares. The local frequency values are also shown. They still tend to over-estimate abundance but as the squares are smaller the frequency values are closer to the cover values.

Species	Touches	% Cover	Present	% Freq.
	8 / 25	= 32	15 / 25	= 60
	4	16	11	44
	3	12	6	28
	10	40	18	68
	0	0	4	16

Species	Touches	% Cover	Present	% Freq.
	32	32	43	43
	16	16	29	29
	11	11	16	16
	40	40	56	56
	1	1	7	7

Figure 6.12 Point sampling can fail to record rare species, especially when a small number of points are looked at. To overcome this problem either look at more points or record local frequency

Density

With plants which grow as discrete individuals, estimates of **density** are possible. If, for example, you were looking at the regeneration of trees within a wood, then counting the number of oak seedlings in a series of 1 m × 1 m or 2 m × 2 m quadrats would indicate the density (number per unit area) of those seedlings. Many species, however, grow in close, intertwined mats, making it impossible to distinguish individuals, as you will see if you try counting the number of grass plants in an area of lawn.

Biomass

In one or two instances you may want to look at the **biomass** of vegetation within a series of quadrats. Estimates of biomass are probably most often used where you are interested in the yield of a plant or in energy-flow studies. Essentially, the vegetation within a quadrat is harvested, sorted into different species and the samples dried (105 °C to constant mass) and then weighed. Sometimes a crude 'wet weight' biomass estimate can be used as an approximation. This method is destructive and has limited use at A level. Appendix III provides a summary of all the methods of describing vegetation.

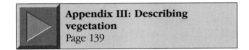

Appendix III: Describing vegetation
Page 139

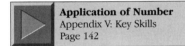

Application of Number
Appendix V: Key Skills
Page 142

Sampling animals

Several different types of data can be obtained for animal populations. The simplest to understand are **direct counts** of density, measured as the number of individual animals per unit area or volume (or per log, tree, plant or other object). Many animal populations are highly mobile so these types of data are often hard to collect, and sometimes a **relative estimate of abundance** is all that is possible. Techniques vary according to the habitats being studied.

Aquatic habitats

Compared with terrestrial habitats, it is relatively simple to obtain direct counts of the **density** of invertebrates from aquatic systems such as streams, rivers and ponds. Sampling normally needs some form of net. A kick-sampling technique is more or less standard practice in **flowing** water. A suitable pond net is positioned in the stream or river and the substrate upstream disturbed. The easiest way to do this is by kicking, though it might be necessary to remove any particularly large stones (replacing them carefully afterwards) and wash these in the mouth of the net first. Two factors influence the number of organisms caught, but these can easily be controlled. The size of quadrat and length of time spent kicking both need to be standardised. As a starting point, try kicking for 1 minute in a 50 cm × 50 cm area as defined by a quadrat. As most pond nets are only 25 cm wide you will probably need to sample the area in two sections (Figure 6.13) and then put all the animals in one sampling pot. You may need to adjust the area of stream bed sampled according to the number of animals you catch. Sampling depends on disturbing the substrate, so you should always work upstream when collecting a series of samples from a section of stream or river.

The numbers of animals vary with season and substrate type. In general, more animals are found in fast-flowing riffle sections where the bed is made of moderately sized stones and cobbles, than in slower sections with depositing substrates (silt and other sediments). Leaf packs trapped behind large branches or boulders are especially rich. As oxygen levels tend to be higher in winter than in summer, many animals show a distinct seasonality. High oxygen-requiring groups like stoneflies, mayflies and some caddis flies are more abundant in the winter months, whilst freshwater shrimps, beetles and the larvae of many Diptera have higher numbers in the summer.

Ponds are three-dimensional and without appreciable flow, so kick sampling will not work. To sample still water, some form of sweep sample is needed. This can be for either a fixed length of time or over a fixed distance, or you can use a cut off, bottomless, plastic dustbin to define a known volume of water to be sampled (Figure 6.14). As with streams and rivers there are variations in the number and types of invertebrates in different microhabitats. Areas of pond with emergent and/or submerged vegetation are usually richer than margins with no vegetation.

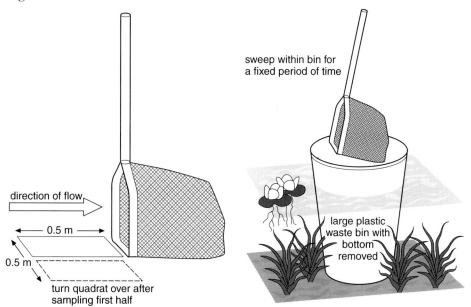

sweep within bin for a fixed period of time

direction of flow

0.5 m

0.5 m

turn quadrat over after sampling first half

large plastic waste bin with bottom removed

Figure 6.13 Kick sampling for aquatic invertebrates

Figure 6.14 Sweep sampling for aquatic invertebrates in still water

The sorting of samples is probably best done in shallow, white trays. White plastic teaspoons, fine paint brushes or wide-mouthed pipettes are useful for handling animals. Keys are available to help with identification of freshwater invertebrates. Identification is possible to family level for many groups, but for the more difficult groups, keys stop at order or class level. Identification beyond family level requires specialist keys and is normally too advanced for A-level studies. Most

FIELD WORK TECHNIQUES

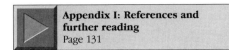
Appendix I: References and further reading
Page 131

lamp with 25–40 watt bulb to slowly dry the sample

tin can with top and bottom removed

piece of net curtain held in place by elastic band retains sample of soil or leaf litter in tin

as the sample dries animals move down, eventually falling into funnel and then into the specimen tube

specimen tube is half filled with water with one or two drops of detergent to break the surface film

Figure 6.15 Tullgren funnel for extracting invertebrates from soil samples

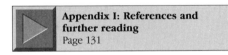
Appendix I: References and further reading
Page 131

lid made from small square of wood resting on three stones to prevent rain entering or larger animals 'stealing' catch

plastic cup sunk into ground forms trap

Cup can either be empty or contain water with a few drops of detergent as wetting agent. It should be slightly raised above the ground surface to prevent rain running in.

Figure 6.16 Pitfall trap

freshwater invertebrates can be identified to family level whilst alive. See Appendix I for suitable keys. Samples should then be returned to the stream.

Safety

When working in any freshwater habitat it is important to be aware of certain safety issues. There are obvious problems associated with working in fast-flowing or deep water or from steep, slippery banks. Less obvious is the risk of picking up gastrointestinal infections or Weil's disease. Even apparently clean water can carry a risk, so it is important that cuts are covered and contamination through the mouth, eyes and nose is avoided. Wear rubber washing-up gloves to handle samples and, after finishing, wash your hands thoroughly before eating.

Terrestrial habitats

Soil and leaf litter

There are two basic choices of method for sampling invertebrates in leaf litter or soil. Firstly, a known mass or volume of litter can be sorted by hand. This works for the larger soil animals such as earthworms, woodlice and the bigger centipedes, but for smaller invertebrates some form of extraction method is needed. The standard approach is to use a **Tullgren funnel** (Figure 6.15). These are simple to construct from old tin cans, plastic funnels and net curtain material. Samples are best dried slowly under a low wattage lamp for a standardised period, at least 2 days, and should be from a quadrat of known area, or the sample should be of known mass or volume. Keys are available to help with the identification of terrestrial invertebrates, including those likely to be found in soil and leaf litter.

Animals active on the soil surface can be caught in **pitfall traps** (Figure 6.16). Without knowing what area the traps are collecting animals from, it is impossible to estimate the actual population density, so direct counts from pitfall traps provide a relative index of abundance. Plastic cups or beakers, or even jam jars make good traps. Traps can be left dry or can contain a small amount of water containing washing-up liquid to break the surface tension. If left dry, it is likely that some of the large carnivores such as ground beetles will eat some of the smaller organisms. An advantage of dry trapping is that it may be possible to use a mark-release-recapture method to obtain an estimate of the total population size, rather than just a relative index of abundance. Appendix I has details of suitable keys.

Mark-release-recapture methods

A sample of a population of animals is caught, marked and released back into the wild. After a period of time, which allows the marked animals to mix randomly with the rest of the population, a second catch is taken. Some of this catch will already have been marked and some will be new captures. You know the number of animals marked, the size of the second catch and the number already marked. You can use the formula in Figure 6.17 to make an estimate of the population. This estimate is known as the Lincoln Index. There are a number of important assumptions (Table 6.4).

Table 6.4 *Assumptions underlying the Lincoln Index*

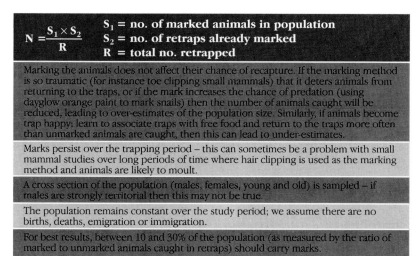

$N = \dfrac{S_1 \times S_2}{R}$	S_1 = no. of marked animals in population S_2 = no. of retraps already marked R = total no. retrapped

Marking the animals does not affect their chance of recapture. If the marking method is so traumatic (for instance toe clipping small mammals) that it deters animals from returning to the traps, or if the mark increases the chance of predation (using dayglow orange paint to mark snails) then the number of animals caught will be reduced, leading to over-estimates of the population size. Similarly, if animals become trap happy; learn to associate traps with free food and return to the traps more often than unmarked animals are caught, then this can lead to under-estimates.

Marks persist over the trapping period – this can sometimes be a problem with small mammal studies over long periods of time where hair clipping is used as the marking method and animals are likely to moult.

A cross section of the population (males, females, young and old) is sampled – if males are strongly territorial then this may not be true.

The population remains constant over the study period; we assume there are no births, deaths, emigration or immigration.

For best results, between 10 and 30% of the population (as measured by the ratio of marked to unmarked animals caught in retraps) should carry marks.

The method works well with:
- carabid beetles (ground beetles) caught in pitfall traps
- woodlice collected from under logs or stones or sheets of hardboard left covering patches of ground left for a few days
- snails collected as they become active in a garden at night.

Marking can be done with a tiny blob of quick-drying correction fluid, or cellulose paint applied with a very fine paint brush. You must be careful not to harm the animals in the process.

Mark-release-recapture methods have commonly been used on small mammal populations caught in Longworth traps. To work successfully, about 40 traps are needed in a 40 m × 40 m area. The traps are costly and this can become a very expensive study. Cheaper plastic alternatives to Longworth traps are available but have a short life span. There are also potential problems in terms of handling the animals. Small mammals carry Weil's disease; some experience is needed in handling animals and if your traps are likely to catch shrews, a licence is required from English Nature (CCW in Wales or Scottish Natural Heritage in Scotland). Insufficient bedding or food can lead to the death of animals. For an A-level study it is, therefore, more appropriate to work on invertebrate populations.

Animals on vegetation

Limited methods are available for sampling animals living on vegetation. Either some form of **sweep net** (Figure 6.18) or a **beating**

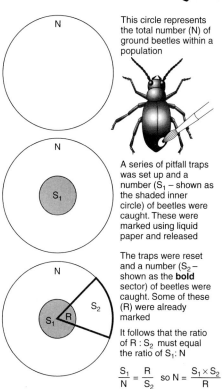

This circle represents the total number (N) of ground beetles within a population

A series of pitfall traps was set up and a number (S_1 – shown as the shaded inner circle) of beetles were caught. These were marked using liquid paper and released

The traps were reset and a number (S_2 – shown as the **bold** sector) of beetles were caught. Some of these (R) were already marked

It follows that the ratio of R : S_2 must equal the ratio of S_1 : N

$$\frac{S_1}{N} = \frac{R}{S_2} \quad \text{so } N = \frac{S_1 \times S_2}{R}$$

Figure 6.17 Mark – release – recapture methods

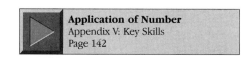

Application of Number
Appendix V: Key Skills
Page 142

Communication
Appendix V: Key Skills
Page 142

FIELD WORK TECHNIQUES

Figure 6.18 A typical sweep net. This can be used to sample animals from low-growing vegetation

Figure 6.19 Beating tray being used to collect animals from the branches of a tree

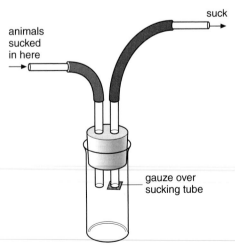

Figure 6.20 Pooter for the collection of small invertebrates

tray (Figure 6.19) can be used. The sweep nets need to be tough, so it is probably best to use a commercially made net, but for beating trays a simple white sheet held under a branch will do. The branch above is shaken or tapped to dislodge the animals, which then fall onto the sheet and they can then be collected using a pooter (Figure 6.20). To identify animals beyond the Order level you will need to anaesthetise or kill them. Use a gas injection 'Sparklets' type cork remover to give them a quick squirt of CO_2 to temporarily anaesthetise them, or slow them down by putting them into a fridge for an hour or so.

With both sweep nets and beating trays it is important that you adopt a standardised method. For instance, when sweeping animals from the vegetation in a meadow you could use a set number of sweeps over a set time or distance. When using a beating tray the branches could be tapped a fixed number of times or shaken for a given period. The numbers of animals you catch are likely to vary a lot, so a large number of replicates in a given area would be needed. It is difficult to use either of these methods when the vegetation is wet or the weather is windy, so the number of animals you catch will also depend on the weather.

Sea shore habitats

Rocky sea shores often lend themselves well to ecological fieldwork and a range of common and easily identifiable animals can be sampled quantitatively.

The density of immobile or slow-moving animals, such as barnacles, anemones, limpets and other snails, can be counted directly within quadrats. On uneven shores with many boulders or rock pools, quadrats are less useful. A timed search method can be used where a particular area of the shore is searched thoroughly and systematically for a particular species over a set period of time, for example 2 minutes. Mark-release-recapture methods can also be used for snails in rock pools or in clumps of seaweed and for animals such as sandhoppers living under rotting seaweed or under stones on the higher shore.

Rocky shores can be dangerous and fieldwork should not be carried out alone. Local knowledge and tide tables should be used to make sure you do not get cut off by incoming tides. The risk is reduced if you only work on out-going tides and during calm weather.

Using animal data

Pyramids of numbers and biomass

By reference to standard texts, it is usually possible to classify most families of invertebrates as belonging to different feeding types (carnivores, herbivores and detritivores). Table 6.5 gives both an example for a freshwater stream and a pyramid of numbers for the site studied.

Table 6.5 *Freshwater data for a north Wales stream showing the feeding types and a pyramid of numbers for the site*

Order	Family	Common name	Feeding type	Number m⁻²
Amphipoda	Gammaridae	Freshwater shrimp	D	67
Hydracarina	Hydrachnellidae	Freshwater mite	C	4
Ephemeroptera	Baetidae	Swimming mayfly	H	23
	Ecdyonuridae	Flat mayfly	H	23
Plecoptera	Perlodidae	Bighead stonefly	C	12
	Taeniopterigidae	Drifter stonefly	D	12
	Nemouridae	Neckgill stonefly	D	34
	Leuctridae	Long-thin stonefly	D	6
	Chloroperlidae	Very long-thin stonefly	C	6
Trichoptera	Glossosomatidae	Conical cased caddis	D	1
	Limnephilidae	Mobile rubbish tip	D	6
	Rhyacophilidae	Green caseless caddis	C	12
	Hydropsychidae	Brown caseless caddis	C	4
	Philopotamidae	Yellow caseless caddis	D	21
	Polycentropidae	Pink caseless caddis	C	8
Diptera	Simuliidae	Blackfly	D	78
	Dixidae	Meniscus midge	D	2
	Tipulidae	Cranefly	D	6
	Chironomidae	Bloodworm	D	21
Coleoptera	Helodidae	Hello beetle	D	21
	Dytiscidae	Diving beetle	C	3
Neuroptera	Sialidae	Alderfly	C	1
		Carnivores (C) =		50
		Herbivores (H) =		46
		Detritivores (D) =		275

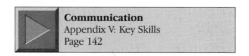

Communication
Appendix V: Key Skills
Page 142

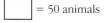 = 50 animals

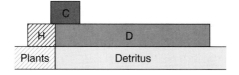

A crude estimate of biomass can be obtained by weighing the animals wet:
- sort the sample into carnivore, herbivore and detritivore pots
- empty the pots into fine sieves – tea strainers work well
- weigh the sieve plus animals
- return the animals, alive, to a sample pot containing water
- subtract the mass of the sieve from the mass of the sieve plus animals.

These wet weight biomass figures can then be used to construct a pyramid of biomass.

Question Would you expect the pyramid of biomass to have the same shape as the pyramid of numbers?

FIELD WORK TECHNIQUES

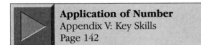

Application of Number
Appendix V: Key Skills
Page 142

Diversity indices

Diversity indices are another way in which quantitative counts of animals can be summarised. A widely used one is Simpson's index which has the formula

$$\text{Simpson's index} = \frac{N(N-1)}{\sum n(n-1)}$$

where N is the total number of animals found and n is the number of individuals of each species or other taxa.

Diversity indices are designed to take into account two components of diversity:

- richness – the number of taxa (families, species or other level to which identification was carried out)
- evenness – the spread of individuals between the component taxa.

Consider two sets of data from different sites. Both were equally rich with 10 species present and had equal numbers of individuals ($N = 100$ for each site). At site A, the 100 individuals were spread equally amongst the 10 species, whilst at site B, most of the individuals were recorded as belonging to one of the species.

Site A species	A	B	C	D	E	F	G	H	I	J
Number (n)	10	10	10	10	10	10	10	10	10	10

Site B species	A	B	C	D	E	F	G	H	I	J
Number (n)	1	1	1	1	1	1	1	1	1	91

The two sites cannot be separated in terms of richness, but the first is more diverse because the number of individuals is more evenly spread. Calculating the Simpson's diversity index for each site gives values of 11 for site A and 1.2 for site B, so a higher index indicates higher diversity.

Habitats which show a pattern similar to that of site B usually have some form of 'environmental' stress. Freshwater sites polluted by either organic waste or effluent from heavy metal mines would give a similar pattern, as would the data for plants in communities at the early stages of sand-dune succession. With plant data, the index should really only be applied to cases where there are direct counts of the number of individuals per unit area (density).

Question A worked example of the calculation of Simpson's diversity index is given in Table 6.6. Use this method to calculate the indices for the data for sites A and B above.

Table 6.6 *Calculation of Simpson's diversity index*

Common name	n number / m^{-2}	$n(n-1)$
Freshwater shrimp	67	4422
Freshwater mite	4	12
Swimming mayfly	23	506
Flat mayfly	23	506
Bighead stonefly	12	132
Drifter stonefly	12	132
Neckgill stonefly	34	1122
Long-thin stonefly	6	30
Very long-thin stonefly	6	30
Conical cased caddis	1	0
Mobile rubbish tip	6	30
Green caseless caddis	12	132
Brown caseless caddis	4	12
Yellow caseless caddis	21	420
Pink caseless caddis	8	56
Blackfly	78	6006
Meniscus midge	2	2
Cranefly	6	30
Bloodworm	21	420
Hello beetle	21	420
Diving beetle	3	6
Alderfly	1	0
Σ (sum) =	371	14426

$$S = \frac{N(N-1)}{\sum n(n-1)} = \frac{371(371-1)}{14426}$$

$$= \frac{137270}{14426} = 9.52$$

Biotic indices

Many pollution studies summarise freshwater invertebrate data using a **biotic index**. These give high scores for animals which indicate good quality streams and rivers and low scores for those which tolerate pollution. The most generally used index for freshwater systems is the BMWP (biological monitoring working party) system. Details can be found in most text books dealing with pollution.

Environmental measurements

The distribution and abundance of plants and animals is determined by a number of **abiotic** and **biotic** components within ecosystems. The relative importance of different abiotic factors will vary with the nature of the ecosystem and will be considered in the following groupings:

- soil or **edaphic** factors – temperature, pH, humus content, moisture content and mineral content
- **aquatic** – pH, water velocity, salinity, oxygen
- **climatic** – light, temperature, wind speed and relative humidity.

Edaphic factors

Soil forms when mineral particles, usually resulting from the weathering of a parent material, interact with living organisms, air and water. The processes which define the structure and composition of a soil are:

- interactions with living organisms – production of **leaf litter**, **decomposition** of dead organic matter by bacteria and fungi, breakdown (**comminution**) by earthworms and other soil invertebrates and **nitrogen fixation**
- interactions with the atmosphere – **nitrogen fixation, oxidation** and **reduction**
- interactions with water – **leaching** and **chelation**
- **human process** – ploughing, drainage, etc.

In terms of measurable environmental factors, the results of these processes will be seen as variations in:

- the depth of soil layers
- moisture content
- humus content
- pH
- mineral content.

Soil layers

The structure of a generalised soil is shown in Figure 6.21(a). Keys are available which will identify soil types and horizons. From a practical point of view the following measurements are useful:

- total soil depth
- depth of organic layers [L, F and H horizons or O horizon in a peaty soil (Figure 6.21(b))]
- depth of A horizon.

See Appendix I for references which will help you describe soil structure and types.

These measurements can either be taken from a soil pit or by using a **soil auger**. The auger is screwed into the soil to the depth of the

(a)

L (or A$_l$) horizon – litter layer
F (A$_f$) horizon – fermentation layer
H (A$_h$) horizon – humus layer

A horizon – a mix of weathered mineral particles and organic matter. This is the layer within which most biological activity takes place. Soil samples for the analysis of humus content, moisture content and pH should come from this layer.

B horizon – subsoil consisting of weathered mineral particles with little organic matter and usually lighter, therefore, in colour than the A horizon.

C horizon – parent material from which the mineral part of the soil developed

(b)

O horizon – organic layer

E$_a$ horizon – leached layer

B$_f$ horizon – iron pan

B horizon

C horizon

Figure 6.21 (a) Generalised structure of a soil (b) Structure of a podzol

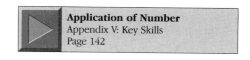

Application of Number
Appendix V: Key Skills
Page 142

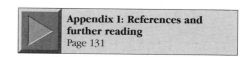

Appendix I: References and further reading
Page 131

screw thread and carefully pulled out, bringing a sample of soil with it. Changes in the colour of the soil indicate the changes in horizons.

Moisture content

The moisture content of a soil can vary from less than 1 per cent for a very young sand-dune soil to over 90 per cent for a wet, peat soil. Values between 20 and 30 per cent are typical for most 'average' soils. Soil moisture will vary with:

- particle size – clay soils will have more than sandy soils
- humus content – peaty soils will have more than brown earths
- current climatic conditions – large day-to-day changes can take place
- slope, aspect, drainage, etc.

The total moisture content of a soil can be split into a number of components; the amount of free-draining or **gravitational water**, the **field capacity** and **available water**.

The field capacity can be estimated using the following procedure:
- take a sample of soil by carefully pushing an open-ended tin can (Figure 6.22, of mass M1) into the soil
- immerse the can, with soil, in a bucket of water; the soil will become fully saturated
- remove the can, invert and allow to drain for 20 minutes (this removes the free-draining water and leaves water retained by adhesion and capillary forces)
- weigh the sample (to give M2)
- dry in an oven for 8 hours at 105 °C
- reweigh and subtract this mass (M3) from M2 to give the mass of water making up the field capacity moisture in the soil
- divide this mass by the mass of wet soil [M2 – mass of can (M1)] and multiply by 100 to give a percentage.

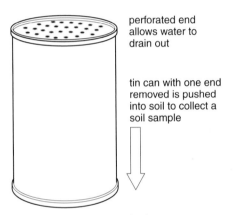

perforated end allows water to drain out

tin can with one end removed is pushed into soil to collect a soil sample

Figure 6.22 Tin can sampler for collecting soil samples

Not all of this moisture is available to plants. Some is held within the soil by capillary and adhesion forces so strong that it cannot be taken up by plants. If a sample of soil is initially prepared as above and then dried in a desiccator at room temperature for 8 hours, the loss in mass represents the **available water content**. This is probably the most meaningful measure of soil moisture; it is the water available to plants. In practical terms, as one sample is not necessarily representative of an area, it becomes a time-consuming exercise to collect a replicated series of samples, saturate them and then dry them in desiccators. For this reason the 'current' moisture content of a soil is usually measured (Table 6.7).

Samples should be taken from the A horizon as this is the layer in which plants are rooted and from which they take up water. If the soil is very peaty, plants will actually be rooted in the peat rather than in the A horizon and samples from the O horizon should be taken. If you are trying to relate changes in vegetation or animal populations to soil conditions, it is probably best to take an average soil sample from each

Table 6.7 *Procedure for determining soil moisture and humus conetent*

Soil moisture
• weigh porcelain crucible (W1)
• add approximately 10 g of soil and reweigh crucible (W2)
• dry in a drying oven at 105 °C for 8 hours
• reweigh crucible
• dry at 105 °C for a furthur hour and reweigh
• repeat last step until no further loss in mass takes place and record final mass (W3)
• calculate % moisture as
$$\% \text{ moisture} = \frac{W2 - W3}{W2 - W1} \times 100\%$$

Assumptions
• all soil moisture has been lost during drying
• only soil moisture has been lost

Soil humus
• burn dried sample in a furnace at 450 °C for 2 hours
• allow to cool in a desiccator and reweigh
• replace crucible in furnace for another hour and reweigh
• repeat until no further loss in mass occurs and record final mass (W4)
• calculate % humus as
$$\% \text{ moisture} = \frac{W3 - W4}{W3 - W1} \times 100\%$$

Assumptions
• all soil humus has been lost during burning
• only soil humus has been lost

quadrat examined. This can be done by bulking several smaller samples from the area covered by the quadrat rather than by taking a single sample from one position in the quadrat. The sample to be dried should not contain any large stones.

A microwave oven can be used as an alternative to a drying oven, though it is more difficult to ensure that only water is being lost. There is a risk that if the sample overheats then ignition of organic matter can take place. The risk of this can be reduced by keeping a small beaker of water in the oven. As a guideline, a 700 watt oven set on medium heat will dry ten 10 g soil samples in about 20 minutes. You will need to experiment a little to find the optimum settings for your oven. Make sure you use porcelain crucibles.

Humus content

An 'average' soil will contain between 20 and 30 per cent humus. The amount, however, can vary from less than 1 per cent in a young dune soil to over 95 per cent in a wet, peaty soil. The amount of humus will depend on:

- the input of litter – either in the form of leaf fall or general death of plants growing in the soil
- the 'decomposability' of litter – conifer litter is less easily broken down than deciduous litter
- rates of decomposer activity – bacteria and fungi function less well in waterlogged soils and in acidic conditions bacteria are less important than fungi
- leaching of humus particles by through-flow of water.

The method for determining humus content is shown in Table 6.7.

pH

The pH of soils is dependent on the nature of the underlying parent material and on the input of material from outside. Acidic leaf litter produced by many conifers and some deciduous trees can lower the pH of soils. The range of pH values found will vary from 3 for acidic peat-based soils to over 8 on soils over chalk or with a high shell sand content. Soils which are at either extreme tend to have more specialised plant communities and acidic soils, in particular, tend to have lower invertebrate populations. There are two approaches to measuring soil pH. A colorimetric test based around universal indicator is widely used:

- place 1 cm of soil in a graduated soil tube or test tube
- add 1 cm of barium sulphate to flocculate clay particles
- add 10 cm^3 of deionised or distilled water and shake the tube
- add three drops of universal indicator and gently invert the tube to mix the sample
- compare the colour against the colour chart – use a white background.

The alternative is to make a standardised 'soil solution' by:
- placing soil up to the 25 cm^3 mark of a 50 cm^3 plastic beaker
- adding deionised or distilled water to the 50 cm^3 mark
- stirring the 'solution' thoroughly
- using an electronic meter and pH electrode to measure pH.

This method is, perhaps, slightly more accurate, though some of the small differences detected by pH meters are unlikely to be ecologically significant; a soil with a pH of 5.64 is probably just as good for plants as one of pH 5.59.

Mineral ions

Commercially available kits (NPK kits) are available to measure nitrogen, phosphorous and potassium but their accuracy is limited. Estimating the soil humus content will probably give a better measure of soil fertility. An exception would be for agricultural soils where chemical fertilisers rather than organic matter provide most mineral nutrients. In saline soils, a conductivity meter can be used to estimate salt content. Using a 'soil solution' prepared as above, a simple conductivity meter can be used to measure the conductivity. This will vary with the concentration of soluble ions present. In habitats such as sand dunes and salt marshes, most of those ions are likely to be sodium and chloride ions, so conductivity becomes an indirect measure of salinity.

Temperature

In habitats with an open plant community (lots of bare soil devoid of vegetation) the surface soil temperature will vary greatly over a period of time. On hot, sunny days the temperature of open sandy soils can exceed 40 °C, dropping to less than 10 °C at night. These conditions can make germination difficult. On well-vegetated soils the soil is insulated by a layer of air trapped above the soil, and temperature fluctuates less. Thermometers with a range –10 °C to 50 °C are ideal for soil use. Use either a digital thermometer or a glass thermometer inside a protective aluminium or brass casing, to measure soil temperature 2 to 5 cm below the surface (this is the level at which germination takes place).

Question In Table 6.8 there are data for various soil factors measured along a transect across a dune system, together with the number of plants species recorded and total vegetation cover. Why do the soil moisture and humus content increase along the transect? Why do the temperature and conductivity readings decrease?

Table 6.8 *Changes in soil factors and vegetation along an interrupted belt transect across the dunes at Morfa Harlech. The number of plant species were recorded from 100 points lowered into the vegetation at each site. Total vegetation cover is the number of points at which vegetation was touched.*

	High drift line	Embryo dune	First dune ridge	First dune hollow	Second dune ridge	Second dune hollow	Highest dune	Dry dune slack	Wet dune slack	Dune scrub
Soil temperature / °C	25.6	25.7	24.6	21.3	17.5	17.9	17.3	17.8	17.8	17.9
Conductivity / μS	489	125	54	48	61	28	66	49	54	89
Soil pH	8.2	8.1	8.0	7.6	7.7	7.3	7.0	6.9	6.8	5.4
Moisture content (%)	1.45	0.99	0.99	1.98	1.54	5.61	3.44	13.56	45.61	23.21
Humus content (%)	0.42	0.10	0.80	1.25	1.28	2.86	1.54	10.23	43.18	21.45
Number of plant species	0	2	4	11	13	16	16	17	15	8
Total vegetation cover (%)	0	21	84	100	98	100	100	100	100	100

Environmental factors in aquatic habitats

Most studies of freshwater ecosystems concentrate on invertebrate communities. Figure 6.23 illustrates some of the interactions which exist within the invertebrate community of a stream, river or pond and some of the environmental factors which will determine the type and abundance of species within that system. The interactions can be complex but measurable environmental factors can be considered as follows:

- substrate type
- water velocity
- temperature
- dissolved oxygen
- water chemistry
- light.

Substrate

The nature of the substrate is dependent to some extent both on water velocity and geology. Depositing substrates are the norm in slow-flowing and still water, where fine particulate matter and detritus settle out. The silts and muds deposited are often low in dissolved oxygen due to the decomposition of organic matter by microorganisms. Invertebrates such as bloodworms (Diptera of the family Chironomidae) can be present in high densities due to their ability to tolerate low oxygen conditions.

FIELD WORK TECHNIQUES

Communication
Appendix V: Key Skills
Page 142

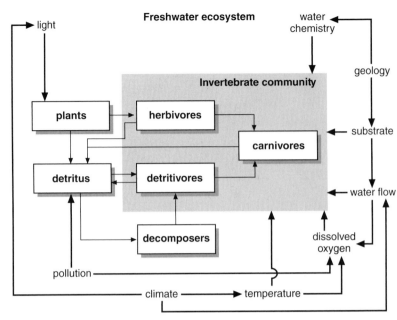

Freshwater ecosystem

Figure 6.23 *The interactions between organisms and their environment in freshwater ecosystems. Most freshwater studies are carried out on invertebrates. The thin arrows represent the flow of energy within the system and the thick arrows some of the environmental factors which have an effect on the composition of the invertebrate community.*

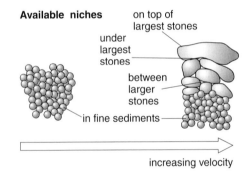

Figure 6.24 *The effect of increasing stream velocity on substrate and niche availability*

Communication
Appendix V: Key Skills
Page 142

Substrate size increases with increased water velocity, providing, initially, an increasingly complex series of microhabitats (Figure 6.24). Beyond a certain velocity, the stream bed becomes unstable and at very high velocities only large boulders and sheets of rocks will be present, leading to a reduction in diversity of microhabitats. The size and shape of the rocks forming the bed of the stream will also depend on how easily weathered the underlying rocks are.

The presence of plants will also be affected by substrate size and water velocity. Whereas slow-flowing areas will allow the colonisation of rooted macrophytes, only algae and mosses will be present in fast, turbulent areas.

Assessing substrate size and type is difficult. By taking a sample of stones from the stream or river bed, or by emptying the contents of the sampling net into a sorting tray, it may be possible to assess the relative proportion of stones falling into each of the size categories in Table 6.9. The percentage of the sorting tray covered with organic detritus is another useful measure. Deposit-feeding detritivores such as freshwater shrimps (*Gammarus pulex*) will be more abundant in samples with a high leaf-litter content than they will be in litter-poor samples.

Table 6.9 *Classification system for stream and river sediments. The dimensions are of the smallest axis of each stone measured.*

Boulder	>256 mm
Cobble	64–256 mm
Pebble	16–64 mm
Gravel	2–16 mm
Coarse sand	0.5–2 mm
Finer sands, silt and clay	<0.5 mm

Velocity

Velocity can be measured with a flow meter or with some form of float. Flow meters are usually based on some form of impeller held facing into the current and a counter which counts the number of revolutions over a set period of time. This is then converted into a velocity expressed as m s^{-1}. Flow meters measure velocities just above the stream bed, so they will not represent the actual flow experienced by stream invertebrates living on or under stones on the stream bed. They will, however, allow measurements to be taken from individual quadrats. Floats take an integrated measure of the flow over a section of stream or river. Oranges and dog biscuits seem to be the most widely used floats because they sit low in the water rather than sitting on the surface itself. By timing how long it takes the float to travel a set distance, an average velocity for the section of stream can be obtained.

Temperature

Temperatures will vary with season and also with light and shade (Figure 6.25). If studies are taking place over a short stretch of stream with little variation in light and shade, the temperature is unlikely to vary greatly between sampling sites. Studies which compare sites with big differences in the amount of overhanging canopy, or studies taking place over long periods of time, may well show large temperature differences between sites or sampling occasions. There could also, therefore, be differences in the levels of dissolved oxygen.

Information Technology
Appendix V: Key Skills
Page 143

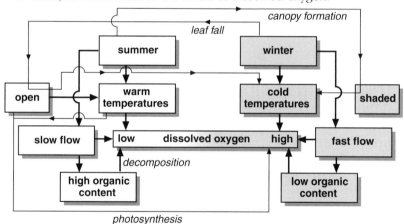

Figure 6.25 The interaction between various biotic and abiotic factors within a stream ecosystem and their effect on dissolved oxygen levels. Key interactions are shown as thick arrows, less important ones as thin arrows. Some biological processes are labelled in italics.

Pollution studies which are looking for a reduction in dissolved oxygen levels in polluted sites need to be carefully designed to eliminate any variations in water flow, shading and temperature. A polluted site with slow flow, in open sunlight and, therefore, warmer temperatures, will have less oxygen than a clean site in shade with faster flow, irrespective of any pollution effect.

Dissolved oxygen

The amount of dissolved oxygen in water is of fundamental importance in the ecology of freshwater systems. Levels of oxygen are

FIELD WORK TECHNIQUES

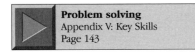

Problem solving
Appendix V: Key Skills
Page 143

affected by a number of abiotic and biotic factors (Figure 6.25). The simplest method of determining oxygen levels is to use a dissolved oxygen meter. They have a number of advantages over the traditional Winkler titration method:

- it is easier to take readings close to the bed of the stream, or even within very soft substrates
- it eliminates the need to carry a lot of glass sampling bottles and chemicals into the field
- it avoids the use of concentrated hydrochloric acid and Winklers reagent (a mix of concentrated sodium hydroxide and potassium iodide) needed for the Winkler titration, both of which have safety and pollution risks.

The only disadvantages are that oxygen meters can be expensive and cheaper ones, in particular, need careful maintenance and use.

Water chemistry

The chemistry of streams, rivers and ponds is dependent on the nature of the underlying geology and surrounding land use. Streams running over chalk- or limestone-based soils will be more alkaline with a higher calcium carbonate concentration (hardness) than those running over slates or other acidic rocks. The amount of calcium carbonate has an effect on the type of invertebrates found. Molluscs and crustaceans depend on calcium carbonate for their shells and exoskeletons. Soft-water streams will, therefore, have fewer snails and shrimps than hard-water streams.

Hardness can be estimated by measuring the conductivity of a water sample. The correlation between calcium carbonate concentration and conductivity is very good (Figure 6.26). In marine work, conductivity can also be used to estimate salinity.

pH paper or a pH meter can be used to measure the pH of water samples, though they are unreliable in very soft water, in which there are very few dissolved ions.

A wide range of commercial water-testing kits is available to measure other mineral ions. The best ranges are the Merckoquant®, Aquamerck® and Aquaquant® kits which cover, amongst others:

- heavy metals – lead, zinc, aluminium and iron kits are useful in heavy metal pollution studies
- ammonium and nitrate – for studies of organic pollution
- dissolved oxygen – an alternative to using oxygen meters or the Winkler titration
- hardness and pH.

Figure 6.26 The relationship between conductivity and hardness

Light

Light is important in allowing the growth of plants in freshwater systems. In deep ponds there may be insufficient light to allow plant growth on the bottom. Light penetration can be measured using a Secchi disc (Figure 6.27). In streams and most rivers, the depth of water is not usually enough to limit light availability. Incident light will affect the temperature and hence, oxygen concentration of water bodies. Measurements of incident light will be covered in the section on climatic environmental measurements.

Climatic factors

Climatic variables are usually easy to measure but highly variable over short periods of time. This makes the link between the abundance or distribution of plants and animals and climatic factors difficult to study. There is no guarantee that the levels of the variables measured on one day are limiting in terms of the plants or animals being studied. There are, however, instances when it might be useful to measure:

* incident light
* temperature
* wind speed
* relative humidity.

Incident light

A photographic light meter can be used to measure light intensity. It is best to measure incident light, that is the light falling onto the subject, rather than the strength of the light source. To measure incident light, place a sheet of white paper against the subject (Figure 6.28) and point the light meter directly at it. The readings will only be comparative; they will not distinguish between light sources with different proportions of various wavelengths of light.

Temperature

Temperature can provide a measure of exposure and the likelihood of desiccation taking place. Two rock faces with different aspects, one north facing and one south facing, will have different degrees of exposure to direct sunlight and therefore provide different conditions for the growth of mosses and lichens. Differences in temperature will reflect the differences in exposure to sunlight. A thermometer taped directly to the surface will give a measure of the variation in temperature. By using a maximum–minimum thermometer, differences in the variability of temperatures at sites can be studied. To give a fair comparison between sites it is important to take measurements of light, and other climatic data, under identical conditions and as close together in time as possible.

Wind speed

Various **anemometers** based around rotating cups or impellers are available to measure wind speed. Wind speed, as with temperature and light, can show differences in the levels of exposure to drying conditions.

Humidity

Relative humidity is defined as the amount of moisture carried in the air as a percentage of the maximum that could be carried at a given temperature. Various types of **hygrometer** can be used to measure relative humidity. Traditionally a **whirling hygrometer** was used. This

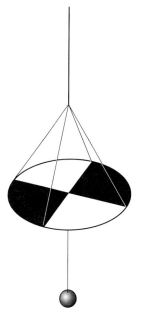

Figure 6.27 A Secchi disc used for making comparative measurements of light penetration into water.. The disc is lowered into water until you can no longer distinguish between the black and white sections and the depth is recorded.

Figure 6.28 Taking an incident light reading from the trunk of an oak tree. Hold a sheet of white paper against the trunk to integrate light from a wide area and point the light meter directly towards the paper, making sure it is held a constant distance away.

FIELD WORK TECHNIQUES

is a rotating frame holding a wet-bulb and a dry-bulb thermometer. As the frame is whirled around, water evaporates from a wick covering the bulb of the wet-bulb thermometer, causing cooling to take place. The amount of evaporation depends on the humidity of the air. If the air is dry, a lot of water will evaporate and the temperature will be considerably lower than is recorded by the dry bulb. If the air is humid, less evaporation takes place and the depression in temperature is less. The humidity can be worked out from measurements of the wet- and dry-bulb temperatures using a conversion table. The advantages and disadvantages of the various hygrometers are shown in Table 6.10.

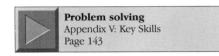

Problem solving
Appendix V: Key Skills
Page 143

Table 6.10 *The advantages and disadvantages of three types of hygrometer*

Whirling hygrometer	Disc hygrometer	Electronic hygrometer
Based on wet-and dry-bulb thermometers	Based on hair, paper or advanced polymer springs which absorb moisture	Based on electronic sensor
Advantages • quick response • accurate	Advantages • can fit in small spaces • cheap • do not use mercury	Advantages • can fit in small spaces • accurate (expensive models) • do not use mercury
Disadvantages • thermometers can be hard to read • cannot be used in small spaces • thermometers fragile • contain mercury	Disadvantages • slow to respond • not very accurate	Disadvantages • good ones are expensive • electronics can fail in wet conditions

Information Technology
Appendix V: Key Skills
Page 143

Long term measurements

A range of environmental probes with data-logging facilities are available. Some of these are suitable for field use and can be left out to record changes in climatic or other factors over long periods of time. They are still relatively expensive, but can allow meaningful links to be made between the abundance and distribution of organisms and abiotic factors.

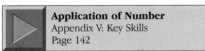

Communication
Appendix V: Key Skills
Page 142

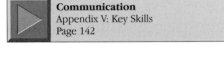

Application of Number
Appendix V: Key Skills
Page 142

Question Figure 6.29 shows the variation in moss and lichen cover along a transect up the trunk of an oak tree, together with light, humidity and temperature readings. What do you know about the biology of mosses which could explain some of these patterns?

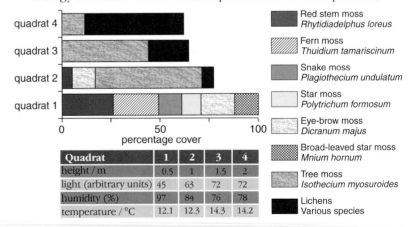

Quadrat	1	2	3	4
height / m	0.5	1	1.5	2
light (arbitrary units)	45	63	72	72
humidity (%)	97	84	76	78
temperature / °C	12.1	12.3	14.3	14.2

Figure 6.29 Changes in the percentage cover of mosses and lichens and certain environmental measurements up a tree trunk. Data for mosses and lichens were obtained by point sampling within a 50 cm × 50 cm quadrat subdivided into 100 5 cm squares. Light was measured using a light meter held 15 cm from the trunk. Humidity, with disc hygrometers taped in the middle of each quadrat and left for 30 minutes. Temperature was measured with a digital thermometer held against the trunk.

7 Investigations: statistics and planning

Problem solving
Appendix V: Key Skills
Page 143

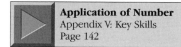

Application of Number
Appendix V: Key Skills
Page 142

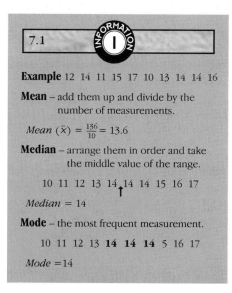

7.1

Example 12 14 11 15 17 10 13 14 14 16

Mean – add them up and divide by the number of measurements.

Mean ($\bar{x}$) $= \frac{136}{10} = 13.6$

Median – arrange them in order and take the middle value of the range.

10 11 12 13 14 14 14 15 16 17

Median = 14

Mode – the most frequent measurement.

10 11 12 13 **14 14 14** 5 16 17

Mode = 14

Example 1
28 15 26 19 27 14 17 20 11 16
No mode – all values are different

Example 2
8 11 12 12 13 11 8 11 13 8
Two modes – 8 and 11, both occur three times

Figure 7.1 *Using mode as a summary of small sets of data, and some problems*

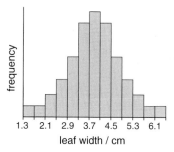

Figure 7.2 *Frequency histogram for a set of normally distributed leaf width data*

Quantitative experimental work involves the collection of data, and it is often of value to know whether or not the measurements we have taken are of any significance. Perhaps, more importantly, we should consider what measurements we need to take before we start our experimental work, spending more time at the planning stage, so that we do not waste time collecting data which adds little to our understanding of the problem under investigation.

In this chapter, ways of summarising data are considered and a number of statistical tests are described. The choice of a suitable test is discussed and illustrated by means of a flow chart and reference to a number of case studies.

Summarising data

Averages – mean, median and mode

Because of the variable nature of biological measurements, for most experimental work measurements need to be replicated and then summarised in some way. If asked to summarise, mathematically, a set of data, most students suggest taking an average and by this they are referring to the **mean**. For many sets of data this is entirely appropriate but for others, the **median** or **mode** would be more appropriate. Information box 7.1 shows you how to calculate the different averages.

The mode (the most frequent value) is least useful for the type of data collected in A-level practicals or student investigations, where small sets of data are often collected and either all the values are different or there are two or more modal values (Figure 7.1). To decide whether to use the mean or median, you need to understand a little about the ways in which numbers are distributed.

The normal distribution

If you take a large sample of people (several hundred at least and ideally adults of the same sex) and measure their heights, or take a large sample of ivy leaves and measure their widths, and then plot a frequency histogram, you would probably end up with a symmetrical, bell-shaped graph (Figure 7.2). This is known as a **normal distribution**. For this type of distribution, the mean, median and mode are the same. It is unlikely that you will be able to take measurements from such a large sample. With smaller sets of data, a tally chart can indicate whether your data are normally distributed or not. Figure 7.3 shows a smaller set, of 20 measurements, which seem to be normally distributed, and the mean ($\bar{x}$) gives a good summary.

INVESTIGATIONS: STATISTICS AND PLANNING

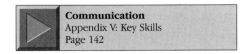

Communication
Appendix V: Key Skills
Page 142

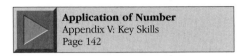

Application of Number
Appendix V: Key Skills
Page 142

Information Technology
Appendix V: Key Skills
Page 143

Width /cm		Mean (x̄)	3.67	
x	*x*	Median	3.65	
		Mode	3.5	
2.3	3.5	Min	1.7	
4.2	3.6	Max	5.6	Tally
1.7	3.1	Interval	0.39	chart
3.7	3.5	Size class	1.70–2.09	I
2.9	3.9		2.10–2.49	I
5.6	4.0		2.50–2.89	I
4.1	5.1		2.90–3.29	III
2.7	3.0		3.30–3.69	IIII
5.0	3.5		3.70–4.09	IIII
3.7	4.3		4.10–4.49	III
			4.50–4.89	
			4.90–5.29	II
			5.30–5.69	I

To help decide if the data are normally distributed we have drawn a simple tally chart. The range of measurements was split into ten equal size classes; the intervals found by dividing the difference between the maximum and minimum values by ten.

Figure 7.3 *A set of 20 leaf widths approximating to a normal distribution*

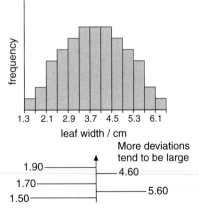

Figure 7.4 uses:
3.30
2.94 — 4.06
2.58 — 4.40 Most deviations from the mean are small
Mean = 3.75

Figure 7.4 *The data quite tightly clustered, giving small deviations. The fact that the mean is different from that in Figure 7.3 can be accounted for by the much larger number of measurements shown here*

Figure 7.5 uses:
More deviations tend to be large
1.90 — 4.60
1.70
1.50 — 5.60

Figure 7.5 *Data more widely spread giving large deviations and hence a larger* **standard deviation**

Standard deviation

The other figure we use in our summary of normally distributed data is the **standard deviation**. This gives a measure of how clumped the individual measurements are around the mean value.

Any set of normally distributed data is made up of a series of individual values, each of which deviates by a measurable amount from the mean. If the data are tightly clumped, then most values are going to be in size classes close to the mean, so the deviations are small (Figure 7.4). If the data are less clumped, the deviations will be larger (Figure 7.5).

It might seem that adding all these deviations would give a measure of the spread of data around the mean, but because the distribution is symmetrical, every positive deviation is balanced exactly by an equivalent negative deviation, so the sum would be zero. To overcome this problem, the deviations can be squared and then summed. The size of that sum will depend on the number of measurements taken, so we need to divide the sum of the squared deviations by the number of samples measured. Finally, as the deviations were squared initially, we take the square root to give a figure of the same order of magnitude as the original measurements.

Expressing this mathematically we have:

Step 1	calculate deviations	$\bar{x} - x$
Step 2	square the deviations	$(\bar{x} - x)^2$
Step 3	sum the squared deviations	$\sum(\bar{x} - x)^2$
Step 4	divide by number of samples	$\dfrac{\sum(\bar{x} - x)^2}{n}$
Step 5	take square root	$\sqrt{\dfrac{\sum(\bar{x} - x)^2}{n}}$

In practice we rarely use this formula. Calculating a whole series of individual deviations tends to be very time-consuming. Using n (the number of measurements) as the divisor leads to an under-estimate of the true standard deviation when we take a small sample from a much bigger population. To overcome these difficulties, mathematicians have devised an alternative formula:

$$\text{Standard Deviation } (s) = \sqrt{\frac{\sum x^2 - \frac{(\sum x)^2}{n}}{n-1}}$$

By using $n - 1$ as the divisor, we boost the standard deviation a little; so it gives a better representation of the true standard deviation of the population. If you are using a calculator or spreadsheet on a computer to calculate standard deviations, you will need to check to see that it is using the correct formula (Information box 7.2).

Calculating standard deviation

An example of the calculation of the standard deviation for a sample is shown in Figure 7.6.

Step 1   check to see if the data are normally distributed.

Step 2   calculate x^2 values

Step 3   calculate $\sum x$ and $\sum x^2$ values

Step 4   substitute values of $\sum x$, $\sum x^2$ and n into the equation

$$\text{Standard Deviation } (s) = \sqrt{\frac{\sum x^2 - \frac{(\sum x)^2}{n}}{n-1}}$$

What the standard deviation tells us

The standard deviation is a measure of dispersal around the mean value. If you compare Figure 7.5 with Figure 7.4 you should see that in Figure 7.4 we had quite tightly clustered data, and if we had calculated a standard deviation for this set it would have been fairly small. Compare this with Figure 7.5, in which the data are more widely spread, the individual deviations larger and the standard deviation would be much bigger. Statisticians tell us that, by definition, 67 per cent of measurements within a set of normal data lie within the range of mean ±1 standard deviation and 95 per cent within the range mean ±2 standard deviations (Figure 7.7).

Confidence limits

If we take a sample of leaves from an oak tree, we can estimate the mean size of all the leaves on the tree. If we take a second sample, it is

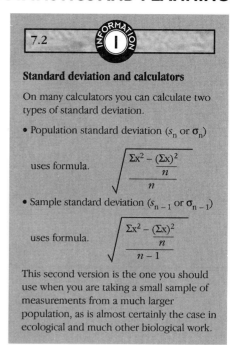

7.2

Standard deviation and calculators

On many calculators you can calculate two types of standard deviation.

- Population standard deviation (s_n or σ_n)

uses formula.
$$\sqrt{\frac{\sum x^2 - \frac{(\sum x)^2}{n}}{n}}$$

- Sample standard deviation (s_{n-1} or σ_{n-1})

uses formula.
$$\sqrt{\frac{\sum x^2 - \frac{(\sum x)^2}{n}}{n-1}}$$

This second version is the one you should use when you are taking a small sample of measurements from a much larger population, as is almost certainly the case in ecological and much other biological work.

Step 1

Size Class	Tallies
1.70–2.09	I
2.10–2.4	I ✓ seems OK
2.50–2.89	I
2.90–3.29	III
3.30–3.69	IIII
3.70–4.09	IIII
4.10–4.49	III
4.50–4.89	
4.90–5.29	II
5.30–5.69	I

Step 2
Calculate x^2 values

Leaf	Width / cm	Step 2
n	x	x^2
1	2.3	5.29
2	4.2	17.64
3	1.7	2.89
4	3.7	13.69
5	2.9	8.41
6	5.6	31.36
7	4.1	16.81
8	2.7	7.29
9	5.0	25.00
10	3.7	13.69
11	3.5	12.25
12	3.6	12.96
13	3.1	9.61
14	3.5	12.25
15	3.9	15.21
16	4.0	16.00
17	5.1	26.01
18	3.0	9.00
19	3.5	12.25
20	4.3	18.49

Step 3
Calculate $\sum x$ and $\sum x^2$ values

Step 3
	$\sum x$	$\sum x^2$
Sum =	73.4	286.10

Step 4
Substitute $\sum x$ and $\sum x^2$ values

$$s = \sqrt{\frac{\sum x^2 - \frac{(\sum x)^2}{n}}{n-1}}$$

$$s = \sqrt{\frac{286.10 - \frac{(73.4)^2}{20}}{20-1}}$$

$$s = 0.94$$

Figure 7.6 *Example of calculation of **standard deviation**. Data are maximum widths for a sample of 20 ivy leaves*

INVESTIGATIONS: STATISTICS AND PLANNING

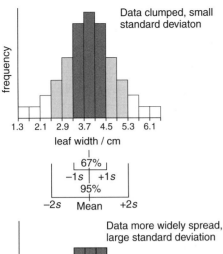

Data clumped, small standard deviaton

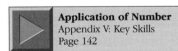

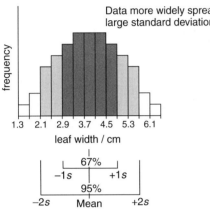

Data more widely spread, large standard deviation

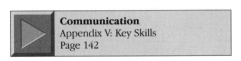

Figure 7.7 Two distributions showing the percentage values which lie within ±1 standard deviation (±1 s) and ±2 standard deviations (±2 s) of the mean

Communication
Appendix V: Key Skills
Page 142

Application of Number
Appendix V: Key Skills
Page 142

Information Technology
Appendix V: Key Skills
Page 143

unlikely that the mean will be identical. **Confidence limits** give a measure of the accuracy of the mean. They let us say how sure we are that the true mean (of the whole population) lies within a certain distance of the mean estimated from a sample of the whole population. To calculate 95 per cent confidence limits from a large (more than 30 measurements) sample, we use the following formula:

$$95\% \text{ confidence limits} = \bar{x} \pm t\,\frac{s}{\sqrt{n}}, \text{ where } t = 1.96$$

The value given by $\frac{s}{\sqrt{n}}$ is known as the **standard error** of the mean and the value of *t* was calculated by a statistician who published his work in 1908 under the pseudonym 'Student'. Mathematically, *t* is a way of expressing deviations from the mean in units of standard deviation and is used in a number of statistical tests. For our purposes we simply need to accept that it is a way of linking probability and sample size. With smaller samples, we have to adjust the value of *t* to take into account the inherent unreliability of smaller samples. We do that using the table below.

n	10	11	12	13	14	15	20	25	30
t	2.26	2.23	2.2	2.18	2.16	2.15	2.09	2.06	2.04

Taking the data from Figure 7.6, we had 20 measurements giving a mean of 3.67 and a standard deviation of 0.94. The 95per cent confidence limits therefore are:

$$95\% \text{ confidence limits} = 3.67 \pm 2.09 \times \frac{0.94}{\sqrt{20}}$$
$$= 3.67 \pm 0.44$$

We can now say that we are 95 per cent certain that the mean of all the oak leaves in the whole population (from which we took and measured a sample of 20) lies within the range 3.67 cm ± 0.44 cm. Confidence limits, or standard errors, are often plotted on graphs as vertical lines extending on either side of the mean value, or presented in the format (used above) of: mean ±95 per cent confidence limits.

See Chapter 3, page 33, for an example of a graph with standard errors.

Non-normal data
Many sets of measurements do not match the normal distribution (Figure 7.8). Measurements such as percentages or proportions are unlikely to be normally distributed. Data obtained by a student looking at the percentage cover of heather (*Calluna vulgaris*) in a series of randomly placed quadrats are shown in Table 7.1.

Most of the quadrats contained little cover of heather but one or two had much greater percentage covers. The mean of this set of data is 10.1. This does not represent the bulk of the measurements; only two

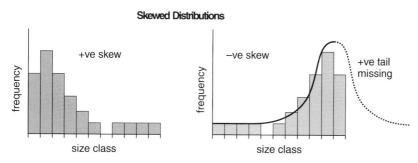

Skewed Distributions

Table 7.1 *The percentage cover of heather (Calluna vulgaris) in eighteen randomly placed quadrats*

Quadrat	1	2	3	4	5	6	7	8	9
% cover	6	5	3	3	1	8	10	5	2
Quadrat	10	11	12	13	14	15	16	17	18
% cover	4	4	8	10	1	47	1	7	52

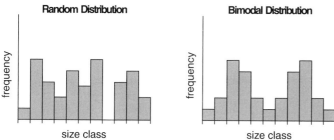

Figure 7.8 Some non-normal distributons

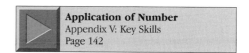

values (47% in quadrat 15; 52% in quadrat 18) are larger, all the other 16 values are smaller.

The data have a skewed distribution. You can see that the 47 per cent and 52 per cent values are not balanced by equally small values at the other end of the distribution. The mean is, therefore, being disproportionately influenced by the extreme values. In fact, as we cannot get less than 0 per cent cover, it is impossible for this type of data to show the symmetrical shape of the normal distribution (Figure 7.9).

For data which do not at least approximate to a normal distribution, it is better to use the median and, rather than calculating standard deviations (which are calculated from deviations from the mean value),

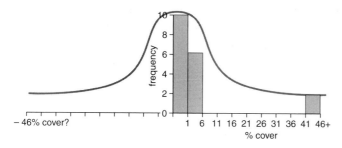

Figure 7.9 The distribution of data in Table 5.1. A free hand line has been drawn to show that the data could approximate to a normal distribution only if –ve percentage covers were possible.

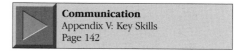

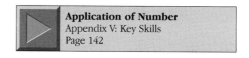

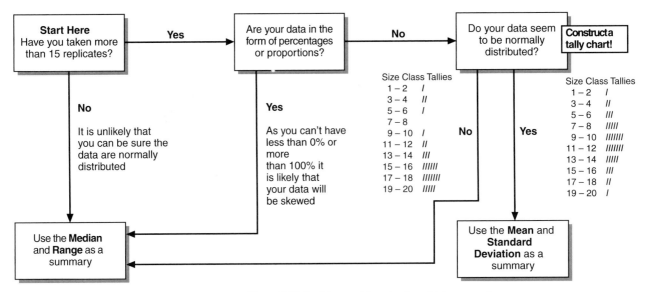

Figure 7.10 Decision-making chart – which average?

quote the median and range as the summary. With small sets of data there is often insufficient evidence to show that the data are normally distributed and if you have fewer than 15 measurements in a data set, it is safer not to assume normality and again use the median as a summary. The flow chart in Figure 7.10 can be used to decide which average you should be using.

Statistical tests – the basis for planning investigations

Deciding which statistical test to use is probably the most difficult aspect of many student investigations. By including a consideration of statistics early in the planning stage, some of the problems usually associated with student investigations can be avoided. Figure 7.11 is a flow diagram which can be used to help plan investigations which incorporate appropriate statistical tests.

The process of carrying out an investigation can be broken down into a series of steps. The case studies which follow on from this section should help lead you through some of these ideas and provide worked examples of the various statistical tests available.

- **Observation or idea** – the best investigations come from observations made directly by students, or from ideas which arise from previous practical work.
- **Background research** – is needed to provide a biological context for the work you are about to do and to help with the next stage in the process.
- **Identify variables** – some variables can be thought of as **key variables** – they are likely to cause the effect you are looking at; others as **control variables** – whose effects can be eliminated by careful design.

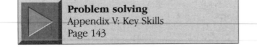

Application of Number
Appendix V: Key Skills
Page 142

Problem solving
Appendix V: Key Skills
Page 143

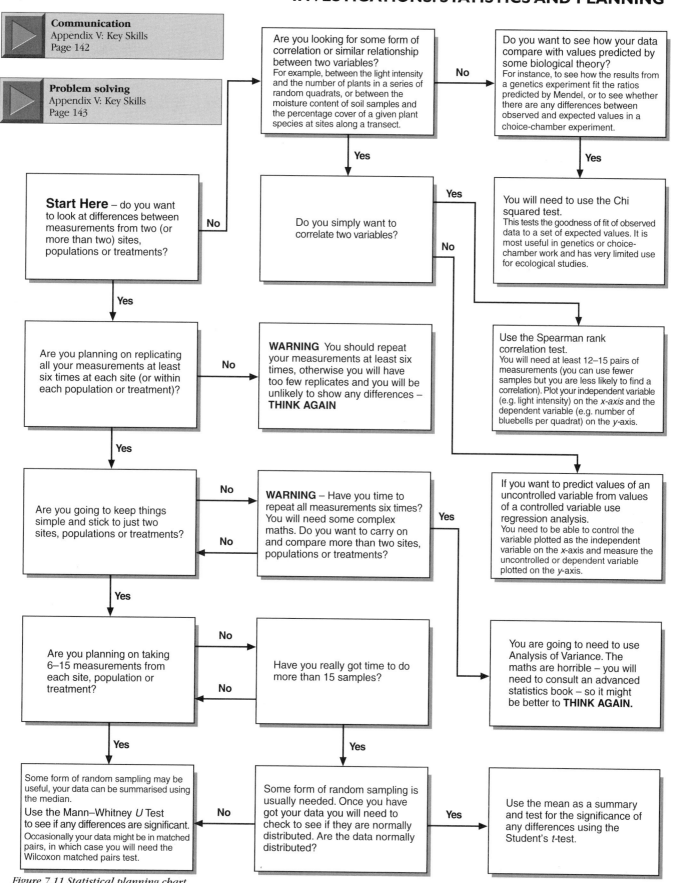

Communication
Appendix V: Key Skills
Page 142

Problem solving
Appendix V: Key Skills
Page 143

Are you looking for some form of correlation or similar relationship between two variables?
For example, between the light intensity and the number of plants in a series of random quadrats, or between the moisture content of soil samples and the percentage cover of a given plant species at sites along a transect.

Do you want to see how your data compare with values predicted by some biological theory?
For instance, to see how the results from a genetics experiment fit the ratios predicted by Mendel, or to see whether there are any differences between observed and expected values in a choice-chamber experiment.

Start Here – do you want to look at differences between measurements from two (or more than two) sites, populations or treatments?

Do you simply want to correlate two variables?

You will need to use the Chi squared test.
This tests the goodness of fit of observed data to a set of expected values. It is most useful in genetics or choice-chamber work and has very limited use for ecological studies.

Are you planning on replicating all your measurements at least six times at each site (or within each population or treatment)?

WARNING You should repeat your measurements at least six times, otherwise you will have too few replicates and you will be unlikely to show any differences – **THINK AGAIN**

Use the Spearman rank correlation test.
You will need at least 12–15 pairs of measurements (you can use fewer samples but you are less likely to find a correlation). Plot your independent variable (e.g. light intensity) on the x-axis and the dependent variable (e.g. number of bluebells per quadrat) on the y-axis.

Are you going to keep things simple and stick to just two sites, populations or treatments?

WARNING – Have you time to repeat all measurements six times? You will need some complex maths. Do you want to carry on and compare more than two sites, populations or treatments?

If you want to predict values of an uncontrolled variable from values of a controlled variable use regression analysis.
You need to be able to control the variable plotted as the independent variable on the x-axis and measure the uncontrolled or dependent variable plotted on the y-axis.

Are you planning on taking 6–15 measurements from each site, population or treatment?

Have you really got time to do more than 15 samples?

You are going to need to use Analysis of Variance. The maths are horrible – you will need to consult an advanced statistics book – so it might be better to **THINK AGAIN.**

Some form of random sampling may be useful, your data can be summarised using the median.
Use the Mann–Whitney U Test to see if any differences are significant.
Occasionally your data might be in matched pairs, in which case you will need the Wilcoxon matched pairs test.

Some form of random sampling is usually needed. Once you have got your data you will need to check to see if they are normally distributed. Are the data normally distributed?

Use the mean as a summary and test for the significance of any differences using the Student's t-test.

Figure 7.11 Statistical planning chart

- **Formulate hypotheses** – these should be testable, think of them as questions to be answered; and predictive. Statisticians like us to use a **null hypothesis** (which is then rejected or accepted) as the basis for statistical tests. Most investigations will be looking for some form of difference, correlation or other association. The null hypothesis is the reverse of what you expect. So if your hypothesis predicts that ivy leaves from a shade bush will be wider than those from a sunlit bush, the null hypothesis would be that there is no difference in average leaf width.
- **Consider statistics** – essentially most investigations will look for **differences** (Case studies 1, 2 and 3), **correlations** (Case studies 4 and 6) or test the **goodness of fit** of data to a series of expected values (Case study 5).
- **Design methods** – Figure 7.11 will help to make sure that methods are adopted which will give data which can be analysed statistically; details of the proposed analysis should be included in the **plan**.
- **Pilot study** – this will sort out any unforeseen problems; in particular whether there is enough time/equipment to replicate measurements adequately.
- **Modify methods** – if necessary.
- **Collect data** – provided students have been thorough in their planning and have taken consideration of the results of their pilot study, the subsequent steps should be straightforward.
- **Analysis** – the subsequent case studies should help to give ideas for appropriate analysis.
- **Write up** – advice on how to write up and present investigations is given in Chapter 3.

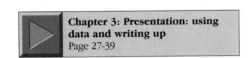

Chapter 3: Presentation: using data and writing up
Page 27-39

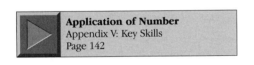

Application of Number
Appendix V: Key Skills
Page 142

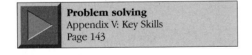

Problem solving
Appendix V: Key Skills
Page 143

Significance levels

Decisions about the significance of the results of any statistical test are based around the 5 per cent significance level. Results are said to be significant if they could occur by chance less than 5 per cent of the time (in other words a probability of $p < 0.05$). This is an arbitrary decision which is accepted by all scientists and statisticians, but in some situations we might need to be more critical. If a medical researcher concluded that there was a 5 per cent chance of a drug causing harmful side-effects then no one would ever use it. In these situations we might want to use a 1 per cent ($p < 0.01$) or 0.1 per cent ($p < 0.001$) significance level before accepting the results.

Tables of critical values, for most statistical tests, are available for several significance levels. If your result is significant at the 5 per cent level, you can then reject the null hypothesis and accept the alternative hypothesis (the one you really wanted to test). If your result is significant at a higher level (1% or 0.1%) then it means that you are more certain of your conclusions. An example of a table of critical values with 5 per cent and 1 per cent significance levels is given in Case study 5. For the other tests, only tables of critical values for the 5 per cent level have been given. The critical value will vary with the sample size. For some tests you will need to calculate **degrees of freedom**. These are simply the way in which some tests take into account sample size. The way we do this varies from test to test.

Mann–Whitney *U* test

Case study 1 – the density of bluebells

A student was interested in comparing the abundance of bluebells in two areas of woodland. One area (Site A) was densely shaded by mature oaks (*Quercus petraea*) whilst the other (Site B) had a much more open canopy dominated by birch (*Betula pubescens*) with a few hazel (*Corylus avellana*). The student decided to count the number of bluebell plants in 50 cm × 50 cm quadrats to obtain a measure of density.

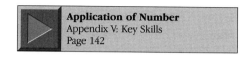

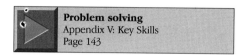

As well as estimating bluebell density, measurements of light (the **key variable**) and pH, soil moisture content and soil organic content were to be taken. The student felt she was clearly looking for a **difference** between the two sites.

A pilot study indicated that to measure all the variables for one quadrat would take **30 minutes**. As she had allowed **6 hours** for her field work, this would give time for **12 quadrats** to be sampled. The initial plan had been to compare four different sites within the wood but with the time available this would have allowed only three quadrats to be sampled at each site. The student felt this was an inadequate level of replication for two reasons. Firstly, three quadrats would not give a reliable average and secondly, most statistical tests do not allow a decision with so few samples. Ideally she would have liked to look at more quadrats at each site as the density figures seem quite variable, but time became a limiting factor.

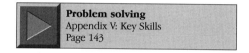

The other problem with comparing more than two sites is the number of statistical tests that would need to be done. For four sites she would have needed to compare A v. B, A v. C, A v. D, B v. C, B v. D and C v. D and these would need to be done on all of the variables she had measured. The alternative would be to use Analysis of Variance (see Figure 7.11) which is complex mathematically and difficult to understand.

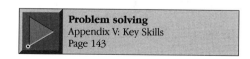

As there was only enough time to collect data from six quadrats per site it would be difficult to make any decision about how close the data were to being normally distributed. The best way to summarise the data would be to use the median and use the **Mann–Whitney *U* Test** (Route 7.1) to test for the significance of any differences between the two sites.

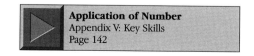

Route 7.1 *Mann–Whitney U test*

Mann–Whitney *U* test – example

Data – density of bluebells (no./0.25 m² quadrat) at two sites

Quadrat	1	2	3	4	5	6	7	8
Site A	26	14	8	6	26	20	11	13
Site B	28	16	26	25	25	24	16	28

Start Here – do you want to look at differences between measurements from two (or more than two) sites, populations or treatments?

↓ **Yes**

Are you planning on replicating all your measurements at least six times at each site (or within each population or treatment)?

↓ **Yes**

Are you going to keep things simple and stick to just two sites, populations or treatments?

↓ **Yes**

Are you planning on taking 6–15 measurements from each site, population or treatment?

↓ **Yes**

Some form of random sampling may be useful, your data can be summarised using the median.
Use the Mann–Whitney *U* Test to see if any differences are significant.
Occasionally your data might be in matched pairs, in which case you will need the Wilcoxon matched pairs test.

Step 1 calculate the median for each set of data

Site A	6	8	11	13	14	20	26	26
Site B	16	16	24	25	25	26	28	28

Median density at Site A $= 13.5$

Median density at Site B $= 25.0$

If the medians are identical there is no point in continuing with the analysis.

Step 2 arrange the data in order and rank the values so that the smallest value gets the lowest rank and the largest the highest rank (Figure 7.12). Tied values get the average of those ranks available. By doing this we can examine and then measure the amount of overlap between the two sets of data which is the basis of the Mann–Whitney U test (Information box 7.3).

Application of Number
Appendix V:
Key Skills
Page 142

Step 3 sum the ranks for each set of data.

$\Sigma R_{Site\ A} = 1 + 2 + 3 + 4 + 5 + 8 + 13 + 13 = 49$

$\Sigma R_{Site\ B} = 6.5 + 6.5 + 9 + 10.5 + 10.5 + 13 + 15.5 + 15.5 = 87$

Step 4 calculate U_1 and U_2 using the formula:

$U_1 = n_1 \times n_2 + \frac{1}{2} n_2(n_2 + 1) - \Sigma R_{Site\ B}$

$U_2 = n_1 \times n_2 + \frac{1}{2} n_1(n_1 + 1) - \Sigma R_{Site\ A}$

where n_1 and n_2 are the number of Site A quadrats and Site B quadrats respectively.

$U_1 = 8 \times 8 + \frac{1}{2} 8(8 + 1) - 87 = 100 - 87 = 13$

$U_2 = 8 \times 8 + \frac{1}{2} 8(8 + 1) - 49 = 100 - 49 = 51$

Step 5 compare the smallest *U* value against the critical value (Table 7.2) for eight samples per data set. If the smallest *U* value is less than or equal to the critical value, then we accept that there is a significant difference between the two median values (statisticians prefer us to accept significance by rejecting a null hypothesis that there is no difference). As our smallest *U* value of 13 equals the critical value for eight samples per data set, we can reject the null hypothesis and accept that there is a significant difference (Information box 7.4) between the median density of bluebells at Site A and Site B.

7.3 INFORMATION

the Mann–Whitney *U* test measures the overlap between two sets of data

- if there is no overlap it would be easy to accept that there really is a difference between the two sets of data.

- the *U* value (the smaller of the U_1 and U_2 values) for this ideal situation would be 0.

- a bigger *U* value tells us there is more overlap and means we are less certain there is a difference.

- the critical value lets us choose a cut-off point along the scale.

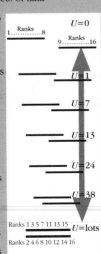

Table 7.2 *Critical values (at* $p = 0.05$*) of U*

Number of samples per data set	Critical value of U	Number of samples per data set	Critical value of U
4	0	13	45
5	2	14	55
6	5	15	64
7	8	16	75
8	13	17	87
9	17	18	99
10	23	19	113
11	30	20	127
12	37		

This table only works for instances where there are equal numbers of replicates in each data set. Other tables are available (*The O.U. Project Guide*, Neil Chalmers & Phil Baker, Occasional Publication No. 9, Field Studies Council 1989) for instances where there are uneven sets of data.

7.4 ⓘ INFORMATION

- Critical values are the U values which could arise by chance one time in 20 due to random variation within two sets of data.

- A U value less than the critical value could therefore only occur by chance one time in 20 (or 5% of the time).

- So if our U value is less than the critical value we can be 95% certain that there is a true (or significant) difference between the two medians.

- $p < 0.05$ is used to indicate a significant difference.

- $p > 0.05$ indicates a non-significant difference.

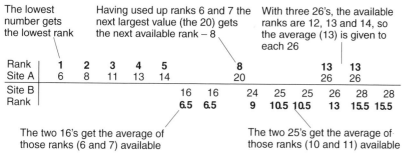

Figure 7.12 Ranking the data for the Mann–Whitney U test

Wilcoxon matched pairs test

Case study 2 – the growth of yeasts

As part of a biotechnology practical, a student had compared the growth of a yeast (*Saccharomyces cerevisiae*) using two different sugar solutions (glucose and lactose). A haemocytometer was used to count the number of cells produced and the results had been very clear cut. Over a 24 hour period the yeast had produced 0.3 million cells per cm^3 on glucose but only 0.1 million cells on lactose.

The student was aware that there were a number of different species and strains of yeasts, some of which were better able to use lactose as a substrate. He only had 12 flasks to use as culture vessels and had access to six species or strains of yeast and wanted to design an experiment which would test the hypothesis that 'All yeasts grow better on glucose than lactose'. He decided that the hypothesis was really concerned with the **difference** between sugars as sources of nutrients for yeasts. Because of the limited amount of equipment available, he could not replicate each yeast on each sugar six times. There were a number of experimental possibilities (Figure 7.13).

Only one of these seemed to answer his original hypothesis. In Design A, only one species of yeast was used but this was replicated six times. Designs B and C were better in that they used two and three species respectively but

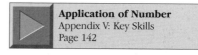

Application of Number
Appendix V: Key Skills
Page 142

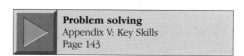

Problem solving
Appendix V: Key Skills
Page 143

Route 7.2 *Wilcoxon matched pairs test*

Start Here – do you want to look at differences between measurements from two (or more than two) sites, populations or treatments?

↓ **Yes**

Are you planning on replicating all your measurements at least six times at each site (or within each population or treatment)?

↓ **Yes**

Are you going to keep things simple and stick to just two sites, populations or treatments?

↓ **Yes**

Are you planning on taking 6–15 measurements from each site, population or treatment?

↓ **Yes**

Some form of random sampling may be useful, your data can be summarised using the median.
Use the Mann–Whitney *U* Test to see if any differences are significant.
Occasionally your data might be in matched pairs, in which case you will need the Wilcoxon matched pairs test.

7.5 INFORMATION

Matched pairs

- To be considered as matched pairs, there must be a single, unique way in which a value from one data set can be linked to a value in the second set.

- In the yeast example, each culture was split into two halves and one half grown on lactose, the other on glucose.

- So a cell count for a yeast grown on lactose can only be matched against the count for the same yeast grown on glucose.

Other examples of matched pairs might be:

- Pulse rates of a set of students before and after exercise; the before exercise rate of one student can only be matched against the after exercise rate for the same student.

- The percentage cover of lichens from quadrats on the north and south sides of a set of oak trees or gravestones; the % cover on the north side of one tree can only be matched against the % cover on the south side of the same tree.

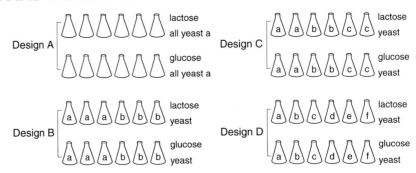

Figure 7.13 Eperimental designs available with 12 culture flasks and 6 yeast strains (for simplicity labelled a, b, c, d, e and f).

only had a limited number of replicates. Design D used all the available yeasts but there was no replication. As the initial question had been to do with the difference between sugars, he decided to use Design D (where the yeasts themselves acted as replicates) and analyse the data using the **Wilcoxon matched pairs** test (Route 7.2) (see Information box 7.5 for more details of **matched pairs**).

Wilcoxon matched pairs test – example

Data – the number of cells (million per cm^3) for five strains [*Kluyveromyces lactis* (Kl), *Saccharomyces rouxii* (Sr), *Saccharomyces diastichus* (Sd), *Saccharomyces carlsbergensis* (Sca), *Saccharomyces cerevisiae* (NCYC974) (974) and *Saccharomyces cerevisiae* (Sce)] of yeast grown on glucose and lactose (source National Centre for Biotechnology Education & Field Studies Council).

Yeast	Kl	Sr	Sd	Sca	974	Sce
Glucose	0.3	1.4	2.1	1.2	2.1	0.3
Lactose	0.3	0.4	0.7	0.1	0.3	0.1

Step 1   calculate **differences** between the measurements

Yeast	Kl	Sr	Sd	Sca	974	Sce
Glucose	0.3	1.4	2.1	1.1	2.1	0.3
Lactose	0.3	0.4	0.7	0.1	0.3	0.1
Diff.	**0.0**	**+1.0**	**+1.4**	**+1.0**	**+1.8**	**+0.2**

Step 2   ignoring the signs, **rank** the non-zero differences so that the smallest difference gets the lowest rank and the largest the highest rank. Differences which are the same get the average of ranks available.

We have two yeasts (Sr and Sca) which show a difference of 1.0 between the cell counts.
We rank them equally as 2.5 (the average of 2 and 3).

As the difference is 0 this yeast is excluded

Yeast	Kl	Sr	Sd	Sca	974	Sce
Glucose	0.3	1.4	2.1	1.1	2.1	0.3
Lactose	0.3	0.4	0.7	0.1	0.3	0.1
Diff.	0.0	1.0	1.4	1.0	1.8	0.2
Rank (*R*)	**–**	**2.5**	**4**	**2.5**	**5**	**1**

Step 3 put the **signs** back in and calculate the sum of the +ve ranks and of the –ve ranks.

Yeast	Kl	Sr	Sd	Sca	974	Sce
Glucose	0.3	1.4	2.1	1.1	2.1	0.3
Lactose	0.3	0.4	0.7	0.1	0.3	0.1
Diff.	0.0	1.0	1.4	1.0	1.8	0.2
Rank (R)	–	2.5	4	2.5	5	1
Sign		+ve	+ve	+ve	+ve	+ve

$\sum R$ –ve = 0

$\sum R$ +ve = 2.5 + 4 + 2.5 + 5 + 1 = 15

As a **check** – if your calculations are correct then:

$\sum R$ +ve +$\sum R$ –ve = 0.5 $N_D(N_D + 1)$

Where N_D is the number of non-zero differences; 5 here.

15.0 + 0 = 15 and 0.5 × 5(5 + 1) = 15 check ✓

Step 4 compare the smallest of the $\sum R$ values against the critical value for the number of non-zero differences (N_D) (Table 7.3). If the smallest $\sum R$ value is less than or equal to the critical value then we can reject the null hypothesis and accept that there is a difference between the two sets of data. Our $\sum R$ –ve value is 0, but as we only have five non-zero differences, the test will not allow us to make a decision (Information box 7.6).

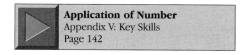
Application of Number
Appendix V: Key Skills
Page 142

Table 7.3 *Critical values (at p = 0.05) for Wilcoxon matched pairs test*

N_D	Critical Value	N_D	Critical Value
5	–	18	40
6	0	19	46
7	2	20	52
8	3	21	58
9	5	22	65
10	8	23	73
11	10	24	81
12	13	25	89
13	17	26	98
14	21	27	107
15	25	28	116
16	29	29	126
17	34	30	137

Reject the null hypothesis if the smallest $\sum R$ value is less than or equal to the critical value for the appropriate number of non-zero (N_D) differences

Student's *t*-test

Case study 3 – nettle leaves

A walk around the school grounds led to the observation that nettle (*Urtica dioica*) plants in shaded areas seemed to have larger leaves than those in more open areas. As a pilot study, a student collected 10 leaves from plants at two sites. One site was open and completely unshaded whilst the other received shade from a large, overhanging oak tree. In order to eliminate the effect of age, the student (using gloves and a pair of blunt forceps) took a leaf from the fourth pair of leaves down the stem – these were the first fully expanded leaves on the plants.

The student was interested in looking at the **difference** between the two sites and as it was simple to measure the maximum length of leaves there was no problem in measuring at **least six leaves** from plants at each site. In fact, after having looked at 10 leaves, he felt that the leaves were very variable in size, so he decided to plot a graph showing the **running mean** for the

7.6

- With less than six replicates, the Wilcoxon matched pairs test will not allow you to make a decision about the significance of your results.

- With six, seven or eight replicates, the data need to be nearly perfect – the differences need to be mostly in the same direction (i.e. all +ve or all –ve).

- To give yourself a chance of showing a difference, you will need a minimum of eight replicates.

- The test can cope with a maximum of 30 values.

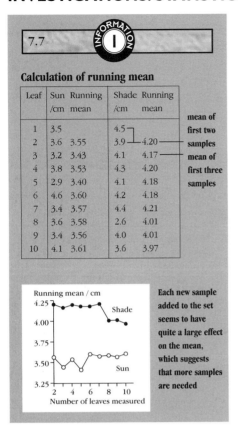

data sets (Information box 7.7). What he found was that the mean was still fluctuating after 10 leaves – each new leaf added to the data set had a big effect on the mean. As it was so quick to measure the leaves he decided to measure 30 leaves (Table 7.4) and plot graphs to see how well the running mean had stabilised and to see how well the data matched the normal distribution. From these graphs (Figure 7.14) he decided that 30 leaves were sufficient, the running mean had stabilised, and that the data were normally distributed, so he used the **Student's *t*-test** (Route 7.3) to test for the difference between the mean values.

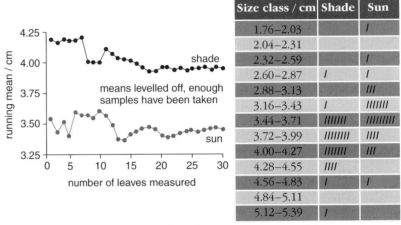

Size class / cm	Shade	Sun
1.76–2.03		I
2.04–2.31		
2.32–2.59		I
2.60–2.87	I	I
2.88–3.13		III
3.16–3.43	I	IIIIIII
3.44–3.71	IIIIII	IIIIIIIII
3.72–3.99	IIIIIIII	IIII
4.00–4.27	IIIIIII	III
4.28–4.55	IIII	
4.56–4.83	I	I
4.84–5.11		
5.12–5.39	I	

Figure 7.14 Checking data for 'levelling off' of running mean and for normal distribution

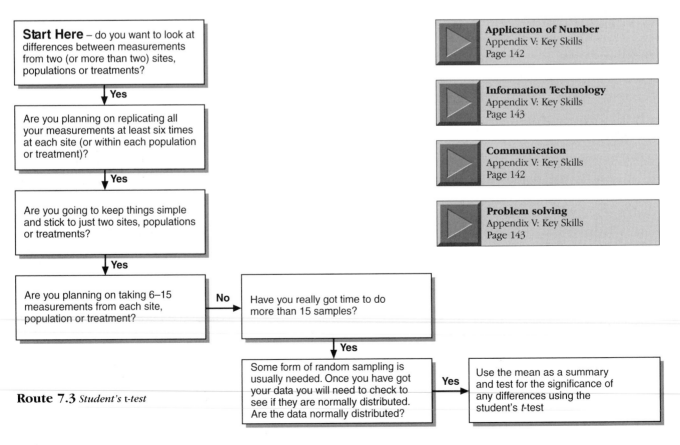

Start Here – do you want to look at differences between measurements from two (or more than two) sites, populations or treatments?

Yes ↓

Are you planning on replicating all your measurements at least six times at each site (or within each population or treatment)?

Yes ↓

Are you going to keep things simple and stick to just two sites, populations or treatments?

Yes ↓

Are you planning on taking 6–15 measurements from each site, population or treatment? **No** → Have you really got time to do more than 15 samples?

Yes ↓

Some form of random sampling is usually needed. Once you have got your data you will need to check to see if they are normally distributed. Are the data normally distributed? **Yes** → Use the mean as a summary and test for the significance of any differences using the student's *t*-test

Route 7.3 *Student's t-test*

	Application of Number Appendix V: Key Skills Page 142
	Information Technology Appendix V: Key Skills Page 143
	Communication Appendix V: Key Skills Page 142
	Problem solving Appendix V: Key Skills Page 143

Student's t-test – example

Step 1 check data are normally distributed (a simple tally chart is enough, see Figure 7.14).

Step 2 calculate $\sum x$ and $\sum x^2$ for each set of data.

$$\sum x_a = 3.5 + 3.6 + 3.2 + \ldots\ldots + 3.3 = 104.1$$

$$\sum x_a^2 = 12.25 + 12.96 + 10.24 + \ldots + 10.89 = 369.61$$

$$\sum x_b = 3.5 + 3.9 + 4.1 + \ldots\ldots + 3.7 = 118.7$$

$$\sum x_b^2 = 20.25 + 15.21 + 16.81 + \ldots + 13.69 = 475.89$$

Step 3 calculate mean values ($\bar{x}_a$ and $\bar{x}_b$).

If these are identical there is no evidence to suggest any real difference and no point in continuing further analysis.

$$\bar{x}_a = \frac{104.1}{30} = 3.47 \text{ and } \bar{x}_b = \frac{118.7}{30} = 3.96$$

Step 4 calculate standard deviations using:

$$\text{Standard deviation } (s) = \sqrt{\frac{\sum x^2 - \frac{(\sum x)^2}{n}}{n-1}}$$

Application of Number
Appendix V:
Key Skills
Page 142

$$s_a = \sqrt{\frac{369.61 - \frac{104.1^2}{30}}{30 - 1}} = 0.54$$

$$s_b = \sqrt{\frac{475.89 - \frac{118.7^2}{30}}{30 - 1}} = 0.46$$

Step 5 substitute means and standard deviations (s) into the formula:

$$t = \frac{|\bar{x}_a - \bar{x}_b|}{\sqrt{\frac{s_a^2}{n_a} + \frac{s_b^2}{n_b}}} \qquad t = \frac{|3.47 - 3.96|}{\sqrt{\frac{0.54^2}{30} + \frac{0.46^2}{30}}}$$

$$= \frac{0.49}{\sqrt{0.0097 + 0.0071}} = 3.78$$

Step 6 compare the value of t against the critical value (Table 7.5) for the number of degrees of freedom (d.f.) calculated using the formula:

$$\text{d.f.} = n_a + n_b - 2$$
$$= 30 + 30 - 2 = 58$$

Table 7.4 *The maximum lengths of 30 nettle leaves from sun and shade sites*

Sun leaves		Shade leaves	
x_a	x_a^2	x_b	x_b^2
3.5	12.25	4.5	20.25
3.6	12.96	3.9	15.21
3.2	10.24	4.1	16.81
3.8	14.44	4.3	18.49
2.9	8.41	4.1	16.81
4.6	21.16	4.2	17.64
3.4	11.56	4.4	19.36
3.6	12.96	2.6	6.76
3.4	11.56	4.0	16.00
4.1	16.81	3.9	15.21
3.2	10.24	5.3	28.09
2.6	6.76	3.6	12.96
2.0	4.00	3.7	13.69
3.3	10.89	3.9	15.21
4.2	17.64	3.9	15.21
3.7	13.69	3.6	12.96
3.9	15.21	3.4	11.56
3.7	13.69	3.5	12.25
3.1	9.61	3.9	15.21
2.4	5.76	4.6	21.16
3.0	9.00	3.9	15.21
3.7	13.69	3.6	12.96
4.0	16.00	4.0	16.00
3.8	14.44	3.9	15.21
3.7	13.69	4.1	16.81
3.2	10.24	3.9	15.21
3.7	13.69	4.2	17.64
3.7	13.69	3.6	12.96
3.8	14.44	4.4	19.36
3.3	10.89	3.7	13.69

Table 7.5 *Critical values (at p = 0.05) for the t test*

d.f.	c.v.	d.f.	c.v.
18	2.10	26	2.06
19	2.09	27	2.05
20	2.09	28	2.05
21	2.08	29	2.04
22	2.07	30	2.04
23	2.07	40	2.02
24	2.06	60	2.00
25	2.06	∞	1.96

Reject the null hypothesis if your value of *t* is greater than or equal to the critical value for the appropriate degrees of freedom (d.f.), calculated as d.f. = $n_1 + n_2 - 2$.

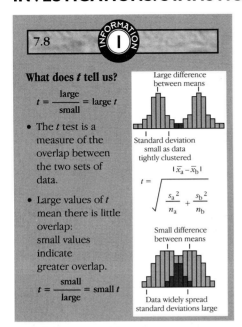

7.8

What does *t* tell us?

$$t = \frac{large}{small} = \text{large } t$$

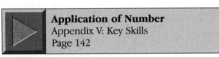

- The *t* test is a measure of the overlap between the two sets of data.

- Large values of *t* mean there is little overlap: small values indicate greater overlap.

$$t = \frac{small}{large} = \text{small } t$$

Large difference between means

Standard deviation small as data tightly clustered

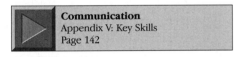

$$t = \frac{|\bar{x}_a - \bar{x}_b|}{\sqrt{\dfrac{s_a{}^2}{n_a} + \dfrac{s_b{}^2}{n_b}}}$$

Small difference between means

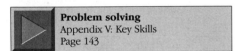

Data widely spread standard deviations large

Application of Number
Appendix V: Key Skills
Page 142

Communication
Appendix V: Key Skills
Page 142

Problem solving
Appendix V: Key Skills
Page 143

---

t measures the amount of overlap between two data sets (Information box 7.8). The larger the value of *t*, the more certain we are that there is a difference. As *t* (3.78) is greater than the critical value of 2.00 (Table 7.5) for 60 d.f. (the closest value to 58 d.f.), we can reject the null hypothesis and accept that there is a significant difference ($p < 0.05$) between the mean length of nettle leaves at sites A and B.

Spearman rank correlation test

Case study 4 – clotting of milk by Rennilase®

A student had been looking at the activity of enzymes and had decided to investigate the effect of varying calcium chloride concentrations on the clotting of milk by the enzyme Rennilase®. She decided that there were two practical approaches to this question. She could select two calcium chloride concentrations and replicate each concentration six times and then use the Mann–Whitney *U* test to test for differences between the median time it took the enzyme to clot the milk. Alternatively, she could use a greater range of calcium chloride concentrations and look for a **correlation** between concentration and clotting time using the **Spearman rank correlation test**.

She decided to adopt the second approach (Route 7.4) and generated the hypothesis that 'as the concentration of calcium chloride increases, the length of time for Rennilase® to form a clot will decrease'. Effectively she was looking for a negative correlation between the calcium chloride

Route 7.4 *Spearman rank correlation test*

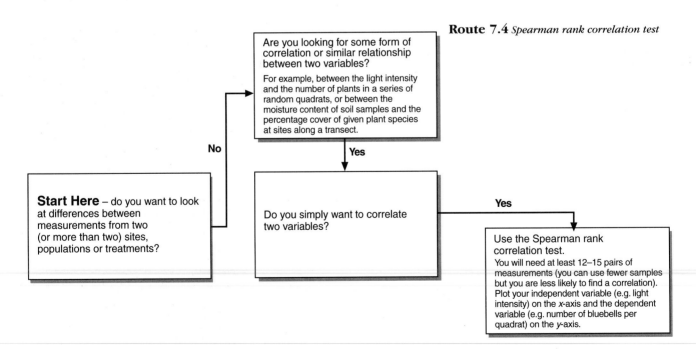

Are you looking for some form of correlation or similar relationship between two variables?

For example, between the light intensity and the number of plants in a series of random quadrats, or between the moisture content of soil samples and the percentage cover of given plant species at sites along a transect.

No

Yes

Start Here – do you want to look at differences between measurements from two (or more than two) sites, populations or treatments?

Do you simply want to correlate two variables?

Yes

Use the Spearman rank correlation test.
You will need at least 12–15 pairs of measurements (you can use fewer samples but you are less likely to find a correlation). Plot your independent variable (e.g. light intensity) on the *x*-axis and the dependent variable (e.g. number of bluebells per quadrat) on the *y*-axis.

concentration (the **independent variable**) and the time for a clot to appear (the **dependent variable**). She decided to use **12** concentrations of calcium chloride. Her data are plotted as a scattergraph in Figure 7.15 and shown in columns 1 and 3 of Table 7.6. There seemed to be a reasonable correlation so she proceeded with the analysis.

Spearman rank correlation – example

Step 1 draw a scattergraph (Figure 7.15) to show the relationship between your two variables. If the graph shows a 'U' or inverted 'U' shape, don't proceed.

Step 2 rank the data (Table 7.6). It is probably easiest to rearrange the data so that one of the variables is in order and then rank both sets independently with the lowest value getting the smallest rank and the biggest the largest rank. **Tied numbers** get the average of those ranks available. For example, for the two **144** values in the 'Time' column, ranks 7 and 8 are available, so both get **Rank 7.5**.

Step 3 calculate the differences between the ranks; for the first pair of measurements the D value is: $1 - 12 = -11$ (Table 7.6). As a check, the sum of the all the D values should be zero.

$$\Sigma D = -11 - 5.5 - 8 - .... + 8 + 11 = 0 \checkmark$$

Step 4 square the D values and calculate a ΣD_2 value (Table 7.6).

$$\Sigma D^2 = 121 + 30.25 + 64 + ... + 121 = 518.5$$

Step 5 substitute the value of ΣD^2 into the equation below and calculate the Spearman rank correlation coefficient (r_s), where n is the number of samples, in this case the 12 $CaCl_2$ concentrations used.

$$\text{Spearman rank correlation coefficient } r_s = 1 - \frac{6 \, \Sigma D^2}{n(n^2 - 1)}$$

$$r_s = 1 - \frac{6 \times 518.5}{12(12^2 - 1)} = 1 - \frac{3111}{1716} = 1 - 1.813$$

$$r_s = -0.813$$

Step 6 r_s is a measure of the strength of a correlation (see Information box 7.9). Compare the r_s value against the critical value (Table 7.7). If the value (ignoring any sign) is greater than or equal to the critical value for that number of samples, then we accept that there is a significant correlation between the two variables.

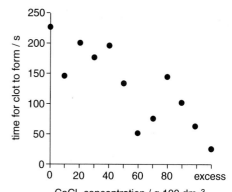

Figure 7.15 *The relationship between calcium chloride concentration and the clotting of milk be Rennilase®*

Table 7.6 *Steps 2, 3 and 4 in the calculation of the Spearman Rank correlation coefficient*

$CaCl_2$ /g 100 dm^{-3}	Rank Step 2	Time /s	Rank Step 2	D Step 3	D^2 Step 4
0	1	231	12	–11	121
10	2	**144**	**7.5**	–5.5	30.25
20	3	202	11	–8	64
30	4	177	9	–5	25
40	5	193	10	–5	25
50	6	133	6	0	0
60	7	54	2	5	25
70	8	75	4	4	16
80	9	**144**	**7.5**	1.5	2.25
90	10	105	5	5	25
100	11	66	3	8	64
excess	12	28	1	11	121
				Σ 0	518.5

Table 7.7 *Critical values for the Spearman Rank correlation coefficient at the p = 0.05 level*

n	5	6	7	8	9	10	12	14
Critical value	1.000	0.886	0.786	0.738	0.683	0.648	0.591	0.544
n	16	18	20	22	24	26	28	30
Critical value	0.506	0.475	0.450	0.428	0.409	0.392	0.377	0.364

Application of Number
Appendix V: Key Skills
Page 142

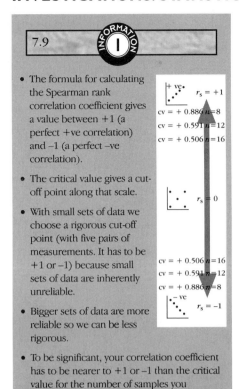

- The formula for calculating the Spearman rank correlation coefficient gives a value between +1 (a perfect +ve correlation) and –1 (a perfect –ve correlation).

- The critical value gives a cut-off point along that scale.

- With small sets of data we choose a rigorous cut-off point (with five pairs of measurements. It has to be +1 or –1) because small sets of data are inherently unreliable.

- Bigger sets of data are more reliable so we can be less rigorous.

- To be significant, your correlation coefficient has to be nearer to +1 or –1 than the critical value for the number of samples you looked at.

- For our example, the r_s value of –0.813 is more (ignoring the sign) than the critical value of 0.591, so we say there is a correlation.

If the sign is +ve, then we say there is a positive correlation; if it is –ve, then there is negative correlation. As our value of $r_s = -0.813$ is bigger (ignoring the sign) than the critical value of 0.591 (for 12 pairs of samples) we can reject the null hypothesis (that there is no correlation) and conclude that there is a significant negative correlation ($p < 0.05$) between calcium chloride concentration and the length of time it takes for Rennilase® to clot milk.

Chi^2 (χ^2) test

Case study 5 – size of cockles

As part of a sea-shore study, students had been looking at the size (maximum length) of cockles (*Cerastoderma edule*). They were using size as a measure of age so they could examine the age structure of a population of cockles on the shore. The class results are shown in Figure 7.16 as the data for shore 1. One student wanted to look at the age structure of a cockle population on a second shore which had a large wintering population of oystercatchers (*Haematopus ostralegus*) and compare it with that of the first shore. His hypothesis was that the oystercatchers would take the larger, older cockles in preference to smaller, younger cockles, leading to a distortion of the size structure towards the smaller size classes. Effectively he was using the age structure of cockles on the first shore as a model distribution (his expected values) and wanted to test the **goodness of fit** (Route 7.5) of the data from the second shore (his observed values) to that model.

Size class / cm	Shore 1 Exp.	Shore 2 Obs.
0.5–0.9	96	111
1.0–1.4	36	40
1.5–1.9	12	12
2.0–2.4	10	3
2.5–2.9	8	8
3.0–3.4	6	4
3.5–3.9	10	8
4.0–4.4	9	6
4.5–4.9	6	2
5.0–5.4	7	6
Total	200	200

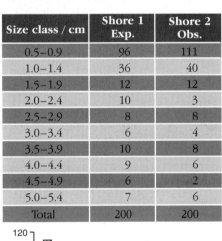

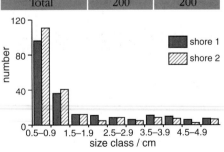

Figure 7.16 *The size distribution of samples of 200 cockles collected from each of the two shore sites*

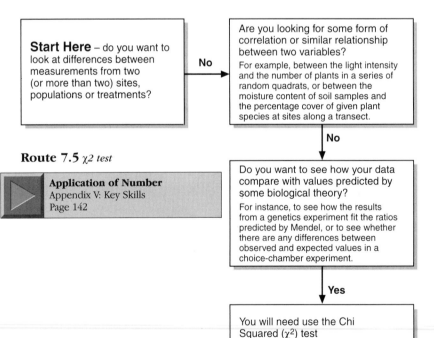

Start Here – do you want to look at differences between measurements from two (or more than two) sites, populations or treatments?

No →

Are you looking for some form of correlation or similar relationship between two variables?

For example, between the light intensity and the number of plants in a series of random quadrats, or between the moisture content of soil samples and the percentage cover of given plant species at sites along a transect.

No ↓

Route 7.5 χ_2 *test*

> **Application of Number**
> Appendix V: Key Skills
> Page 142

Do you want to see how your data compare with values predicted by some biological theory?

For instance, to see how the results from a genetics experiment fit the ratios predicted by Mendel, or to see whether there are any differences between observed and expected values in a choice-chamber experiment.

Yes ↓

You will need use the Chi Squared (χ^2) test

This tests the goodness of fit of observed data to a set of expected values. It is most useful in genetics or choice-chamber work and has very limited use for ecological studies.

The χ^2 test can be used for this type of situation. It also has applications in **genetics** where it is used to test the fit of **observed** data to **expected** 9:3:3:1 ratios, and in behavioural work where animals in **choice chambers** are presented with various options. In ecological work, use of the χ^2 test is limited to situations similar to that above or to **association analysis**. It should not be used to test for the difference between series of measurements from two sites, populations or treatments (see Information box 7.10). Some of the books listed in Appendix I have examples of the other applications of the χ^2 test.

χ^2 test – example

Step 1 for each pair of observed and expected values calculate the difference $(O - E)$ (Table 7.8).

Table 7.8 *Steps 1, 2 and 3 in the calculation of the χ^2 test*

Size class / cm	Shore 1 Exp.	Shore 2 Obs.	Step 1 $O - E$	Step 2 $(O - E)^2$	Step 3 $\dfrac{(O - E)^2}{E}$
0.5–0.9	96	111	15	225	2.34
1.0–1.4	36	40	4	16	0.44
1.5–1.9	12	12	0	0	0.00
2.0–2.4	10	3	–7	49	4.90
2.5–2.9	8	8	0	0	0.00
3.0–3.4	6	4	–2	4	0.67
3.5–3.9	10	8	–2	4	0.40
4.0–4.4	9	6	–3	9	1.00
4.5–4.9	6	2	–4	16	2.67
5.0–5.4	7	6	–1	1	0.14

Step 2 square these values to obtain $(O - E)^2$ (Table 7.8).

Step 3 divide the $(O - E)^2$ values by their Expected values (Table 7.8).

Step 4 calculate χ^2 by summing these values.

$$\chi^2 = \sum \frac{(O - E)^2}{E}$$

$$= \frac{(111 - 96)^2}{96} + \frac{(40 - 36)^2}{36} + \frac{(12 - 12)^2}{12} + \cdots + \frac{(6 - 7)^2}{7}$$

$$= \frac{225}{96} + \frac{16}{36} + \frac{0}{12} + \cdots\cdots\cdots\cdots + \frac{1}{7}$$

$$= 2.34 + 0.44 + 0.00 + \cdots\cdots\cdots + 0.14 = 12.56$$

7.10

- You will often see practical work which generates data like that in the table opposite.

Quadrant	No. of woodlice Site A	No. of woodlice Site B
1	1	5
2	2	5
3	1	6
4	1	5
5	1	4
6	47	5
Total	53	30

- It might seem like a good idea to take the average of the two totals to give an expected value. Expected value = 41.5.

- and then use χ^2 to test for the difference between the totals and the expected values.

$$\chi^2 = \sum \frac{(O - E)^2}{E} = \frac{(53 - 41.5)^2}{41.5} + \frac{(30 - 41.5)^2}{41.5}$$

$\chi^2 = 6.37$, critical value = 3.84 (Table 7.8, for 1 d.f.)

- The conclusion would be that there is a significant difference between the two sites; woodlice are more abundant at site A.

- Is this a fair decision? On average woodlice are more abundant at site B.

- The results of the χ^2 test are biased, here, by a single large count. By summing data and basing the analysis on a single figure for each site we lose any benefit of replicating measurements. We should have used the mann–Whitney U test.

Table 7.9 *Critical values at $p = 0.05$ and $p = 0.01$ for the χ^2 test*

Degrees of freedom	$p = 0.05$	$p = 0.01$	Degrees of freedom	$p = 0.05$	$p = 0.01$
1	3.84	6.63	8	15.51	20.09
2	5.99	9.21	9	16.92	21.67
3	7.82	11.34	10	18.31	23.21
4	9.49	13.28	16	26.30	32.00
5	10.07	15.09	20	31.40	37.57
6	12.59	16.81	25	37.65	44.31
7	14.07	18.48	30	43.77	50.89

Reject the null hypothesis (at $p = 0.05$ or $p = 0.01$) if your value of χ^2 is greater than or equal to the critical value for the appropriate degrees of freedom. The method of calculating these varies according to how the test is used. The general formula is (number of rows − 1) × (number of columns − 1)

Step 5   compare the value of χ^2 against the critical value (Table 7.9) for $n - 1$ degrees of freedom where n is the number of pairs of observed and expected values (10 in this example). χ^2 measures the magnitude of the difference between observed and expected values in relation to the magnitude of the numbers being examined (Information box 7.11). If your value is greater than the critical value for p = 0.05 you can reject the null hypothesis and accept that there is a significant difference between the observed and expected values. In our example, the critical value of 16.92 is larger than our χ^2 value, so we must accept the null hypothesis that the observed data (shore 2) matches the expected data from the first site. So there is no difference between the size class (i.e. age) structure of the two populations.

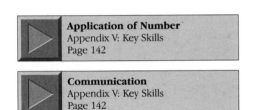

Application of Number
Appendix V: Key Skills
Page 142

Communication
Appendix V: Key Skills
Page 142

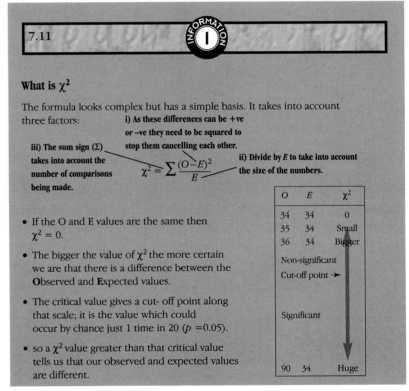

7.11   INFORMATION

What is χ^2

The formula looks complex but has a simple basis. It takes into account three factors:

i) As these differences can be +ve or –ve they need to be squared to stop them cancelling each other.

iii) The sum sign (Σ) takes into account the number of comparisons being made.

$$\chi^2 = \sum \frac{(O - E)^2}{E}$$

ii) Divide by E to take into account the size of the numbers.

O	E	χ^2
34	34	0
35	34	Small
36	34	Bigger

Non-significant

Cut-off point →

Significant

| 90 | 34 | Huge |

- If the O and E values are the same then $\chi^2 = 0$.

- The bigger the value of χ^2 the more certain we are that there is a difference between the **O**bserved and **E**xpected values.

- The critical value gives a cut-off point along that scale; it is the value which could occur by chance just 1 time in 20 (p =0.05).

- so a χ^2 value greater than that critical value tells us that our observed and expected values are different.

Regression analysis

Case study 6 – temperature and oxygen concentration

Problem solving
Appendix V: Key Skills
Page 143

As part of a long-term study of the ecology of a freshwater stream, a group of A-level students were measuring the change in dissolved oxygen concentration and temperature of a small stream within their school grounds. There appeared to be a close relationship between these two variables, so they thought they would try to use the temperature to predict the oxygen concentration. They could then avoid the time-consuming titration for estimation of oxygen (the Winkler titration). Their data are shown in columns B and C of Figure 7.17. If they were going to use temperature to predict oxygen they first needed to be sure that there was a good correlation between the two variables.

Using the Spearman rank correlation they found a value of $r_s = 0.980$. This was highly significant ($p < 0.001$) so they felt confident that by measuring temperature they could accurately predict the oxygen concentration of their stream. To do this properly, they needed an equation for a **best fit line** (see Information box 7.12 for more about drawing best fit lines) and to do this they used **regression analysis** (Route 7.6).

Linear regression – example

Step 1   draw a scattergraph to check that there is a roughly linear relationship (Figure 7.18).

Route 7.6 *Regression analysis*

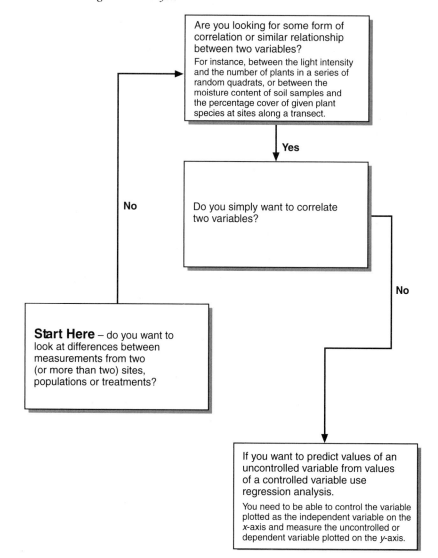

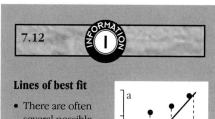

7.12

Lines of best fit

- There are often several possible 'best fit' lines and the temptation is to draw the one (graph a) which emphasises the trend you are trying to describe.

- Regression analysis is a mathematical way of fitting a line to a set of data.

- It does this by adjusting the slope and intercept of the line to minimise the vertical deviations (shown as dotted lines) of points from that line.

- By carefully measuring the dotted lines you can see that graph b has the smaller deviations. This is the mathematically fitted best-fit line.

- Strictly speaking it is the line for the regression of the y variable on the x variable.

- We assume that the x (or independent) variable can be measured with no error so variations are all in the y direction.

Problem solving
Appendix V: Key Skills
Page 143

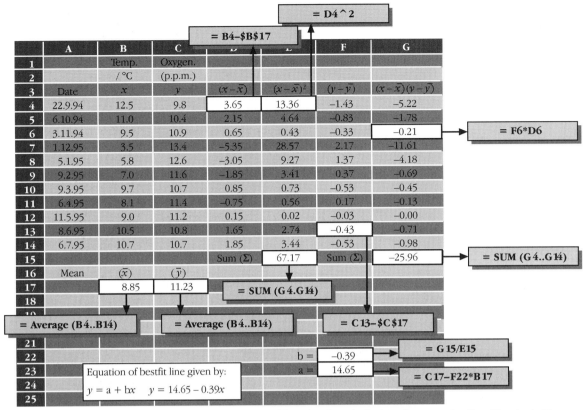

	A	B	C	D	E	F	G
1		Temp.	Oxygen.				
2		/°C	(p.p.m.)				
3	Date	x	y	$(x-\bar{x})$	$(x-\bar{x})^2$	$(y-\bar{y})$	$(x-\bar{x})(y-\bar{y})$
4	22.9.94	12.5	9.8	3.65	13.36	–1.43	–5.22
5	6.10.94	11.0	10.4	2.15	4.64	–0.83	–1.78
6	3.11.94	9.5	10.9	0.65	0.43	–0.33	–0.21
7	1.12.95	3.5	13.4	–5.35	28.57	2.17	–11.61
8	5.1.95	5.8	12.6	–3.05	9.27	1.37	–4.18
9	9.2.95	7.0	11.6	–1.85	3.41	0.37	–0.69
10	9.3.95	9.7	10.7	0.85	0.73	–0.53	–0.45
11	6.4.95	8.1	11.4	–0.75	0.56	0.17	–0.13
12	11.5.95	9.0	11.2	0.15	0.02	–0.03	–0.00
13	8.6.95	10.5	10.8	1.65	2.74	–0.43	–0.71
14	6.7.95	10.7	10.7	1.85	3.44	–0.53	–0.98
15				Sum (Σ)	67.17	Sum (Σ)	–25.96
16	Mean	$(\bar{x})$	$(\bar{y})$				
17		8.85	11.23				
18							

Formula annotations (shaded boxes):
- $= D4\char94 2$
- $= B4 - \$B\$17$
- $= F6*D6$
- $= SUM (G4..G14)$
- $= SUM (G4.G14)$
- $= C13 - \$C\$17$
- $= Average (B4..B14)$
- $= Average (B4..B14)$
- b = –0.39 $= G15/E15$
- a = 14.65 $= C17 - F22*B17$

Equation of bestfit line given by:
$y = a + bx$ $y = 14.65 - 0.39x$

Figure 7.17 *Spreadsheet for the calculation of a regression line. The shaded boxes show the formulae used to calculate the figures shown on the table.*

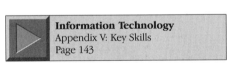

Information Technology
Appendix V: Key Skills
Page 143

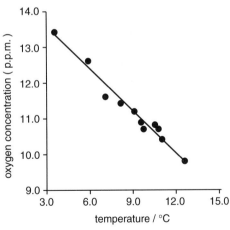

Figure 7.18 *The relationship between temperature and dissolved oxygen for monthly samples taken from a small stream. The best fit line has been fitted using regression analysis and has the equation:*
y = 14.65 – 0.39 x where y is the oxygen concentration and x is the temperature.

Step 2 – to calculate the line of best fit we use the standard formula for a straight line of:

$$y = a + bx; \text{ estimate } b \text{ as: } \frac{\sum(x-\bar{x})(y-\bar{y})}{\sum(x-\bar{x})^2} \text{ and } a \text{ as: } \bar{y} - b\bar{x}$$

These formula involve considerable mathematical manipulations which are probably most easily done on a spreadsheet (Figure 7.17).

The equation of our best fit line is: $y = 14.65 - 0.39x$ and this can be plotted on the scattergraph as in Figure 7.18. It is possible to test the significance of the regression but it is sufficient at A level to use regression analysis to calculate lines of best fit and use the Spearman rank correlation test to test the significance of any relationship. The regression equation can be used to predict values of y from those of the independent variable $– x$. If the temperature of the stream was, for example, 16 °C then we would expect the oxygen concentration to be:

oxygen = 14.65 – 0.39 × temperature = 14.65 – 0.39 × 16 = 8.44 p.p.m.

8 Preparing for the examination

To the student

During your course you will have covered the syllabus topics and done experimental work which will have helped you to develop your practical skills. You will have.acquired an understanding of, and we hope developed an interest in, biology. You must also focus on the examination. Prepare well ahead, planning your approach to your revision. Look at examination questions and think about why questions are being asked and about your responses to the styles of questions. Advice in this chapter will help you prepare for the examination.

The syllabus (specification)

All A level Biology (and to some extent, Human Biology) syllabuses contain a common body of biological knowledge. They also share common aims, assessment objectives and requirements relating to practical skills. You will find these listed in the syllabus, so at some stage you should read them. There are minor variations in the way in which the question papers of the different examining boards are set out and in the style of the questions. However, similar principles apply to question papers set by all examination boards, so the comments below give general advice, which is relevant for whichever Biology syllabus you are following. You should obtain a copy of the syllabus so that you are familiar with the papers that you will sit during, or at the end of, your course. Remember also that syllabuses and the examination format do change from time to time, so keep yourself up to date by looking at your *current* syllabus and recent specimen or question papers. In the syllabus, you will find a list of the component modules, or sections of syllabus content, together with a description of the scheme of examination. This tells you about the different question papers, practical assessment requirements, and gives you an indication of the different styles of questions you could expect to find on each paper. In addition, you will find notes on the background required in physical science and mathematical skills, as these might also be needed to answer questions set in the examinations.

The examination – the question papers

You should make yourself familiar with the format of the question papers well before you sit the examination. In the examination room there is no time for surprises – you need to get on with the job of answering the questions, and to do this in the time allowed for the examination. The Examiner's job is to produce a fair examination, consistent in style and comparable with equivalent papers in previous years and which tests the biology contained in the syllabus. At the same time your ability in a range of different skills is being assessed. Most of these skills crop up also in other subjects, although some may be rather special to Biology.

8.1 INFORMATION

From the year 2000 onwards, 'syllabuses' will be described as 'specifications' to conform with terminology used by QCA. These specifications should not be confused with the 'specification grid' used for question papers and other components of the assessment scheme. This specification grid is discussed on page 124 onwards and it defines the balance of marks allocated, for example, to knowledge and understanding, skills, mathematics and so on. In this chapter, the more familiar term 'syllabus' has been retained.

PREPARING FOR THE EXAMINATION

The specification grid for the question papers

If you are aware of some of what goes on behind the setting of the papers, you should be better prepared to tackle the questions on the examination day. The Examiners write the question papers to match a fairly tight specification and they fill in a specification grid as they prepare the questions. This specification grid helps to keep the papers consistent from one examination to the next. You will find an outline of the specification grid in the syllabus.

Some questions or parts of questions are designed to test your **knowledge and understanding** of the syllabus content – material you should have studied when covering different syllabus topics. You need to know and recall biological facts, understand the meaning of, and use, biological terms correctly, give names of structures (recognised perhaps in a drawing or a photograph) and describe their functions, understand how biological processes are carried out and explain how one process relates to another. You also need to be familiar with and to describe certain experimental procedures and the apparatus which would be used.

Other questions are designed to test **skills and processes** and expect you to apply your biological knowledge and understanding to other situations, some of which may be unfamiliar. You may be required to handle numerical or written biological information, then to analyse or evaluate it, to interpret data or to explain the relevance of results of experiments. Numerical data may be given in graphs or tables of figures. You may be asked to design an experiment, given an outline of the problem to be investigated. You are also assessed on your ability to communicate biological information in different ways – sometimes as free prose, or by means of diagrams, or by presenting numerical data in other forms, including plotting graphs, or in tables. In addition, you may be asked to do calculations. These may be quite simple arithmetical processes, such as percentage change in a set of experimental results, or working out the rate of a reaction, or you may be asked to work through a statistical analysis of some results to determine their significance in relation to an hypothesis.

All syllabuses aim to promote an awareness and appreciation of the significance of biology in 'personal, social, environmental, economic and technological contexts'. So you will certainly find some questions which are designed to test **applications** of biology, in terms of our everyday lives. Instead of providing data about plants grown in a research laboratory, the question may refer to a crop plant, or to microorganisms used in industrial processes, or even something as familiar as yoghurt manufacture or brewing beer. This would also include environmental, health and even ethical issues – such as use of genetically modified organisms, or relate to decisions to be made in control of fertility and genetic counselling in humans. With ethical issues of this sort, you must be clear that the question paper would be testing your understanding of the *biology* involved and your awareness of some of the arguments surrounding an issue and possible consequences in a biological framework, rather than expecting you to give your personal opinions.

In a complete examination, there is a consistency in the balance between marks allocated to knowledge and understanding and those allocated to certain skills, as described above. Relatively few marks are likely to be allocated to calculations and there will usually be at least some questions (or parts of questions) testing applications. Depending on your syllabus, some papers may contain more questions testing knowledge and understanding and in other papers the balance may require more questions testing skills. You can check this balance in your syllabus, and then analyse a question paper to see if you agree with the specification grid given in the syllabus. Above all, it should be clear to you that you **must** learn some facts in your biology, but also be prepared to link your background understanding to unfamiliar situations and to the interpretation of novel data. To be successful, you must do some **learning** and some **thinking** and also be able to **apply** that knowledge.

The question styles – structured and free prose or essays

When you look through any question paper, you immediately see a range of question styles. It would be very dull if every question started 'Write something you know about . . . .'. Instead, the variety makes you think in different ways, and really enables the Examiners to test your competence in several different skills. Again, you can look through sets of past papers, and you may produce a list similar to that given in Information box 8.2. Those at the top of the list tend to be the shorter structured questions and test mainly knowledge and understanding, whereas further down the list, the styles are likely to be linked with the longer structured questions, and tend to give greater weight to testing a range of skills. Free prose questions or longer essay questions certainly test your knowledge and understanding but also qualify for some skills marks because you need to select relevant material to answer the question and then organise the material and communicate it in a coherent way.

How to answer the questions – a little advice from the Examiners

Key words

When you look at a question paper, you will see there are various words which key you in to how you approach the question. As you read the question through, you should note these **key words** and let them guide you into the style of your answer. Always, you need to read the questions very carefully, then to think about your response and select the appropriate answer.

- **name, state, give** – generally short, factual answers are expected, with precise use of biological terms or the name of a structure. Often one-word answers are sufficient

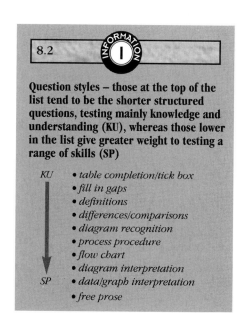

8.2 INFORMATION

Question styles – those at the top of the list tend to be the shorter structured questions, testing mainly knowledge and understanding (KU), whereas those lower in the list give greater weight to testing a range of skills (SP)

KU
- *table completion/tick box*
- *fill in gaps*
- *definitions*
- *differences/comparisons*
- *diagram recognition*
- *process procedure*
- *flow chart*
- *diagram interpretation*
SP
- *data/graph interpretation*
- *free prose*

PREPARING FOR THE EXAMINATION

- **give . . . . the function of** – again, short and factual responses are required, though at A level, usually more than one-word answers are appropriate

- **label . . . on the diagram** – make sure the end of the label line is neat and precisely touches the structure or region to be labelled. Sometimes a bracket label around a zone is more appropriate

- **compare, contrast, distinguish between, . . . how X differs from Y** – you are looking at two (or more) structures, functions, processes, events, or sets of data, and in your answer you should say something about both. **Compare** generally indicates that *similarities* as well as *differences* are expected, whereas **contrast, distinguish between** or **differs from** would expect you to focus on *differences*. Make sure you select equivalent features and keep them together, if you are presenting them in an account or in a table. If you write two separate accounts, the Examiner has to do the work for you, i.e. make the comparison or pick out the differences, and you may not earn your marks. Often it is appropriate to use comparative verbs, e.g. . . . X is bigg**ER** than Y . . ., and also you must make it quite clear which feature you are referring to

- **advantages, disadvantages** – as with comparisons or differences, you are effectively comparing one process or whatever with another, e.g. the effect of using pesticides **compared** with using biological control. Make sure your answers are comparative and that you make it clear which feature you are referring to when making your statements

- **describe** – this may be related to a biological event or process, or to data presented, say in a table, graph or other form. Your description should be concise and straightforward, using relevant biological terms rather than vague generalisations. If relating to unfamiliar data, you may be expected to notice the trend and to present this in words or translate into another form. If interpreting numerical data, it is often appropriate to refer to the figures, and these should be 'manipulated' in some way – quantify the trends, say the rate is twice as fast, or perhaps calculate the percentage difference over a specified period of time

- **explain, give explanations, give reasons** – you would be expected to draw on other biological knowledge to give reasons or explanations for the results of an investigation, or a description of biological events. Usually 2- or 3-mark answers are required and your answer should go beyond just a repetition or reorganisation of the information presented

- **using the information in the diagram, . . . features visible in the diagram . . .** – make sure you refer only to the information presented to you and not to other examples or features, which may be perfectly correct, but are not shown so are not what the Examiners were asking for in this question

- **suggest** – implies that the answer may include material or ideas you would not have learnt directly from studying your syllabus material, but you should be able to respond by making a reasonable suggestion, using your biological knowledge and understanding of related topics. Sensible answers in a biological context are likely to earn you marks, so always make an attempt at these questions

- **comment** – is a word the Examiners do not often use, and you may be unsure as to what is required. You can think of it as 'describe and explain' as you are usually expected to make observations or describe a trend, based on the data or information provided, and then to offer a little more, taking the discussion a stage further and perhaps give an explanation or relate the trend to other biological processes.

If you now look down this list of key words, you should recognise a trend – those at the beginning are expecting mainly knowledge and understanding, with more skills as you move down the list. Check back through a question paper and see how far this agrees with your analysis of the questions.

A few more hints on tackling different question styles

- **tick box questions** – read the instructions and make your intentions quite clear with either a tick (✓) or a cross (✗). If you change your mind, do not try to change a cross into a tick, or vice versa. Cross out your original answer and replace it clearly with your new answer. A tick crossed through is treated as an error when the Examiners are marking
- **fill in the gaps** – in answering these questions, read the whole passage through before starting to answer as this helps you see the context and the sense of the passage. When you have selected your words to fill the gaps, read the passage again to make sure it makes sense
- **calculations** – your answer should include appropriate units, unless this has been precluded by the way the question is phrased. You are usually asked to 'show your working', so you should include some intermediate stages in the calculation – for example, write down the figures read off from a graph and indicate how you manipulate these to get the answer. Maybe you will need to show how you substitute figures into a formula or how you calculate a percentage change. If you do it all on a calculator, without indicating any of the steps you are taking, you will get a mark for the answer (if it is correct) but not for showing the stages in your working. This system for marking can work in your favour if you give the wrong figures but are using a correct method
- **graphs** – marks are awarded for the correct labelling of the axes (including appropriate units), the choice of a sensible scale (try to use more than half the graph paper provided) and for careful plotting of the points. You should join the points neatly, with **straight lines** between the points, and **DON'T** extrapolate (go beyond the data given). Freehand curves and lines of best fit are usually inappropriate for the data given in examination questions and should be avoided, unless you are specifically instructed otherwise

PREPARING FOR THE EXAMINATION

- **genetic diagrams** – read the instructions in these questions very carefully and make sure you use the same notation and letters for alleles as those used in the question. Always give a line for the gametes as well as the genotypes of the parents and offspring, and note whether you need to give ratios of genotypes and/or phenotypes

- **spelling** – good spelling of ordinary words is important for your general presentation, particularly in the essay question. Examiners are generous in working out your intentions, but it is essential to be precise with biological terms, as errors can give a word with a different meaning. Words that are often confused (and would be marked wrong if used incorrectly) include: ure**TER** and ure**THRA**; m**IT**osis and m**EI**osis; th**Y**mine and th**IA**min(e); lact**OSE** and lact**ASE** . . . .the list could be extended, but we hope you get the words right and are aware of some of the pitfalls!

- **mark allocation** – the number of marks allocated to each question part acts as a precise guide as to how much information you are expected to give in your answer. Try answering some structured questions, then check back with a published mark scheme, and see that you are making a suitable number of points to earn enough marks. Often the mark scheme gives more points than the mark allocation, but that means there is some flexibility in the way the question is answered, and you do not necessarily need to give all the information to gain full marks

- **number of lines** – in structured questions, these are linked carefully to the mark allocation. For 2 marks, you are usually given 3 or 4 lines, for 3 marks, 5 or 6 lines, and so on. Sometimes, if one-word answers are expected, you may be given one line for one mark. When giving your answer, there is no need to start off by rewriting the question, but get on with the answer. Particularly in structured questions, you need to think critically about what is being asked, then carefully select what you write down. Often Examiners read answers where the first three lines really say nothing, then the candidate begins to say something worthy of a mark, but by then there are no more lines, so the writing goes up round the edge, into the margin . . . a bit of crossing out, then a rethink and confusion! We can all fall into this trap – so read the question carefully, think first, select what is required for the answer and be guided by the number of lines. The layout of the question is intended to help you

- **lines and the list rule** – sometimes you are asked for '*two* ways', or '*three* precautions', or '*two* examples . . .' of something, and the available lines are numbered 1, 2, 3, etc. Make sure you start each fresh answer on a new numbered line. If you jumble several ideas onto the same line, it is not the Examiner's job to choose which is correct – the Examiners will not do the work for you and they usually apply the '**list rule**'. This means that they mark the first idea on the numbered line (or in a box in a table) and ignore the rest. Suppose you put two correct ideas on one line and nothing on the next, you would score marks only for the first idea. Suppose

the first idea on the line was incorrect, followed by a correct idea –
you would score no marks, because it is the first idea only which is
marked. So, be wary, and, as has been said several times – **THINK**
first, before writing down your answer!

'Essay' or free prose questions – These are designed to be
answered by writing in continuous prose. Such questions have a mark
allocation which is larger than the sections within a structured
question - probably 10 marks or more, perhaps up to 20. They are
likely to start with 'Give an account of . . . . .'., or 'Write an essay
on . . . . .'. So the brief is more open and you are expected to do the
work of selecting the material and organising the structure of the
answer. As a start, it is essential to read the question carefully to make
sure you are setting off on the correct topic – if the question says
desertification, you will not get many marks for an account of
deforestation and, similarly, if the question says *water* pollution you
will not get many marks for an account of *air* pollution. If the title
refers to plants and animals (or living organisms), make sure you do
include information about both and not just about animals. (Don't be
side-tracked into writing the answer to the question which was set in
the last examination, or which you practised in your recent revision.)
Then quickly jot down your ideas and begin to organise them into a
list or 'plan' with a logical sequence. You can probably group different
ideas together and you are beginning to get the sub-sections or
paragraphs for your answer. You should write your answer in 'free prose',
which means using complete and coherent sentences. Concise notes,
lists or tables for comparisons can be helpful for planning your answer
and organising the information, but then you should expand this
structure into a free prose format. Diagrams can be useful, but they
need to be labelled or well annotated, and should complement your
answer, rather than just repeating information you have given in your
written description.

Depending on which syllabus you are following, and perhaps even
which paper within a scheme of examination you are preparing for, you
may find different styles of free prose questions. It is sensible also to
look at some of the published mark schemes, so that you know the
approach which is used in marking. In some free prose questions, you
are expected to give a fairly straightforward account, relating to the title
given. You may find there are many more mark scheme points than the
maximum for the question which means there is some flexibility in how
you present your account. The mark scheme points may also be quite
brief, but the Examiners are often expecting a bit of elaboration on the
key idea – give one or two examples, or further explanation or
qualification. Compared with the short structured questions, be
prepared to give a little more information to illustrate the points you are
making, but you should still be concise and make sure you use suitable
biological terms correctly. Probably two sides of the examination paper
are more than enough to cover an answer for, say, a 10 mark question –
sometimes candidates write three or four pages, and have perhaps only
one or two points worthy of marks on each page.

In longer free-prose questions, usually described as essays, your skills at organising the material and presentation as well as the factual content are being assessed. The ideal essay starts with a brief introductory paragraph which sets the context of the subject matter or the argument to be followed, then works through several areas of material relevant to the topic. It would end with some sort of rounding off paragraph, that perhaps gives a general conclusion or shows how the topic developed through the essay. In some examination boards, the mark schemes for essays are organised differently from those for the shorter free prose questions. In such essays, you do not earn marks for each correct point made, but rather a judgement is made on the quality of the scientific content which must, of course, be relevant to the topic of the essay. Again, you would select and organise your material as you did for the shorter free prose questions, but in essays you are expected to explore the different areas more fully or at greater depth. It is important to cover a range of areas relevant to the topic – you might give an excellent account of one part of the topic, but leave out other important material. This would not earn high marks. You need to keep a balance, and you may get marks, in a separate category, for the overall balance within the topic. You are also judged on your communication skills – for your presentation. This includes your written style, which should be well organised, coherent, written in sentences, with good grammar and spelling. This needs practice, but the key to success is to select your material, then to organise it in a coherent way.

Organising your time in the examination

If you look at the total number of marks in a paper and the time allocation, you will be able to calculate the relationship between the time and the marks. Very roughly, there is likely to be about a minute (or more) for each mark. Some of the marks you can get quickly, whereas others need longer to think through. Make sure you answer something in every question or question part. It is often easier to get the first one or two marks than the third or fourth, or the first five in a free prose than the last five. You have plenty of time in the examination – it is not a race, but it pays you to read the question, think, select then write. Remember to do plans for your free prose and essay answers. Time spent thinking and planning is time well used. You waste time writing material that is irrelevant to the answer, and waste much more time writing a wrong answer that you have to come back to at the end of the paper. It is then that the panic starts! Allow a little time to go back and read over the paper at the end. This may help you to correct silly mistakes, that were just slips rather than something you did not know. Don't, when you reach the end, panic and be tempted to change something you thought about earlier in the examination to an incorrect answer! Remember above all, the examination is designed to find out what you know from your study of the biology syllabus. If you work through the paper steadily and systematically, reading each question carefully before you start an answer, you should do yourself justice.

Appendix I: References and further reading

Titles which are now OUT OF PRINT are indicated as such in the list below, but you may find them in school and college libraries and they still represent useful reference material.

Chapter 1 - Laboratory techniques

Laboratory techniques and suggestions for practicals

Aldridge, S. (1994) *Practical Biochemistry for Advanced Biology*. Cambridge University Press (ISBN 0 521 437822)

Jones, A., Reed, R. and Weyers, J. (1998) 2nd edition *Practical Skills in Biology*. Addison Wesley Longman (ISBN 0 582 29885 7)

Roberts, M.B.V., Reiss, M. and King, T.J. (1994) *Practical Biology for Advanced Level*. Nelson (ISBN 0 17 448225 6)

Aspects of laboratory safety

Control of Substances Hazardous to Health Regulations (COSHH) 1994 (ISBN: 0 7176 1308 9)

The CLEAPSS (Consortium of Local Education Authorities for the Provision of Science Services) Laboratory Handbook. Details from: CLEAPPS School Science Service, Brunel University, Uxbridge, UB8 3PH; Tel: 01895 251496; e-mail: science@cleapss.org.uk

Topics in Safety (1998) Revised second edition, published by the Association for Science Education (ISBN: 0 86357 104 2)

Chapter 2 – Microscopy and observation

Bradbury, S. and Bracegirdle, B. (1998) *Introduction to Light Microscopy*. Royal Microscopical Society Handbook No. 42. BIOS Scientific Publishers (ISBN 1 85996 121 5)

Garvin, J.W. and Boyd, J.D. (1990) *Skills in Advanced Biology - Observing, Recording and Interpreting*.
Stanley Thornes (ISBN 0 8595 0 817X)

Jones, A., Reed, R., and Weyers, J. (1998) 2nd edition *Practical Skills in Biology*. Addison Wesley Longman (ISBN 0 582 29885 7)

Bracegirdle,B. and Miles, P.H. (1971) *An Atlas of Plant Structure Volume 1*. Heinemann (ISBN 0435 60312 4) OUT OF PRINT

APPENDIX I

Bracegirdle, B. and Miles, P.H. (1973) *An Atlas of Plant Structure Volume 2*. Heinemann (ISBN 0435 60314 0) OUT OF PRINT

Freeman, W.H. and Bracegirdle, B. (1966) *An Atlas of Histology*. Heinemann. OUT OF PRINT

Freeman, W.H. and Bracegirdle, B. (1976) *An Advanced Atlas of Histology*. Heinemann Educational Books (ISBN: 435 603175).

Roberts, M.B.V., Reiss, M., and King, T.J. (1994) *Practical Biology for Advanced Level*. Nelson. (ISBN 0 17 448225 6)

Chapter 3 – Presentation: using data and writing up

It would be useful for students to read accounts of investigations and experiments and reference to such accounts in *School Science Review* and the *Journal of Biological Education* would be valuable.

Chapter 4 – Quantitative techniques in biology

Aldridge, S. (1994) *Practical Biochemistry for Advanced Biology*. Cambridge University Press (ISBN 0 521 437822)

Hewitt, W. and Vincent, S. (1989) *Theory and Application of Microbiological Assay*. Academic Press (ISBN 0 12 346445 5)

Jones, A., Reed, R. and Weyers, J. (1998) 2nd edition *Practical Skills in Biology*. Addison Wesley Longman (ISBN 0 582 29885 7)

Meidner, H. (1984) *Class Experiments in Plant Physiology*. George Allen & Unwin (ISBN 0 04 581016 8) OUT OF PRINT

Reed, R., Holmes, D., Weyers, J. and Jones A. (1998) *Practical Skills in Biomolecular Sciences*. Addison Wesley Longman (ISBN 0 582 29826 1)

Roberts, M.B.V., Reiss, M. and King, T.J. (1994) *Practical Biology for Advanced Level*. Nelson (ISBN 0 17 448225 6)

Chapter 5 – More advanced tools and techniques

Jones, A., Reed, R., Weyers, J. (1998) *Practical Skills in Biology*. 2nd edition. Longman (ISBN 0 582 29885 7)

References relating to practical work with DNA, including safety

A guide to the genetically modified organisms (contained use) regulations (1992) as amended in 1996 by the Health and Safety Executive (1996). Her Majesty's Stationery Office, London (ISBN 0 7176 1186 8)

Alberts, B., Bray, D., Johnson, A., Lewis, J., Raff, M., Roberts, K., Walter, P., (1998) *Essential Cell Biology - An introduction to the molecular biology of the cell*. Garland Publishing Inc. (ISBN 0 8153 2045 0)

Kreuzer, H., Massey, A., (1996) *Recombinant DNA and Biotechnology. A guide for students*. American Society for Microbiology Press / Carolina Biological Supply Company (ISBN 1 55581 110 86)

Madigan, M. T., Martinko, J. M., Parker, J. (1997) *Brock Biology of Organisms* Prentice Hall (ISBN 0 13 571225 4)
Parkin, D. (1996) DNA fingerprinting of birds of prey. *Biological Sciences Review*, **9**(1), pp. 33–35.

Richardson, J (April 1995) Practical work with DNA. *Education in Science*, p. 16.

Tully, G. (1996) Forensic analysis of mitochondrial DNA. *Biological Sciences Review*, **8** (3), pp. 7–10.

Walker M.R.and Rapley, R. (1997) *Route Maps in Gene Technology* Blackwell Science (ISBN 0 632 03792 X)

References relating to PCR

Bloom, M.V., Freyer G.A., Miklos, D.A. (1995), *Laboratory DNA Science – An introduction to recombinant DNA techniques and methods of genome analysis*, pp 281–288, Benjamin Cummings [ISBN 0-8053-3040-2] [Description of manual method for PCR].

Brown, B. (1998) What is... ? PCR (polymerase chain reaction). *Biological Sciences Review*, 11(1), pp. 18–19.

References relating to fermentations

NCBE (1993) *Practical Biotechnology, a guide for schools and colleges*. National Centre for Biotechnology Education, University of Reading, UK.

Schollar, J., Watmore, B., (due 1999) Practical fermentation, a guide for schools and colleges. National Centre for Biotechnology Education, University of Reading, UK and The Society for General Microbiology (available through NCBE: consists of pack with Student Guides and Teacher Guides)

References relating to tissue culture protocols

Fuller, M.P. and Fuller, F.M. (1995) Plant tissue culture using Brassica seedlings. *Journal of Biological Education*, 29(10), pp. 53–59.

Hanley-Browne, M. (1998) Fast tissue culture. *Biological Sciences Review*, 10(3), pp. 2–6.

Fuller MP, Hanley-Browne M and Fuller F (1997) *Tissue Culture Workshop Protocols*. SAPS, Homerton College, University of Cambridge, UK

APPENDIX I

References relating to rapid-cycling brassicas ('fast plants')

Price, R. (1991) Perfect plants for projects. *Biological Sciences Review*, **4**(1), pp 32–36.

Price, R. and Harding, S. (1993) Genetics in the classroom – inheritance patterns of two mutant phenotypes in rapid-cycling *Brassica rapa* (syn. *campestris*). *Journal of Biological Education*, **27**(3) pp. 161–164.

Tomkins, S.P. and Williams, P.H. (1990) Fast plants for finer science – an introduction to the biology of rapid-cycling *Brassica campestris* (*rapa*) L. *Journal of Biological Education*, 24(4), pp. 239–250.

References relating to ELISA

Brown, B. (1998) What is... ? ELISA. *Biological Sciences Review*, **11**(2), pp. 30–31.

Turner, P. C., McLennon, A. G., Bates, A. D., White, M. R. H. (1997) Instant Notes in Molecular Biology. Bios Scientific Publishers (ISBN 1 85996 0561)

Protocols for ELISA, as developed by SAPS (Dr Mary MacDonald) and Dr Molly Dewey (Department of Plant Sciences, University of Oxford)

Chapter 6 – Fieldwork techniques

Identification

The Field Studies Council publishes some excellent keys as part of their AIDGAP project. The ones below are particularly helpful for terrestrial and freshwater work:

Tilling, S.M. (1987) *A key to the major groups of British Terrestrial Invertebrates*. Field Studies Council, Offprint No. 187.
(ISBN 1 85153 187 5)

Croft, S.M. (1986) *A key to the major groups of British Freshwater Invertebrates*. Field Studies Council, Offprint No. 181.
(ISBN 1 85153 181 6)

For seashore work the latest Collins Pocket Guide is very comprehensive:

Hayward, P., Nelson-Smith, T. & Shields, C. (1996) *Collins Pocket Guide - Sea Shore of Britain & Northern Europe*. Harper Collins.
(ISBN 0 00 219955 6)

Soil structure is well summarised in:

Trudgill, S. (1989) *Soil Types - a Field Identification Guide*. Field Studies Council, Offprint No. 196. (ISBN 1 85153 196 3)

Field Studies Council have also published a series of fold-out charts which are very useful identification guides. They provide excellent keys with means of identification for different groups of animals and plants, including: plants common in woodlands, plants common on sand dunes, plants common on moorland, common lichens and air pollution; lichens of rocky shores; waste ground and roadside grasses; British land mammals; water beetles. Available from Field Studies Council (address at bottom of this page)

Chapter 7 – Investigations - statistics and planning

Planning and statistics

The Open University project guide provides more details of some useful techniques and comprehensive statistical tables:

Chalmers, N. & Parker, P. (1986) *The OU Project Guide - Fieldwork and statistics for ecological projects*. Field Studies Council and The Open University, Occasional Publication 9. (ISBN 1 85153 809 9)

For further information on statistical method:

Cadogan, A. & Sutton, R. (1994) *Maths for Advanced Biology*. Nelson. (ISBN 0 17 448214 0)

Appendix V – Key skills

Qualifications and Curriculum Authority (QCA), 29 Bolton Street, London W1Y 7PD Tel: 0171 509 5555 Fax: 01787 312950 (for publication information only), e-mail: webinfo@qca.org.uk
Website: www.qca.org.uk/

Field Studies Council, Head Office, Preston Montford, Montford Bridge, Shrewsbury SY4 1HW Tel: 01743 850674, Fax: 01743 850178 ,
e-mail: fsc.headoffice@ukonline.co.uk ,
website: http://web.ukonline.co.uk/fsc.dalefort/index.html

Appendix II: Reagents and recipes

Suppliers of laboratory equipment, enzymes and reagents, equipment for biotechnology, including DNA extraction kits, living organisms, microbiological media and cultures of microorganisms, biological models, datalogging equipment.

> **Safety note**: Before planning and carrying out any practical work involving genetic modification, you are strongly advised to check the regulations relating to such work in your own country. Some of the practical protocols described on websites and educational kits for biotechnology, particularly those in the USA, are forbidden in schools and colleges within the European Union, unless the national laws that govern genetic modification have been complied with. Within the EU, it is forbidden to transfer genetic material between different species without special permission from the relevant authorities, and without strict health and safety guidelines being adhered to.

Adam, Rouilly Ltd., Crown Quay Lane, Sittingbourne, Kent ME10 3JG, UK. Tel. +44 (0)1795 471378 *[High quality anatomical, botanical and zoological models]*

Bioline, 16 The Edge Business Centre, Humber Road, London NW2 6EW, UK. Tel. +44 (0)181 830 5300 *[DNA polymerases, restriction enzymes, reagents and kits for molecular biology, products for electrophoresis]*
Website: www.bioline.com

Bio-Rad Laboratories Ltd., Bio-Rad House, Maylands Avenue, Hemel Hempstead, Hertfordshire HP2 7TD, UK. Tel. +44 (0)181 328 2000 *[Classroom kits for biotechnology, including bacterial transformation, protein purification (green fluorescent protein, GFP), restriction analysis of DNA, DNA fingerprinting. Electrophoresis equipment and supplies, protein assay kits. Microbiology accessories, including micropipettes. Please note that the transformation and protein extraction (GFP) kits are NOT available in the EU]*
Website: www.bio-rad.com

Blades Biological, Cowden, Edenbridge, Kent TN8 7DX, UK. Tel. +44 (0)1342 850242 *[Range of living and preserved organisms, housing, microbiological media, antibiotic sensitivity discs and cultures of microorganisms, rapid cycling brassica kits, seeds (including several mutants) and individual components for growing rapid cycling brassicas]*

Carolina Biological Supply Company, 2700 York Road, Burlington, North Carolina, 27215-3398, United States. International Customers Tel. +1 336 584 0381 *[Very wide range of laboratory equipment for biology and biotechnology, reagents, specimens, living organisms, visual aids, etc. Kits for plant tissue culture, growth and development of fast plants, bacterial transformation, DNA amplification by PCR, DNA extraction, electrophoresis and protein assay]*
Website: www.carolina.com

Clontech Laboratories UK Ltd., Unit 2, Intec 2, Wade Road, Basingstoke, Hampshire RG24 8NE, UK. Tel. +44 (0)1256 476500 *[DNA and RNA extraction kits with users' manuals]*
Website: www.clontech.co.uk

Culture Collection of Algae and Protozoa, Institute of Freshwater Ecology, Windermere Laboratory, Far Sawrey, Ambleside, Cumbria LA22 0LP, UK. Tel. +44 (0)15394 42468 *[Very large range of species of algae and protozoa. Also supply a culture kit for practical microbiology and biotechnology, and video 'The Microbial Engine']*

Curriculum Warehouse, Unit 11, Tannery Road, Tonbridge, Kent TN9 1RF, UK. Tel. +44 (0)1732 773325 *[Datalogging equipment and curriculum support material]*

Griffin & George, Bishop Meadow Road, Loughborough, Leicestershire LE11 3RG, UK. Tel. +44 (0)1509 233344 *[General laboratory equipment, microscopes and accessories, datalogging equipment, chemicals, biological specimens and models, field studies equipment, visual aids]*
Website: www.fisher.co.uk

National Centre for Biotechnology Education, The University of Reading, Whiteknights, Reading RG6 6AJ, UK. Tel. +44 (0)1189 873743 *[Enzymes, cultures of microorganisms, laboratory fermenters, complete kits for DNA electrophoresis, replacement parts and consumables, bacterial transformation kit and schools' microcentrifuge. Protocols for DNA extraction from plant material and other practicals, including lambda DNA gel electrophoresis and fermenter experiments, are given on the NCBE website]*
Website: www.reading.ac.uk/NCBE

Oxoid Ltd., Wade Road, Basingstoke, Hants RG24 8PW, UK. Tel. +44 (0)1256 841144 *[Microbiological media]*

Philip Harris Education, Lynn Lane, Shenstone, Lichfield, Staffs WS14 0EE, UK. Tel. +44 (0)1543 480077 *[General laboratory equipment, microscopes and accessories, datalogging and videologging equipment, chemicals, biological specimens and*

models, *field studies equipment, visual aids, etc. Kits for electrophoresis, enzyme biotechnology, immunochemistry, growth and development of rapid-cycling brassicas, plant tissue culture. Laboratory fermenters]*
Website: www.philipharris.co.uk/education

Qiagen Ltd., Boundary Court, Gatwick Road, Crawley, West Sussex RH10 2AX, UK. Tel. +44 (0)1293 422911 *[Products for PCR, protein purification, detection and assay. Kits for DNA and RNA isolation and purification]*
Website: www.qiagen.com

Richardsons of Leicester Ltd., Evington Valley Road, Leicester LE5 5LJ, UK. Tel. +44 (0)116 273 6571/2 and +44 (0)116 273 6585 *[Laboratory glassware and equipment, Petri dishes, counting chambers, tally counters, laboratory coats, disposable gloves, safety equipment]*

Science and Plants for Schools (SAPS), Homerton College, Cambridge CB2 2PH, UK. Tel. +44 (0)1223 507168 *[Information about rapid-cycling brassicas and other plants, worksheets for students and teachers' notes, and details of the SAPS programme, workshops for teachers, and newsletter 'Osmosis'. CD ROM 'Investigating Plant Science'. Protocols for plant tissue culture, pollen tube growth, thin layer chromatography for plant pigments, and many other practical activities and ideas for student investigations are given on the SAPS website. A Protocol for ELISA is currently being developed and trialled, and a kit is likely to be available from autumn 1999. For further information, please contact SAPS]*
Website: www-saps.plantsci.cam.ac.uk

Sigma Aldrich Co. Ltd., Fancy Road, Poole, Dorset BH12 4QH, UK. Tel. +44 (0)1202 733114 *[Inorganic and organic chemicals, including enzymes, amino acids, nucleotides and immunochemicals. Tissue culture media and reagents, protein assay kits, laboratory equipment]*

Stratagene Europe, Gebouw California, Hogehilweg 15, 1101 CB Amsterdam, Zuidoost, The Netherlands. Tel. +31 20 312 5600 *[Cloning vectors, nucleic acid extraction and purification kits, products for PCR, instruments including microcentrifuges and electrophoresis apparatus]*
Website: www.stratagene.com

Ward's Biology, 5100 West Henrietta Road, PO Box 92912, Rochester, New York, 14692-9012, United States. International Customers Tel. +1 716 359 2502 *[Very wide range of materials and equipment for biology and biotechnology, including living materials, models, field equipment, computer software, microscopes, chemicals, etc.]*
Website: www.wardsci.com

Appendix III: Describing vegetation

Whole area descriptions

Of limited use only, perhaps as a quick introductory look to see if there are sufficient differences between habitats to justify further study

Species list — No estimate of abundance

ACFOR — Tends to underestimate inconspicuous species, ratings vary from observer to observer

Quadrat based descriptions - subjective estimates

All subjective estimates are quick but their subjectivity is a major limitation, best used for simple descriptive work

% cover — "Guesstimates" can vary wildly from person to person

ACFOR rating — Hard to decide on appropriate rating, and different observers will rate species differently

Domin scale — Semi-quantitative so an improvement on simple guesses

Crapp scales — A scale similar to Domin Scale for use on rocky shore, useful for comparing different organisms

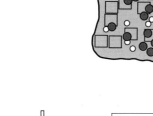

Quadrat based descriptions – objective estimates

For more detailed ecological work involving comparisons of sites or changes along a transect or any statistical work

% frequency — Presence and absence data from open frame quadrats, quick to do but difficult to interpret, frequency depends on quadrat size, useful in association analysis, need to define when a species is in a quadrat

Local frequency — Needs gridded quadrat, better than point sampling at picking up rare species but frequency will still depend on size of subdivisions within a quadrat

% cover — Can be estimated using intersections on a gridded quadrat or point quadrat frame, needs lot of points to give an accurate estimate, can miss rare species

Density — Not all plants occur as discrete individuals so can be difficult to estimate but gives a good measure for things like tree seedlings

Biomass — Requires harvesting so destructive, but useful for investigations where yield or energy content is important

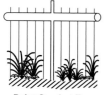

Point Quadrat Frame

Used to measure % cover. Many frames have to be placed within each sample area to obtain accurate data.

Point sampling

% Cover given by $\dfrac{\text{No. of Touches}}{\text{Total No. of Points}}$ times 100

Species	Tallies
🌿	//////
🌿	///
🌿	//////
No touch	/

Gridded Quadrat
Use intersections as locations for point samples to estimate % cover or measure local frequency. Select one corner of each small square within the quadrat and, using a pencil or other sharp object as pointer, record what you touch. If the quadrat has 100 squares then you will have a direct estimate of % cover. If you just count how many of the small squares contain each species then you will have estimated % local frequency.

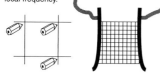

Appendix IV: Planning and statistics review

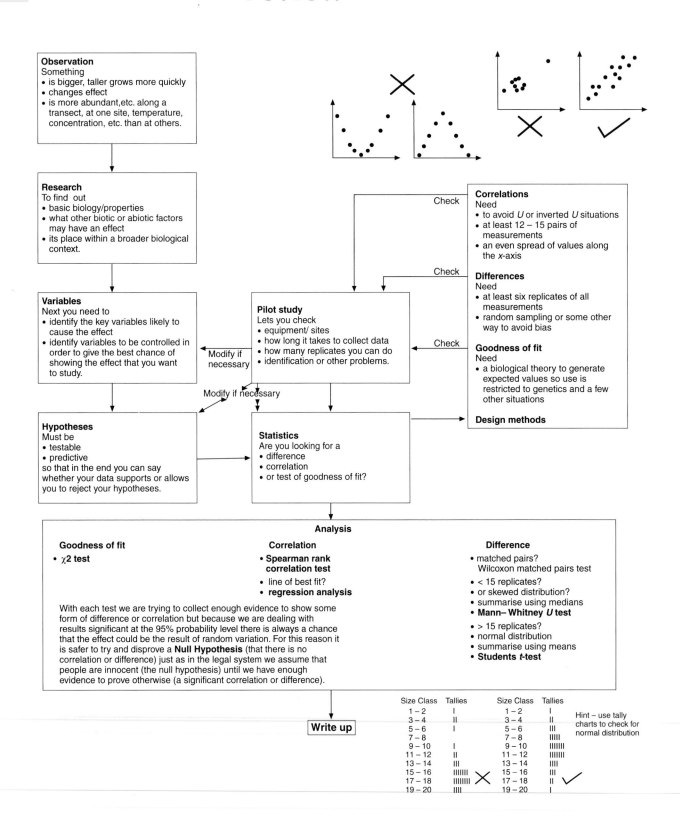

Observation
Something
- is bigger, taller grows more quickly
- changes effect
- is more abundant, etc. along a transect, at one site, temperature, concentration, etc. than at others.

Research
To find out
- basic biology/properties
- what other biotic or abiotic factors may have an effect
- its place within a broader biological context.

Variables
Next you need to
- identify the key variables likely to cause the effect
- identify variables to be controlled in order to give the best chance of showing the effect that you want to study.

Hypotheses
Must be
- testable
- predictive
so that in the end you can say whether your data supports or allows you to reject your hypotheses.

Pilot study
Lets you check
- equipment/ sites
- how long it takes to collect data
- how many replicates you can do
- identification or other problems.

Modify if necessary

Modify if necessary

Statistics
Are you looking for a
- difference
- correlation
- or test of goodness of fit?

Check

Check

Check

Correlations
Need
- to avoid U or inverted U situations
- at least 12 – 15 pairs of measurements
- an even spread of values along the x-axis

Differences
Need
- at least six replicates of all measurements
- random sampling or some other way to avoid bias

Goodness of fit
Need
- a biological theory to generate expected values so use is restricted to genetics and a few other situations

Design methods

Analysis

Goodness of fit
- χ^2 test

Correlation
- **Spearman rank correlation test**
  - line of best fit?
- **regression analysis**

Difference
- matched pairs?
  Wilcoxon matched pairs test
- < 15 replicates?
- or skewed distribution?
- summarise using medians
- **Mann– Whitney U test**
- > 15 replicates?
- normal distribution
- summarise using means
- **Students t-test**

With each test we are trying to collect enough evidence to show some form of difference or correlation but because we are dealing with results significant at the 95% probability level there is always a chance that the effect could be the result of random variation. For this reason it is safer to try and disprove a **Null Hypothesis** (that there is no correlation or difference) just as in the legal system we assume that people are innocent (the null hypothesis) until we have enough evidence to prove otherwise (a significant correlation or difference).

Write up

Size Class	Tallies	Size Class	Tallies
1 – 2	I	1 – 2	I
3 – 4	II	3 – 4	II
5 – 6	I	5 – 6	III
7 – 8		7 – 8	IIIII
9 – 10	I	9 – 10	IIIIIII
11 – 12	II	11 – 12	IIIIIII
13 – 14	III	13 – 14	IIII
15 – 16	IIIIIII	15 – 16	III
17 – 18	IIIIIII	17 – 18	II
19 – 20	IIII	19 – 20	I

Hint – use tally charts to check for normal distribution

Appendix V: Key skills

Introducing Key Skills

During any course of study, students acquire knowledge and understanding of the subject matter and they also develop competence in a range of skills. As part of the overall qualification framework, certain **key skills** can be identified and assessed in a way that will contribute to the achievements of each individual student. Teachers and students should be aware that, from the year 2000, all AS and A level specifications (syllabuses) will 'signpost' areas where there are opportunities for development of key skills. Teachers and students are advised to refer to the documentation published by QCA (Qualifications and Curriculum Authority) for the latest relevant information (*see Appendix I*).

Six main areas of **key skills** are recognised:
- Communication;
- Application of number;
- Information Technology;
- Problem solving;
- Working with others;
- Improving own learning and performance.

While some of these may be assessed by tests which are set and marked externally, all key skills can be assessed internally, during the course of study in a range of different subjects. Within an A level Biology or Human Biology course, there are many opportunities for students to develop key skills. This Appendix can be used as a review of earlier chapters in *Tools, Techniques and Assessment* and it signposts opportunities for students to develop and to be assessed on the different key skills. It will thus enable students to identify work that can be used as evidence of their achievements. Tables V.1 to V.6 outline the framework for the six recognised areas of key skills together with amplification to show the nature of the work which could be produced as evidence. The third column selects examples of some chapter references in the book related to practical work that students might undertake. These opportunities are also flagged by the appropriate symbol in the margin of the earlier chapters in this book. The chapter references on the tables link the key skills opportunities to specific pages, tables, information boxes or figures. Inevitably there are more situations which have not been flagged that could contribute to a key skills programme. However, those which have been signposted give ample guidance to teachers who may then find further suitable opportunities which could provide evidence for achievement in the range of key skills. In addition, some case studies are provided to illustrate how students may explore and exploit key skills in a broader context.

APPENDIX V

Key for symbols in Tables: F = Figure; T = Table; p = page; I = Information box; Ap = Appendix.

References in **bold** have no cross-references in text.

It should be noted that the cross references indicate only the broad category of key skill, such as 'Communication' or 'Application of Number' whereas the tables that follow give further detail which identifies the subset of key skills which would be relevant. Specific chapter references have not been given for 'Working with others' and 'Improving own learning and performance', but the case studies in this appendix illustrate how there are opportunities in many parts of the course which would enable students to fulfil these key skills requirements.

Table V.1 Communication

Amplification of the key skill	Chapter reference						
	1	2	3	4	5	6	7
• participation in group discussion (of a complex subject)					pp 57, 62, 65, 76	p 80, 81	
• presentation with images (of a complex subject)		F 2.7, 2.8, 2.17	F 3.1, 3.2, 3.3, 3.4	p 46 F 4.5, 4.7	F 5.1, 5.10, 5.14	**T 6.8** F 6.1, 6.2, 6.5, 6.7, 6.8, 6.12, 6.17, 6.23, 6.24, Ap III	I 7.3, 7.7, 7.8, 7.11 F 7.9
• selection and synthesis of information (for extended documents and images)	p 9 F 1.3	pp 17, 23 F 2.11	F 3.5	pp 41, 44, 50, 51 T 4.3	pp 57, 58, 59, 60, 61, 63, 65, 67, 73, 75 F 5.4, 5.5, 5.6, 5.14	T 6.3, 6.5	p114 T 7.1 to 7.9, I 7.3, 7.7, 7.8, 7.9, 7.11 F 7.10, 7.11
• writing of documents (complex subject, extended document with images)			p 27 T 3.1 F 3.1, 3.2, 3.3	p 47		T 6.5, 6.8 F 6.12, 6.29	F 7.2 to 7.5, 7.7, 7.8, 7.9

Table V.2 Application of Number

Amplification of the key skill	Chapter reference						
	1	2	3	4	5	6	7
• planning of how to obtain and interpret information (including large data set)				p 49		pp 77, 79, 80, 84, 91	p 101
• doing multi-stage calculations with (a) amounts and sizes	F 1.3, T 1.4		F 3.1	p 51,			
(b) scales and proportions				T 4.3 F 4.1, 4.5 T 4.1			
(c) handling statistics							pp 106, 108, 109, 110, 111, **112**, 113, 114, 115 117, 118, **119**, F **7.6**
(d) rearranging and using formulae (including large data set)	p 10			pp 40, 42 51		p 90 T 6.4, 6.6 F 6.17	pp 110, **112**, 115, 117, **119** I 7.11
• select appropriate method of presentation (including graphs, charts, diagrams), interpretation of results and presentation of findings, justification of methods used	T 1.5 F 1.8		F 3.2, 3.3, 3.4, 3.5	p 47, T 4.2		T 6.8 F 6.7, 6.12	pp 110, 111, I 7.8 F 7.2 to 7.5, 7.7, 7.8, 7.9, 7.14, 7.16

Table V.3 Information Technology

Amplification of the key skill	Chapter reference						
	1	2	3	4	5	6	7
• using different sources for information retrieval				pp 54, 55	pp 56, 57 68, 70 F 5.8(b), 5.9	p 100	
• how to exchange information to meet different purposes				F 4.5	F 5.6(c)		F 7.17
• presentation of information for different purposes (including text, images, numbers)				p 51, F 4.7, 4.10		p 97 F 6.25	pp 114, 122, T 7.7 F 7.2 to 7.5, 7.7, 7.8, 7.9, 7.14

Table V.4 Problem solving

Amplification of the key skill	Chapter reference						
	1	2	3	4	5	6	7
• identification of problem	p 12		F 3.5	pp 54, 55	p 70 T 5.2 F 5.13	pp 80, 82	pp 101, **113**, 116, **118**, 120
• production and comparison of different options in solving the problem, agree method of solution					p 70	pp 80, 82, 96, 98 T 6.10 F 6.6, **6.9**	pp 108, 109, 111, 116, **118**, 121 F 7.10, 7.11 Ap IV
• planning and implemention of selected methods for solving the problem			F 3.5	pp 49	p 70 T 5.2	p 77	pp 101, 106, 111, 114
• review of methods used in solving the problem and evaluate the outcomes						p 79	

Table V.5 Working with others

Amplification of the key skill	Chapter reference						
	1	2	3	4	5	6	7
• planning and participating in activities with others							
• recording your discussions over achieving the targets							
• agreement of targets and monitoring progress							
• production of action plan over extended period							

Table V.6 Improving own learning and performance

Amplification of the key skill	Chapter reference						
	1	2	3	4	5	6	7
• agreement of targets and monitoring progress							
• production of action plan over extended period							

Case Study 1

A presentation by students to a group of local residents, to explain the arguments for and against GM (genetically modified) products being included in foods sold in supermarkets.

Students are to work in groups of four and each should prepare a five minute presentation, representing a different viewpoint. Following their presentation, they will be required to participate in and lead discussion groups.

Key skill opportunities

The subject is 'complex', and allows selection of relevant material for their presentation, which can include images. It would be appropriate to use IT to search for different sources of information, from CD-Rom and websites. The task would enable the students to work together in their planning and organising of the activities, both to collect and present the information and to handle the discussion.

Case Study 2

A presentation by students to other students in the group to illustrate the ultrastructure of cells.

Students are to work in pairs and part of their presentation will be in poster format. The oral presentation is likely to be about five minutes and the students will then need to respond to questions from the group.

Key skill opportunities

The subject is 'complex' as cell organelles are not visible with a light microscope and the students are unlikely to have experience of an electron microscope. Images are essential for the poster. IT skills could be used to provide suitable images or layout on the page. It would be appropriate to use IT to search for different sources of information from CD-Rom and websites. The task would enable the students to work together to gain the necessary understanding and so relate biological structure to function.

Case Study 3

Individual students are expected to devise a programme which will monitor their achievement in a range of practical skills over an extended period of time, such as ten weeks.

Key skill opportunities

The student selects a limited number of skills. These could, for example, include use of a microscope to do biological drawings or collection and presentation of large sets of data. In discussion with a teacher, the student becomes aware of his / her current performance and agrees a means of measuring improvement in the identified skill area. The student then suggests ways of developing the skills and proposes a programme which allows monitoring of achievement at specified intervals. The student agrees targets with the teacher and produces an appropriate action plan.

Working together

On many occasions when doing practical work during the course, there are opportunities for students to work together and plan and participate in activities with others. Laboratory experiments may, for example, allow students to work with enzymes at different temperatures, and their combined results could then be used to form part of a discussion. Similarly, in doing fieldwork, as described in Chapter 6, there are numerous opportunities for initial identification of the problem to be solved and discussion of the most appropriate method to be used, to be carried out in groups. (Further guidance on opportunities for key skills in a fieldwork context may be obtained from the *Field Studies Council – see addresses or references.*) It is often possible to compare different options and agree a method of solution for the problem to be investigated. While such group discussions are valuable for the development of certain skills, teachers and students are advised that, for assessment purposes, it may be necessary for students to work individually in carrying out investigations.

Index

INDEX